The Cadillac That
Followed Me Home

The Cadillac That Followed Me Home

Memoir of a V-16 Dream Realized

CHRISTOPHER W. CUMMINGS

McFarland & Company, Inc., Publishers
Jefferson, North Carolina, and London

LIBRARY OF CONGRESS CATALOGUING-IN-PUBLICATION DATA

Cummings, Christopher W., 1952–
    The Cadillac that followed me home : memoir of a V-16
dream realized / Christopher W. Cummings.
        p.   cm.
    Includes index.

    ISBN-13: 978-0-7864-2808-3
    ISBN-10: 0-7864-2808-2
    (softcover : 50# alkaline paper) ∞

    1. Cummings, Christopher W., 1952–   2. Automobiles—
Conservation and restoration.   3. Cadillac automobile—
Collectors and collecting.   I. Title.
TL152.2.C86 2006   2006026811

British Library cataloguing data are available

On the cover: The author's 1930 Cadillac V-16

Manufactured in the United States of America

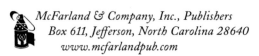

McFarland & Company, Inc., Publishers
    Box 611, Jefferson, North Carolina 28640
        www.mcfarlandpub.com

To my wife Barbara,
who made me reach for a dream
that I thought was gone

Acknowledgments

I would like to thank the many people, living and deceased, who have helped and encouraged me over the years with my cars and my interest in Cadillacs. Many of those people are mentioned in these pages. My wife Barbara deserves a special bow for dancing with me and making my dreams come true. The rest of the honor roll is so extensive that I would certainly miss a few if I attempted to list everyone.

I have learned a great deal from various chroniclers of Cadillac history, including Roy A. Schneider whose books *Cadillacs of the Forties* (Royco Publications, 1976) and *Sixteen Cylinder Motorcars* (Heritage House, 1974) occasioned many daydreams and answered a raft of questions about how these cars came to be, how they were built and how they worked. Maurice Hendry's *Cadillac, Standard of the World: The Complete Seventy-Five Year History* (Automobile Quarterly Publications, 1973) is a masterly history of the Cadillac marque, and my copy is well-worn. Walter M.P. McCall's book *80 Years of Cadillac LaSalle* (Crestline Publishing Company, 1992) is filled with Cadillac factory pictures of every model and body style from 1902 through 1982, together with detailed historical material, organized by model year.

The Standard Catalog of Cadillac (2nd Edition, James T. Lenzke, Editor, Krause Publications, 2000), presents several splendid essays. One, *Where Did All the 16s Go? A documentary study of the 1930-31 Cadillac V-16s* by Alan Merkel (reprinted by permission from *The Classic Car*, the magazine of the Classic Car Club of America) tells how those cars were dispersed around the country and abroad. *Smoothness, Silence, Acceleration and Hill Climbing Ability* by Bill Artzberger describes the competitive pressures and engineering considerations involved in Cadillac's decision to build a sixteen cylinder car. *Cadillac V-16: Worth Its Weight in Prestige* by Robert Ackerson also describes the engineering and economic factors driving the V-16 project and compares the cars with other ultra-luxury brands.

The (New) Cadillac Database is an amazingly all-encompassing collection of material placed on the Internet and maintained by noted Cadillac enthusiast Yann Saunders. Among other fascinating resources, the *Database* includes a chart showing many of the surviving V-16 Cadillacs, with notes about their individual histories and current ownership. Mr. Saunders has given the collection to the Cadillac-LaSalle Club Museum & Research Center, Inc. and has continued to maintain and update the many pages, links and photographs.

The Cadillac-LaSalle Club has been an inestimable help when I first became an old Cadillac owner and to the present day. The monthly newsletter, *The Self-Starter* (named for Cadillac's innovative and award-winning adoption of an electric starter motor), provided a forum for buying scarce replacement parts and wonderfully informative technical articles and accounts of club activities. The Potomac Region of the club has provided a network of fellow old Cadillac lovers interested in showing and driving their cars, sharing their knowledge and experiences and socializing together.

Lastly, my hat is off to the men and women of the Cadillac Motor Car Company who conceived, executed, sold and serviced the beautiful machines that inspired this book.

Contents

A dream of the Roaring Twenties ... materializing at the time the bottom fell out of the stock market—advertised for the "400"—who were now in hiding—and finding instead only empty pocketbooks. Be that as it may, it was an outstanding piece of work.

—Ernest Seaholm, Cadillac Chief Engineer from 1922 to 1943, summing up the Cadillac V-16 automobiles, quoted by Maurice Hendry in *Cadillac—Standard of the World— The Complete Seventy-Year History* E.P. Dutton 1973.

Introduction

This is a story about a decades-long interest in (and desire to possess) an example of a machine that was designed and intended to be bought and owned by the most discerning of well-heeled motorists. As such, it doesn't inspire courage or exhort the reader to heroic virtue. It may even be seen by some as an exercise in venality or cupidity. It does tell, however, the timeless tale of man's admiration for, and his need to touch, great art and fine craftsmanship. Everything set forth here happened pretty much the way I am recalling it. There were many surprises and interesting twists along the way. As I began writing, I never imagined that the goal would be achieved.

The car in question was meant to be what is now called a "halo" car—a model that has no realistic hope of selling enough units to pay for its development and production costs, but that will attract interest, admiration and buyers to the manufacturer's bread-and-butter vehicles. Many automotive historians credit this particular "halo" car with consolidating the Cadillac Motor Car Company's pre-eminence in the United States luxury car field over rivals such as Packard, Pierce Arrow and Lincoln. In any event, it was exclusive, expensive and distinguished, both mechanically and esthetically. Production numbers over the 11-year run of the Cadillac V-16 from 1930 through 1940 totaled less than 4,100 cars, about three-quarters of which were produced in the first two years. But the image and added prestige that this line gave to Cadillac cannot be calculated.

During the teens and twenties, the automobile had grown from a spindly, gawky contraption that people mostly rode "on" to an integrated and enclosed conveyance. Wealthier customers had begun to demand not only comfort and protection from the elements, but luxury. Upholstery in an enclosed car no longer needed to be weather-proof, and neither did the floor coverings and fittings. Cars became bigger and heavier, roads were improving, and the manufacturers began competing with each other to provide swifter and more magnificent coaches for their well-heeled buyers.

1

Weight and speed require power, and the ability to deliver that power was limited in a number of ways. Gasoline chemistry and engine design had yet to converge in a way that permitted higher compression ratios without causing "knock" or detonation. The principal ways open to contemporary carmakers to increase power were supercharging (expensive and noisy) and increasing the size of the engine (whether by expanding the bore and stroke, or by adding cylinders). The first cars had used single-cylinder engines, but fours and sixes soon appeared. Rolls Royce was one of the first to use an in-line six. Cadillac came out with the first mass-produced V-8 engine in 1915, and in the same year, Packard presented a V-12 it called the "Twin Six." After six years, Packard switched to a "Single Six" that was easier to manufacture, and in 1923, a straight 8 that was to be the company's mainstay for years to come.

In the quest to provide an increasingly smoother ride for their sophisticated and increasingly demanding customers, a number of prestige auto manufacturers had begun actively exploring "multi-cylinder" engine designs, moving beyond an 8, or even a 12. Much of the motivation was the fact that more power pulses per revolution of the engine's crankshaft would result in a closer approximation of constantly applied (and therefore smooth) power. A piston engine that gets its power from combustion is a percussion instrument. It goes "bang" rhythmically and shoves a piston to turn a crank, and the passenger senses that as vibration. The closer together the rhythmic bangs are, the more the vibration and bumpiness is smoothed out. More cylinders firing in sequence was a practical way to achieve this increased smoothness, and the introduction of the 90° V-8 engine in the teens had been a quantum leap in the technology of producing increased power with a minimum of roughness. Another reason for more cylinders was old-fashioned prestige and one-upsmanship—it put more distance between one car and the rest and made the salesman's job easier.

The Cadillac V-16 was conceived in secrecy in the middle of the "Roaring Twenties," when incomes were rising, prosperity seemed endless and the car business was beginning to break free from a period of almost ruthless tyranny of function over form. At about the same time, Marmon and Peerless were working on their own sixteen-cylinder engines. As it happened, however, Cadillac beat its rivals to the punch and brought its entry to the market first as a 1930 model, following up with a V-12 in 1931. In 1932, Lincoln, Packard and Pierce Arrow would add V-12s to their existing eight-cylinder offerings. Auburn and Franklin would also offer V-12s.

When the 1920s gave way to the 1930s, nearly everything changed, and not just for the auto industry. The ebullient optimism and flamboyance of the "Roaring Twenties" came to a screeching halt with the onset of what became a worldwide financial depression. In a very short time, most of the market for what the press calls "big ticket luxury items" dried up. Auto manufacturers and their dealers, suppliers and related businesses (such as custom body designers and builders) found themselves suddenly and dramatically out of step with their customer base.

Re-orienting a car maker's product offerings and marketing operation is something like turning an ocean liner around—it takes time and a lot of effort. Many of the major fine car makers didn't survive the Great Depression, and those that did endure relied on luck, strategy, flexibility and in some cases, subsidies from corporate affiliates. In the early 1930s, there were many models that, in retrospect, seem spectacularly inappropriate in a time of widespread financial hardship. But many of these extravagant creations had been imagined, designed and germinated in the mid–'20s when it seemed that good times and the demand for flashy exciting cars could only increase. The Cadillac V-16 and V-12 offerings were examples of this phenomenon, as were the Duesenberg "J" (introduced in 1929) and the Marmon 16. Only after the economic tide had turned did these glittering projects reach the showroom floor, too late to find enough qualified buyers (or buyers bold enough to flaunt wealth in a suddenly bleak landscape).

When the manufacturers were able to react to the new economic climate, many chose the path of discretion, whether by diverting resources to more modest products or toning down the flamboyance of their high-end lines. In the early '30s, to drive a spectacular and obviously expensive automobile, one had to be not only financially well-endowed, but immune to a certain social pressure (sometimes applied by direct means, such as hurled fruit and rocks) from those who disapproved of, or resented the display. This disincentive coincided chronologically with the ascendancy of the stylist as a driving factor in determining what a car looks like. It also coincided with the passion to "streamline" everything, from railroad locomotives to kitchen appliances to cars. The result of these forces was the progressive disappearance of straight lines on car bodies, and the increasing concealment of mechanical and structural elements of the vehicle within enveloping, rounded expanses of sheet metal. Like the maxi-skirts that engulfed women's legs and ankles in the late 1960s, the stylists of the 1930s covered up the frames, suspension parts, and other structures that had always been unself-consciously displayed. The soaring clamshell fenders would morph into pontoons that in some cases threatened to swallow the wheels whole, and bold exposed radiators would become stylized grilles with flat hoods. The puffy late–'40s Packard Clippers represent one extreme of this trend, while the largely indistinguishable "blob" cars of the 1990s are another.

So, in 1930 and 1931, under the influence of such men as Harley Earl, Gordon Beuhrig, Bill Mitchell and Howard Darrin, the car industry turned a corner. In the next few years, the transition from "horseless carriage" to something wholly new would be achieved. The integration of separate parts—fenders, running boards, spare tires, hoods, trunks, bumpers—into a seamless envelope is a trend that started here and that would continue for decades. Some parts would re-emerge—running boards and exposed spare tires on some SUVs, for example. And the trend to swallow the car's rolling wheels would reverse itself to the point that in the 2000s, only one car in the world (the Honda Insight) would sport fender skirts, or, indeed, anything but fully exposed front and rear wheels.

To my tastes, 1930 and 1931 represent an aesthetic high-water mark for car design. My personal favorite is the Cadillac model line for 1931, including for this purpose the 1930 V-16s (which introduced the styling features that the rest of the line would pick up in 1931). In response to the inevitable objections and cries of anguish my position will arouse, let me acknowledge that yes, many subsequent models of various makes are true works of art in their own rights, but I have reasons for my choice. "J" and "SJ" Duesenbergs are magnificent, but they represent a distinct aesthetic (to my mind more belligerent) and each is so individual as to be almost *sui generis* (and in all likelihood, permanently out of my reach!). Packard, aided by Dietrich, Darrin and others, cannot be dismissed, but the Cadillac lines and styling for '30 and '31 are to me more alive than Packard's. Peerless, Marmon, Rolls, Mercedes (and others including Hispano Suiza, Isotta Fraschini, and so on and so forth) have substantial merit in this retrospective contest, but for me, the Cadillacs combine a high level of mechanical sophistication and reliability, true elegance, comfort and overall beauty in a particularly satisfying way.

In the book of Genesis, the loss of our first parents' innocence is accompanied by a sudden awareness of their nakedness, and a need to cover up. Something similar happened in the automobile industry about 1930. Prior to that time, if you looked at a car, you could easily see a lot of the innards, the mechanical workings, without opening the hood or removing any of the parts. Take a look at a car from the teens or the twenties, and you can see the springs, the shock absorbers, the radiator (with or without shutters), large sections of the frame, the brackets that hold the bumpers, steering links and so on and so forth. After 1930, the fig leaves come out, and everything gets covered up. The fenders spread to cover the suspension and brake parts, the frame, and even portions of the wheels. Curves chase away all the straight lines. The radiator disappears behind a grille that will ultimately span the entire front of the car, and its filler cap hides under the hood. The headlights become elongated pods, first faired into the fenders, and ultimately merged into them (until, today, they lie entirely flush with the rounded corner of the front fender). And it all starts around 1932, picking up speed through the following decades.

It was almost as though cars had become collectively uncomfortable with the idea that they were machines, and they felt a need to conceal the fact from the public. One can imagine that they suddenly wished they were airplanes (or aeroplanes in the language of the time). And some of the touring cars and roadsters had passenger compartments that resembled the cockpits of contemporary aircraft (particularly in the way that the windshield was mounted to the cowl, and in the way the top edge of the doors continued along the lip of the cowl over the dash and the body behind the seat). As planes became more streamlined, automobile designers picked up styling cues from that process—rounded edges, smooth transitions from one surface to another. And so, separately defined fenders became less and less defined as the surface of the car body progressively trended toward a seamless envelope enclosing everything.

What I see when I look at the 1931 Cadillacs (and for that matter, most cars from the several years leading up to that year) is a kind of innocent pride. Pride at having achieved acceptance by, and real usefulness to, the general public. No longer an eccentric plaything for the wealthy to tickle their fancy with, the car was becoming an essential appliance, replacing the horse and challenging the railroad as the transportation mainstay of the nation. Men and women, rich and poor, urban and rural, everyone was learning to drive, and the manufacturers were providing products for every taste and pocketbook.

The innocence shows in the calm knowledge that it is a machine, with no need to hide the fact or try to be something else. In subsequent years, cars would pretend to be rockets, jet aircraft, animals or fanciful examples of rolling sculpture. Oh, for sure, there had already been the occasional jackrabbit, ghost, arrow or phantom, but everyone knew they were metaphors, not incarnations. Later cars would sport such innovations as "jet tube" tail lights (mid fifties Fords), P-38 Lightning tail fins ('48-'49 Cadillacs) and prop spinner noses (early fifties Fords and Studebakers). They would become "pony cars" or "land yachts" or various types of liners and cruisers. A few novelty vehicles could be converted by the driver into airplanes or boats that actually flew or swam. Ultimately, the convergence of aerodynamic designs in the eighties and nineties would make many cars seem like all but indistinguishable jelly beans.

Part of what was happening was emulation of the airplane and the identification of aerodynamic lines with speed. Part of it was the newfound power of the designer over the shape and appearance of the automobile, displacing the engineers, who had based form almost entirely on function. And part of it was the changing economic conditions that made anything smacking of ostentation into an unwise course. The immediate result was that the high classic period of automobile design would evolve into something more discreet, more enclosed, more industrial before fading out entirely with the onset of the Second World War. But for that moment in time when radiators last stood upright for all the world to see, and clamshell fenders crested front wheels and the wind as well, a certain ideal had been reached that could never recur.

By the time the Cadillac V-16 reached showrooms in 1930, the age of the stylist was under way, custom body manufacturers were producing elegant coachwork to match increasingly powerful and sophisticated chassis, and the nation was falling headlong into the Great Depression. The miracle is that so many of these extravagant conveyances were sold at all. In 1931 a Chevrolet cost between $475 and $650. A Cadillac V-16, by contrast, cost from about $5,600 on up to around $10,000 or potentially even higher, depending on body style and custom coachwork. Almost overnight, the pool of potential buyers who could afford such luxury shrank dramatically. Moreover, many of those who could still afford the price either felt that their own finances were more precarious than before, or were not inclined to lord their situation over the less fortunate. Of the manufacturers who brought out V-16s, Peerless and Marmon were unable to weather the hard times and they bowed out of auto making altogether. Cadillac had General Motors's broad shoulders to lean on.

These difficulties notwithstanding, Cadillac continued producing V-16s through the end of the decade of the thirties, even introducing a completely redesigned 16-cylinder engine for the last three model years. Even today, these are impressive cars to drive, as well as to look at. Endowed with ample power, even for the heavy chassis and bodies they were built with, they can run comfortably at modern highway speeds. This is truly what was meant by the motto "Standard of the World."

1. Beginnings

In 1965, when I was 12 years old with three younger brothers, my parents bought a house in Albuquerque, New Mexico. The previous owner left behind a neatly-shelved collection of *The Reader's Digest* spanning the years from the mid–1940s through the first half of 1965. Just for good measure, there was a lone 1937 issue, hinting that the collection had once been even more extensive.

My brothers and I devoured those magazines, figuratively and literally. We read them voraciously and we wore them out, passing them back and forth and leaving them all over the house. We thrilled to the *Drama in Real Life* and first-person articles, laughed at the *Humor in Uniform* and other anecdotal features, built our vocabularies and stuffed our brains with myriad new information. As young boys will, we took a terrible toll on the covers and bindings, but we certainly profited from those little books.

In the March 1955 issue I found an article[1] that a man wrote about his teenaged son's purchase (against his father's better judgment) of a 1941 Cadillac sedan, and how the son's determination to restore and renew that car had helped him grow up and find not only himself, but a career in engineering as well. As a car lover myself, I imagined my feet in the son's shoes as I read about him working on the car, getting parts from salvage yards, failing and succeeding, and picking his father up from the Denver airport in the almost re-made Cadillac. The images from that article etched themselves into my imagination and I called them to mind from time to time. I didn't know it then, but the effects that article would have on my life would be profound and lasting.

When my parents asked me what I wanted for my thirteenth birthday, I answered that I wanted a plastic model called the "Visible V-8 Engine." It was a ¼ scale replica of an automobile engine with moving internal parts—crankshaft, pistons, valves and so on—and with clear plastic outside surfaces so that when it was assembled, the modeler would be

1. *Paul Friggens*, Don't Raise Your Son Without a Cadillac. *March 1955 issue, pg. 93.*

7

able to watch how the innards of a real engine move as it runs. I'd had my eye on this particular model for several years, but it was a bit expensive to come right out and ask for. The model is still available today (although it's made by Revell-Monogram now, instead of Renwall) and it goes for about $63.00. As my thirteenth birthday approached, I felt bold enough to make my request. As it turned out, my parents had a better idea.

A few days before my birthday, I noticed a strange car in our garage. That I noticed was unusual, as we only used the garage for storage, parking my parents' car on the driveway. I don't know why I looked through the window into the garage on my way into the house as I came home from school. But there was an old and plain light blue coupe from the 1950s in there, paint worn down to primer in spots. When I asked my mother, she explained that Wesley Haskew, the fellow who had recently sold us our house, had asked us if he could leave it in the garage for a few days. I accepted the story at face value and thought nothing further about it.

On the morning of my birthday, I was presented with a brand new Craftsman toolbox and an assortment of new screw drivers, box, allen and

The Visible V-8 Engine. This is the model I'd asked for for my thirteenth birthday. My parents had another idea.

socket wrenches and other tools. Then I was shown a poster that announced that something else was mine, to take apart, refurbish or otherwise do with as I pleased, and taped to the poster was a set of keys on a ring. My father had gone to a used car lot and purchased a 1952 Ford Mainline coupe (for $52 dollars, as I found out later) and had had it delivered to our garage. My mother's fib about Mr. Haskew notwithstanding, I was now the owner of that car I'd noticed a few days before. But before examining it I would have to wait for the end of the school day, as it was now time to leave.

That evening, my parents joined me as I inspected and investigated this life-sized car model they had given me instead of the plastic scale model kit I had asked for. I was fascinated, intrigued and overwhelmed. It was an example of Ford's basic transportation line for 1952, the Mainline series, although the fender badges indicated that it had the extra-cost optional V-8 engine, instead of the standard inline six. When I raised the hood, I saw my first flathead V-8. To that time I had seen (or seen pictures of) only recent overhead-valve engines. All of those had oblong valve covers, usually embossed or painted with the name of the car (or some

1952 Ford Mainline Coupe. This factory photograph shows a pristine, new specimen of the car my parents gave me for my thirteenth birthday. My car was light blue and substantially the worse for wear (courtesy Ford Motor Company).

other inspiring words, like "Blue Flame" or "Red Ram"). Flatheads went incognito. They just had cast-iron cylinder heads whose flat surfaces were broken only by spark plugs and boltheads. This was also the first time I'd ever seen an old-fashioned oil-bath air cleaner, sitting on top of the engine like a medium-sized metal pumpkin. I still couldn't believe my parents had given me an actual car.

In the trunk were an assortment of used parts, like old brake cylinders and lines, and the jack. Glued to the inside of the trunk lid was the tire changing instruction sheet, showing a gentleman in fedora and overcoat working the properly placed jack. Scattered in all imaginable nooks and crannies were scads of those ubiquitous Albuquerque elm tree seeds. The seats sported vinyl seat covers that were beginning to fray. The car was equipped with an optional heater and an AM radio that worked.

On a Saturday afternoon a few weeks later, my father went out to the garage with me, opened the overhead door and started the car. It roared to life in a respectable fashion and seemed to run smoothly enough. After letting it warm up a bit, my father put the transmission in reverse and let out the clutch. Nothing happened. So he tried first gear (gently, so as not to drive into the wall between the garage and the house!). Still nothing. And nothing in second gear, either. In third gear, the car moved forward when my father eased out the clutch pedal. My father informed me that the transmission gears must have been severely "stripped" with the exception of third gear. Sadly, there was going to be no impromptu neighborhood drive in the '52 Ford that day.

I set about applying my new tools to my automotive subject. I ordered the 1952 Ford shop manual from the company that still makes those books for Ford, and I read up on how things go together and come apart on those cars. I removed the broken parking brake cable, had a neighborhood Philips 66 station order me a replacement, and I installed the new part successfully. I took out the distributor and brought it to my eighth grade science class to show to my classmates as we studied how engines work. I bought a new set of spark plug wires and replaced the old cracked set, and the plugs as well. I did various other light repair jobs on the car, and various acts of purely exploratory surgery. Along the way I found out how a side-valve engine (such as a flathead V-8) works. I learned about basic automobile electrical systems. And I became acquainted with the singularly persistent black grease that auto mechanics have always found so hard to get out from under their fingernails.

I did actually try to address the transmission problem. Slithering underneath the car with an old paint bucket and a wrench, I unscrewed the drain plug from the underside of the transmission and let the plug and the transmission lube drain into the bucket. Instead of hearing a quiet whoosh as the liquid flowed smoothly into the pail, I heard a staccato clatter as a collection of broken gear teeth dropped into the container. Just an additional confirmation that the gearbox was shot and would have to be replaced. I consulted the service manual and was not really encouraged. The way to remove the transmission without taking out the engine at the same time involved first removing a 2-foot long frame cross member.

The manual envisioned two ways that the transmission could be removed from the car. It could be taken out still attached to the engine if the whole power plant was hoisted out through the engine compartment from above, or it could be removed from underneath the car by detaching it from the bell housing at the rear of the engine. The latter method required moving the transmission several inches towards the back of the car to withdraw the splined end of the transmission main shaft from the clutch, and then bringing the transmission down and out of the car. Either method involved removing the drive shaft.

The book recommended taking out the frame cross-member to minimize the amount of wiggling and manipulation required to get the transmission free from the close space between the frame and the car's floorpan. Although it did not say that the transmission absolutely couldn't be removed with the cross-member in place, the manual left the clear impression that life would be much easier if you took it out first. I was already nervous about sliding underneath the car, freeing up a large, heavy mechanism more or less directly over my face, working it free from the car and lowering it gently to the floor without injuring myself. The prospect of removing the frame cross member in the same way only made me more apprehensive. Nevertheless, I set about removing the drive shaft by unbolting the universal joint at the differential pinion shaft, lowering the back end of the driveshaft and pulling it out of the tailpiece of the transmission. I detached the speedometer cable from the side of the transmission tailpiece, but my nerve failed and I left the cross member and the transmission itself in place.

Even though my uncle lent me a scissors jack to use in lowering the transmission, I never felt confident enough to attempt the task, and the 1952 Ford languished there in the garage. In the meantime, I became interested in other, fancier cars. Though I deeply appreciated my parents' decision to give me the real thing when I'd only asked for a model, and though I learned a great deal poking around in the Ford, boys and young men are not very pragmatic about cars. It's more a matter of the heart and the emotions.

In the spring of my eighth-grade year, I got a ride home from school with a classmate, whose parents drove a 1963 Cadillac Sedan De Ville. That was my first ride in a Cadillac. I remember being fascinated by the way the tail fin swept back down the length of the fender to end in a flicker of chrome and a ruby-red taillight. And I remember the feel of the elegant brocade upholstery fabric, and the seriousness and poise of the interior appointments. I was, in a word, impressed. After that, on the bike trips to explore the local new and used car lots that my brother and I would make, I started paying more attention to Cadillacs and other luxury makes. They had more toys to play with, like power door locks, windows, seats and mirrors—and they were really designed to make you feel rich just by getting in and sitting down. And occasionally a used limousine would show up at a dealership, and that was the height of exotic elegance (and an occasion to fantasize about being a government official or a captain of industry riding somewhere in style).

That same year was the first time I seriously considered owning, restoring and driving a *really* old car. On a Sunday morning in late 1965 or early 1966, I was riding my bicycle back home from Mass and I saw at the Shell station on the way a shiny tan 1940 Chevrolet Master Deluxe sedan, looking just like it must have when the new owner took it for a first drive. The whole car was lovingly renovated and it sported red-and-yellow 1940 New Mexico license plates that were as shiny as the car.

Until that morning, I had been sure I'd go looking for a late-model car when I got my driver's license and saved up enough money. I'd seen old jalopies driving around Albuquerque before—metal lasts nearly forever in the dry southwest. They were easy to dismiss as dilapidated, outdated and forgettable. But I hadn't seen what a car from the early 1940s had looked like in its full glory, when someone first bought it. Now I saw what the original buyer saw in the car.

Just to look at that Chevrolet was to take a trip to another age, when cars stood upright and people sat tall in them. You could almost believe that if you opened the door and climbed in you would be transported to 1940, when Albuquerque was a tiny, sleepy desert town where Route 66 crossed the Rio Grande, when life in general moved at a more deliberate pace.

I walked my bike around that car, taking in the details like the inviting wool upholstery, the gleaming whitewall tires and the sparkling chrome trim. I began to imagine what fun it must be to travel around in a vehicle unlike any made today, reminding everyone who saw you of a different time and place.

I never saw that '40 Chevrolet again. But if I would take another way home, there was a grey 1949 Cadillac sedan that lived in front of a house

I would pass. It must have been owned by the man or woman who first bought it. The only things outwardly wrong with it were that the merciless New Mexico sun had caused the red plastic taillight lenses to fade to whitish pink around the edges, and the ivory-colored gearshift handle had broken off, leaving a sad ring of plastic around the threaded end of the chrome selector shaft. In my youthful ignorance I wondered why the owner didn't just buy a new shifter handle. In its own way this car was evocative of different times and tastes. The tailfin design theme had begun for Cadillac the year before, and the fins on this car were mild. And compared to the more aggressive front ends on the Cadillacs that came before and followed after the 1948–1949 model years, this front end looked pushed-in and a little timid to me. But the car still had a distinct personality that would grab you if you let it, a purposeful streamlined styling statement, inspired by the World War II P-38 fighter plane.

Not long after that Sunday morning encounter at the Shell station, I would find and purchase an old car that would stay with me for decades. The moment was one of those points in life where not a great deal seems to be happening at the time, but from the perspective of years, it becomes clear that a threshold was crossed and things were not the same.

✦ ✦ ✦

Most of my knowledge of cars built before World War II had come from three sources. When I was 4 years old, my semi-invalid grandfather sat me on his knee while he cut the assorted old car pictures from a series of matchbook covers and glued them in neat rows for my enjoyment on a couple of the cardboard panels launderers used to fold shirts. I still have one of those panels. He had been a physicist who worked for the U.S. Bureau of Standards. He had been deeply involved in the development of no-knock gasoline, and had known personally many of the pioneers of the auto industry (including Walter Chrysler that I recall) and one of the Wright brothers. He himself had never learned to drive, ironically.

When I was five, my family moved to Albuquerque, and we traveled there by way of my other grandfather's house in Sarasota, Florida. On the way we visited a museum outside Tampa called Cars of Yesteryear. All I remember of it was that the wheels were all large with wood spokes or wire, which I found fascinating, and the colors of the cars were all bright and cheery. My father pointed the different makes out to us, and some of the names were familiar, but others—like Locomobile—were entertaining.

In 1962 we moved again, to Charleston, South Carolina. The movers took a long time to arrive with our furnishings, and four young boys were hard pressed to stay entertained and amused without their accustomed toys and games. As part of the effort to keep us from tearing the new house apart, my father would come home from work with little presents for us. For me there was a series of model car kits with metal parts that you used a file and a screwdriver to fit together. These were replicas of Model A Fords—a "tudor" sedan, a touring car ("phaeton") and a rumble seat coupe— with rubber tires and radiator hoses, detailed engines and interiors, and acetate plastic for the windows. Learning about rumble seats and staring at a car that started with a hand crank fascinated me. Later that year, my brother Phillip and I received for our birthdays similar model kits for a Packard roadster and a touring car, introducing us to the more luxurious veteran cars. I still have the instruction sheet with its capsule history of the Packard Motor Car Company.

My first inkling that V-16 Cadillacs even existed came some four years later from the side panel of the box that another model car came in. The Jo-Han company manufactured ⅟₂₅ scale plastic model car kits for hobby- ists (and assembled promotional models for car dealers to give to prospec- tive customers). I had bought their 1966 Cadillac Coupe DeVille kit while my family was vacationing in Washington, D.C., and on the long car trip back home, my bored eyes fell on the side of the box. There, the company featured two of its other offerings—replicas of two 1931 V-16 Cadillacs, a convertible coupe (cabriolet) and an open touring car (phaeton).

What fascinated me was not just that there was such a thing as a sixteen-cylinder automobile engine, but that 1931 Cadillacs (even from the little pictures on the side of the box) had been such majestic creations. I made up my mind to find out more. I had recently become interested in Cadillac cars, and my mother's cousin, who had worked for a LaSalle dealer in the 1930s, had tipped me off to the idea of writing to Cadillac's public relations office for information about the cars I was interested in. I had requested information from the company twice, now, once about recent (mid–1960s) Cadillac sales materials and the other time about the Series 75 limousines for various years. The public relations folks had sent back in response a generous pile of dealer brochures and press kits with glossy photos. Anticipating those manila envelopes with the red-edged mailing labels added a certain zest to the end of a given school day.

So when I first saw those little pictures of 1931 Cadillacs, I was sur- prised to see that Cadillacs had once sported imposing chrome radiator shells as impressive as any Packard or even Rolls Royce counterpart. And those great headlights flanked by clamshell fenders certainly cut a dis- tinguished figure. I made up my young mind to get myself those '31 V-16 models and to find out more about old Cadillacs. I wrote to Cadillac for information and pictures of the V-16 cars. I visited all of the local hobby stores looking for the models, but to no avail. Then on Christmas 1966, to my delight, I found under the tree the Jo-Han kits for the '31 phaeton and the cabriolet.

As car models go these kits were remarkably accurate and intricately detailed. The engines were finely crafted representations of the magnificently styled mechanical marvel Owen Nacker had designed. The suspension parts and undercarriage were painstakingly reproduced, and the front wheels and steering parts worked. Little design details from the door handles to the parking lights atop the fenders to the goddess on the radiator cap were all faithfully reproduced. I was happy as a clam putting those models together and I learned, as I worked, about how the real car was designed and constructed. Once the model was assembled, you could almost imagine opening the door and climbing in. I itched to see the actual automobiles.

During the summer of 1967, my family (now living in Albuquerque again) vacationed in the Los Angeles area. While we were there, I persuaded my father to take us to the Briggs Cunningham Automotive Museum in Costa Mesa. There I saw an amazing assortment of thorough-

Cadillac V-16 Model Kit. This is the box cover for one of the plastic model kits that first acquainted me with early 1930s Cadillacs generally, and with the V-16 cars in particular.

bred classic automobiles—Duesenberg, Bentley, Rolls, Mercer, Bugatti, the 1950 Cadillac that placed tenth at Le Mans, and a beautiful 1930 Cadillac V-16 roadster. I dutifully looked at the other cars, but I parked myself next to the V-16 for the rest of our visit, until my parents said that we had to leave. The car had one side of the hood propped open to show the gleaming porcelain, polished aluminum, enamel and chrome in the engine compartment. I peered in carefully to see as much as I could, obediently resisting the overwhelming temptation to touch. I didn't drool, I am proud to say. But I would have stayed there for a week if I had been allowed, studying each curve and detail, and trying to memorize that car. I remember a little bronze plate on the rear of the car indicating that the Inglis Uppercu Cadillac dealership in New Jersey had been the original point of sale. The color was a two-toned copper/bronze that went well with the leather upholstery. The chrome-framed wind wings that flanked the windshield had little chrome struts that attached to the doors, so that when the door was opened, the wind wing automatically moved out of the way. Two features of this particular car I later discovered were seldom found on V-16s. Wooden, so-called artillery wheels were officially the standard wheel for those cars, but in practice, the vast majority were ordered with wire wheels. And the single spare tire mounted on the rear of the car was another standard item, although most V-16s had two "side-mount" spare tires, mounted in wells in the front fenders.

Long after we returned from that California trip, I would replay in my mind the mental video of the '30 Cadillac, comparing what I'd seen with the details on the models. Meanwhile, the Cadillac Motor Car Company (they still preserved in their correspondence the polite fiction that they were not just another GM "division") sent me some beautiful factory pictures of V-16 automobiles, including the widely circulated shot of a 1931 dual cowl phaeton by the water. Soon the idea took hold that if I could find a neglected unrestored representative of this breed, I just might be able to buy it and get to work bringing it back to a drivable, presentable condition.

I bugged my father to take me to junkyards to snoop around. Back then it was still possible to find the occasional "diamond in the rough" in an auto graveyard, although most yard owners were getting pretty savvy about what they had. I haunted used car lots and pored over want ads in the newspaper and in car magazines, in the hope I'd find a V-16 that needed someone to restore and care for it. I brought the subject up with anyone who even looked like a car buff, all to no avail. The closest I got was a 1946 Cadillac coupe at a salvage yard west of Albuquerque, but the car was already spoken for—the yard personnel were stripping the old paint for the owner.

1930 Cadillac V-16 Roadster. This is the first V-16 Cadillac I saw in person. At the time it was displayed at the Briggs Cunningham Automotive Museum in Costa Mesa, California. The "stock" wooden wheels were rarely seen on V-16s, which were usually ordered with wire wheels and fender-mounted spare tires (courtesy CH Motorcars, LLC).

By the time I became interested in the V-16 Cadillacs, the prices had already started to move up. I had an afterschool job at a motel on old Route 66 and a bit of an income that I industriously funneled directly into a savings account at the bank across the street. But the likelihood that I'd save enough, quickly enough, to afford even a rough unrestored V-16 was clearly small, even to me. Nevertheless, I tried to enlist every resource I could tap for my quest to find one of these cars.

2. 1941 Cadillac Series 7523 Seven-Passenger Touring Sedan

First Appearance

At about the time I got my first driver's license, I met the car I have been leading up to. It would not be a V-16, as things turned out (it was a year too young in any event, as the V-16's last year was 1940) but it would more than make up for that shortcoming. I saw this particular 1941 Cadillac limousine in the fall of 1967, at a dirt-lot used car sales outfit that is now occupied by a bank branch. The car didn't catch my attention at first because it did not have the "V and Crest" badges I expected all Cadillacs to have. I dismissed it as a large sedan of another GM marque. My father said, "There's an old Cadillac" and I disagreed until we stopped and took a look. Apart from that roadster in California, it was the first pre-war Cadillac I ever remember seeing. This one belonged to the Series 75, Cadillac's limousine series from the late 1930s through the 1976 model year. Although it didn't have a glass window separating the driver's seat from the rear compartment (officially a "Series 7523 seven-passenger touring sedan"), for all intents and purposes it was a limousine and I would always refer to it as such.

The car was sitting apart from the rest of the autos on the lot, because it was on consignment and not part of the regular inventory. It was long, high and massive. The body panels and surfaces were streamlined without making the car appear bulbous. The proportions made sense, and each part seemed to belong harmoniously to the whole. The doors were hung in the manner that since became known as "continental" (front door hinged at the front edge, back door hinged at the back). And there were running boards, serious running boards, and not just decorative attachments. Each was nearly a foot wide, and ran from the front fender all the way back to the rear fender. This was a carriage you literally climbed into.

Outwardly, the car was quite presentable. It wore a set of 1947–48 "sombrero" hubcaps and somewhat elderly wide whitewall 8.20 × 15" tires. The paint was a uniform shiny black, and all of the chrome trim sparkled, with no evidence of rust or pitting. The rear bumper had a crack halfway through in the middle of its length, and one of the bumper guards was missing. But for a 26-year-old car, it looked pretty spiffy. In each of the rear quarter windows was a hand-lettered "For Sale" sign with the owner's phone number. I made a note of it and decided to call when I got home.

I opened the driver's door, sat down and fell in love. Manufacturers of modern SUVs brag about "command seating," the above-the-traffic vantage point that seems to appeal to so many drivers. This car had that, plus a long, tapered hood to look down with a little piece of sculpture at the end of a long chrome-plated center strip.

The interior had clearly suffered from time spent outdoors in Southwestern sunshine. The front seat was draped in a cloth seat cover, and the cover on the steering wheel hid the cracks in the plastic. The faux wood dashboard finish had faded, but the instruments were bright and sharp. The rear seat was still magnificent, even though there were several splits in the grey wool broadcloth. The jump seats were almost like new, having spent most of the years folded away. But the most impressive feature inside the car was the six-inch-wide band of solid wood extending across all of the doors, the back of the front seat, and the trim panels next to the back seat. These were ¾ inch thick boards tapered at the edges, in which the door handles and window cranks were mounted. And each of the windows was outlined by a wooden garnish molding, with the windshield surrounded by gleaming chrome.

When I looked at the instrument panel, there was an inconspicuous little button labeled "START." And there was a clutch pedal, so this was a Cadillac without an automatic transmission (a phenomenon I'd never encountered, excepting of course, that 1930 roadster in California). The original cigarette lighter was still in its socket, and the car had a radio. This must have been a magnificent carriage in its day!

The lot attendant was the one who introduced me to that Cadillac trick of making the hood ornament serve as the release for the hood latch. I had reached into every crevasse of the egg-crate grille and checked thoroughly for a lever under the dash before I went and asked. The hood was massive and cavernous. At first, I wondered if the springs would hold it up, but they proved quite adequate. The engine was clean, painted a dark blue. This was a flathead V-8, the same configuration as my 1952 Ford had

had, but half again as big. Fat black porcelain exhaust manifolds sat on top of the cylinder heads, and the air cleaner looked like two large black tin cans arranged perpendicularly, with a smaller can joined to the end of one of them. The battery hid deep in the bottom of the fender behind the right front wheel.

When I turned the key and pressed the start button, the engine *slowly* turned over—a-rrurrh—rrurrh—rrurrh—rrurrh—and then it caught. Then silence. The car was so quiet at idle, I thought that the engine had died and I tried to start it again (ouch!).

Bringing It Home

When I phoned the owner, I found a very friendly and voluble city policeman, who had bought the car, put in a rebuilt engine, given it a new paint job and loved it for a number of years. Now, with children and other family preoccupations, it was no longer practical to keep the car. He told me how it had sat in a field for years and about the little tool compartment inside the lip of the trunk. He wanted $600 for the car, and I had $702 in my savings account. He wouldn't budge on the price, and I guess he knew he had me hooked. There were a number of visits to the car on the lot while I weighed in my mind whether to go ahead and buy it.

As a newly licensed driver and eager to do things right, I asked to take the car to Galles Cadillac for a diagnostic workup before buying. My father drove the car there and the dealership's service department kept it over the weekend. I remember bicycling down on Sunday and peering in the service department door glass to see the dignified rear end and chrome-framed windows amid the contemporary silhouettes, and thinking how good it looked. Galles reported a number of things that needed attention (e.g., missing headlight trim rings and left rear bumper guard; bad muffler; rear engine main seal; broken rear spring leaves; minor body work). There was nothing deal busting, so I decided to go ahead. My mother drove me to the used car lot and I handed over the cash for the purchase price. After the paperwork was completed, the newly ex-owner, Officer Frank Zaccarias chauffeured me home in my new limousine.

Getting Acquainted

I began a process of getting to know the car, and at the same time, cleaning and refurbishing and exploring nooks and crannies. I would start the car and run the engine and operate the accessories. The vacuum-

The New Acquisition. Shortly after I bought the 1941 limousine, I took some pictures with my father's Polaroid camera. That's our neighbor's house in the background.

powered windshield wipers worked, but slowly and with a rhythmic whoosh-hiss seldom heard even in the 1960s, much less today. One of the fog lights worked (the other bulb was burned out). The heater was a pleasant surprise. It consisted of two units (with fans) under the driver's and passenger's sides of the front seat. How thoughtful to warm up the riders' feet first! Vents behind the front seat shared the warmed air with passengers in the back. I bought a new battery for the car, and learned quickly what "positive ground" means. The fellow who installed the battery wasn't paying attention, and he hooked it up the way most car makers (even by then) had settled upon. I was quite startled to see the ammeter work in reverse (strong *dis*charge when I stepped on the gas). And there was a requirement to repolarize the generator, once the battery had been hooked up the right way (that is, with the positive terminal connected to ground).

Sometimes I would just sit in the driver's seat and study the shapes and contours of the windows, doors, dash and upholstery. I cleaned all the glass and vacuumed out dust and dirt. I poked my head behind the dash

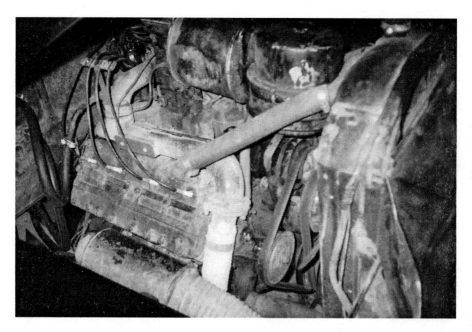

Engine of the 1941 Series 75. The 346 cubic inch flathead V-8 engine of my '41 limousine was rated at 150 horsepower. Unlike modern cars, each of the spark plugs can be seen and easily reached.

and into the hidden corners of the trunk. I investigated the back-seat glove boxes and map pockets, and I tried all of the interior lights and the various accessories. I hosed off the body of the car, washing the dirt out of the fender wells and other hiding places, and I applied a coat of polish and stood back to admire the beast. I took off the Cadillac badges and painted them carefully.

I wrote to Cadillac Motor Car Division, asking them what they could tell me about my car. The public affairs department wrote back that there were 405 Series 7523 cars built in 1941, but they could not tell me where or to whom the car was sold. They enclosed copies of official company photographs of the 1941 model line, as well as copies of pages from the 1941 service manual showing the specifications and the lubrication chart. There was also a suggestion that I write to the Cadillac-LaSalle Club regarding parts and technical assistance. I did join that Club, and it proved to be a wonderful source of parts and information (particularly the shared experiences of fellow restorers who wrote about what worked, what didn't work and what surprises popped up in the process. A picture of my car (together with a brief introduction I penned and submitted) appeared in the November-December 1968 issue of the Club's newsletter *The Self-Starter* (named in honor of Cadillac's history-making incorporation of an electric starter into its production autos in 1912).

Some of the most fascinating aspects of the car were the examples of pre-war optional equipment. The fog lights were operated by a little lighted plastic knob below the dash, and they spilled a pool of orange light on the street in front of the car. The bulbs are an unusual design with a unique pre-focused base (not readily available at the neighborhood parts store). The push-button radio was a source of delight—each button had a label beneath it with Chicago radio station call letters neatly printed there, giving strong evidence of the location where the car was sold new. When turned on, like all radios of that era, it took a while to "warm up." Then you could tune it to any station you desired (AM, of course!).

The cloth covering the seats had become fragile and brittle, but if you were careful, you could still sit in the back, put your feet on the carpeted footrest and look out across the open space between you and the front seat. The wide band of wood below the windows and across the back of the front seat (with a clock in the middle of the seatback), the wooden window moldings, and the brass and chrome door handles and cranks all spoke the language of elegance and quality construction. Each armrest of the back seat had a cigarette lighter, an ash tray and a map pocket, and just above, a door opened out of the wood trim panel to expose a cloth-lined glove box. There were mysterious slots in the front of the armrests that I later found out were meant to carry a notepad and a vanity set (missing from my car, sad to say).

My family insisted that I get new tires, so a trip to Bellas Hess produced a set of Dunlops with disappointingly narrow whitewalls (white stripes, maybe?). Then a visit to Galles for some of the service items they pointed out. The manager of the service department, Herb Klein, quickly became quite fond of the car, and whenever I brought it in to have something seen to, he was very helpful and pleasant. The folks in the parts department were proud to inform me that they had an actual 1941 Cadillac muffler for the car, which they installed. Sadly, though, the new muffler produced a deep chug-chug sound that hadn't been there with the old muffler (I had been seriously impressed at the silence of the car when running. As mentioned before, I had even tried to start it on the lot after it was already running, it was so amazingly quiet in operation. In truth, though, the idle had been set so slow that the ammeter showed a discharge). The rear spring and some of the other items fixed, I was ready to start working on hunting down parts and getting other repair work done.

I discovered that the limousine had originally been equipped with 16-inch wheels (while most of the 1941 model line used 15-inch wheels). My car was one of many, I later found out, that were converted to 15-inch

The 1941 Cadillac Series 75. I posed the car in front of our house in the Spring of 1968. The tires I bought shortly after I purchased the car place it very low to the ground. The late–40s "sombrero" hubcaps that came with the car have been replaced by correct 1941 wheel covers.

wheels in response to wartime tire shortages and the increasing subsequent scarcity of 16-inch tires. This change tended to aggravate the effects of an already low ground clearance. Many times before I owned the car (and not infrequently during my days with it) the underside of the running board on the passenger side scraped noisily on a curb as the driver parked the car just a little bit too close to the sidewalk. And the lower parts of the engine and the flywheel housing were quite vulnerable to roadway debris (or the road itself, if a wheel landed in a significant pothole).

As I indicated, ads placed in the newsletter of the Cadillac-LaSalle Club were a wonderful source of parts for my car. I obtained the correct color lens for one of the fog lights, a windshield washer bottle, a new speedometer cable, and a pristine set of fender skirts. Those fender skirts were a signature 1941 styling feature. Unlike later designs, the fenders of 1941 Cadillacs (except for the distinctive Fleetwood Sixty Special series) appeared finished and complete without fender skirts. The skirts simply covered the wheel opening and some of the surrounding fender surface, adding to the streamlining of the overall body design. Since two of the three attachment points were underneath the lower lip of the fender, the passenger-side fender skirt was susceptible to being knocked loose if the car was parked too close to the curb.

3. Please Don't
Call Them Junkyards

There were other resources for remedying the unavailability through the normal channel of many of the parts I needed. For instance, the local auto parts store could provide new spark plugs (the tips are amazingly small) and other tune-up parts, such as rotors, condensers and distributor caps. Hoses and tubing are stock commodities, easily available. But if I needed a rear bumper guard, the Cadillac dealer would tell me the company no longer stocked those parts. The retail auto parts stores didn't have them either, and there was no such thing as eBay. My choice was to place an ad in the club newsletter or *Hemmings Motor News* and wait for someone to answer. Or I could go hunting through the acres of salvage yards that still existed in the days before the EPA and "clunker legislation." That was an experience and an education no car buff should miss.

Those were the days when junk yards had yet to be attacked by the environmentalists. Some skirmishes had occurred between salvage yard and civic beautification advocates, but generally that only led to the insertion of slats in the chain link fences to conceal the car carcasses from the passing throng. The yellow pages in Albuquerque had plenty of entries for auto graveyards, and I sat down with the phone and a piece of paper. I asked each operator if they had any old Cadillacs in their inventory, and if any of them were 1941s, and if they'd sell parts off of the cars. Many outfits had nothing to offer, but I found a number of promising prospects. On North 2nd Street, General Auto Salvage had a 1946 hearse. Another yard had a 1941 Cadillac sedan. South Coors Wrecking had a couple of 1941s. Before long, I had a supply network and I had a pretty good idea what I could get and where it could be had.

Contrary to their seedy reputation, most of the enterprises derided as junkyards or automobile graveyards were organized, more or less carefully-managed enterprises. The staff knew what makes, models and years they had anywhere on the property and could tell you over the phone. Many had racks with orderly rows of sorted parts (generators in one place, doors in another, and so forth) labeled by the auto of origin. Most importantly, as far as I was concerned, most would let you remove the parts you needed and check your purchase out for you at the front desk like a trip to the grocery store. The prices were generally more than reasonable, because the big run-up in old car prices was still in the future, and to the yard owners, parts were parts and the source didn't much matter. And you never knew what interesting old vehicles you might see way back in some corner of the yard (once I saw the remains of a radar-operated military canon, now reduced to empty consoles and unhooked bundles of cables). And on another occasion I saw a completely disassembled 1923 Durant Star Phaeton spread out in the dried grass.

As a teenager with limited driving rights, the next step was to persuade my father to chauffeur me to one or more of the yards where old Cadillacs rested. God bless 'im, my father was a good sport (aided to some extent by his natural curiosity) and he obliged. Our trips were generally on Saturday afternoons (few yards were open on Sundays), and we'd load my toolbox into the trunk and head out. Most places would let you come into the yard and show you, more or less precisely, where the target car was. They'd let you remove the parts you wanted and then tell you how much they wanted when you brought the parts up to the counter on the way out. This was before insurance paranoia fed by liability lawsuits forced civilians out of the yards (and out of auto service bays at dealers and repair outfits, as well).

When we visited South Coors Wrecking, I got to meet the second and third 1941 Cadillacs I'd ever seen. Both had been set aside by the owner's son and were clearly objects of his affection. One was a Series 62 coupe. Cadillac made two coupes in 1941, the Series 61 fastback as its entry-level, low-cost leader, and the Series 62 which had "notchback" styling. The Series 62 was the standard line, the equivalent of the later DeVille. The coupe had a long gently tapered deck lid behind the rear window of the passenger compartment and its rakish and sporty look was a startling contrast to the stately formality of my Series 75 sedan. This example was a pretty good original car, retaining its apparently original color scheme, red above the belt line and cream below. And it had correct full-disk hubcaps (unlike the postwar hubcaps my Series 75 came to me with).

The other '41 was a Fleetwood 60 Special Sedan, the first I'd ever seen. This series was introduced in 1938 as a bold and innovative styling venture designed by Bill Mitchell (and to my mind, shamelessly copied by Edsel Ford and his boys when they produced the first Lincoln Continental). In the Cadillac product line, the 60 Special stood just under the Series 75 and 67 limousines, and above the Series 61, 62 and 63 lines. For 1941, the 60 Special had unique features not found on other Cadillacs: front fender extensions into the front doors, unique flush-fitting rear wheel fender skirts, doors with only thin chrome window frames above the belt line, and a distinctive elegant roof treatment. This particular black 60 Special was less well maintained than the 62 coupe, needing, among other things, repair to the wood in the front fender extensions.

The yard owner's son was unwilling to sell parts off these cars, offering to sell the entire car, instead. I was very interested in having a set of correct hubcaps for my car (and a gearshift knob, and some other items), but I was not looking for another vehicle. Moreover, I was afraid that any price offered by this fellow would be inflated in proportion to his personal attachment to his Cadillacs. He was, however, willing to sell a loose rear bumper guard, and I was quite willing to buy it and thank him for letting me examine his cars.

General Auto Salvage was located in a largely undeveloped area on the edge of Albuquerque, with an incapacitated Chrysler sedan from the 1940s for a roadside sign. Far back in the lot on the north side was a 1946 Cadillac hearse that had been repainted red and white for ambulance service before ending its career in the tumbleweeds and dust. The hood was gone along with the engine and transmission, but most of the rest of the vehicle was still there. What was left of the maroon velvet upholstery was faded and tattered. Beer cans inside the doors betrayed hints of how it spent its last days. Most of the big rubber rollers that were inset in the floor to help move caskets in and out were still there.

Over the course of several visits, I removed a nice selection of useful parts from this moribund beast—tail light lens, fog light bulb, light switch, vent window and frame, parking brake cable, windshield wiper motor. While I wasn't looking, my father removed some additional items on his own initiative—a chrome taillight fin, a small disk hubcap and a dash knob for a fresh air vent. Unfortunately, my dad didn't always understand the optimal way to remove parts (generally not done by breaking things off instead of unbolting, for example). Decades later, a friend who could drill and replace rivets was able to use the taillight fin, and I still have a nice distinctive and shiny dash knob that doesn't hook up to anything.

Then one day, I discovered that the '46 hearse was gone. When I asked about it, the yard employee told me that it had been cut up for scrap. In this it joined so many of the forgotten and exhausted products of the auto industry over the years.

I don't remember the name of the salvage yard that held a brown

Series 61 sedan, but that was another car I paid multiple calls on. Most of the engine was there, but without a hood. Once upon a time it had been a classy family conveyance, larger, faster and more solid than sedans from GM's other lines (or from most other makes). Now, anyone who saw it would be sure that it had parked for the last time. New Mexico sun and dust had baked and coated it, and it squatted complacently on the ground. Nevertheless, I set to work with my tools and removed various useful pieces. I remember in particular the stamped steel cover that forms the lower part of the bell housing that covers the engine flywheel and clutch. My father removed a rear seat ashtray. I never did figure out how he got the sliding plastic cover out of the metal housing without breaking either of them.

Four or five years after the last visit I made to the brown Series 61 sedan, I was leaving my parents' house, far on the other side of Albuquerque. As I turned onto Candelaria Boulevard, I was startled to see that very car driving up the hill from the other direction. It was still hoodless, but some very clever person had brought it back to life and was driving it up into the foothills of the Sandia mountains. I couldn't believe my eyes. But I knew that the days of browsing junkyards for cheap replacement parts were probably numbered.

On a couple of occasions I visited junkyards that held really noteworthy treasures. My father heard from one of his patients of a yard on Agua Fria Road in Santa Fe, and one day I persuaded him to take me there. It had several Cadillacs from 1941 and adjacent years, as well as Packards, Lincolns and various other highly interesting makes. Unfortunately, the yard owner had a very expansive view of the value of his holdings, and was not about to sell individual parts from his prize specimens.

By the mid–1970s, I had become pretty thoroughly distracted from automotive activities by the exigencies of college studies. But since I was still driving my '41 Cadillac daily, the urgent need for an out-of-production replacement part arose from time to time. Like the time I burned out the differential gears, or the time an axle shaft just sheared in two, or the time that a bearing failed in the steering gear box. A yard in Tijeras Canyon cut the rear end out of another 1946 hearse for me so I could replace the differential gears. I persuaded a machine shop in Albuquerque to modify one of the hearse's axle shafts to serve as a replacement for my limousine's broken counterpart. And my brother and I removed a steering bearing from a 1942 Cadillac sedan in a salvage yard on Atrisco Road, along with two very nice brake and clutch pedal pads. 1942 was a short model year, with the Cadillac factory switched over to war production in February. So I bought that car's distinctive round turn signal lenses as long as I was there.

That was the end of my adventures at the auto recyclers. My sense is that few 1941 Cadillacs remain in junk yards around the country, and those that exist are in the hands of folks who want to sell the entire car (or what's left of it) for top dollar. But for quite a while this resource was invaluable for folks like me, trying to keep an elderly auto on the road despite the auto industry's (however understandable) reluctance to stock a full range of replacement parts. Not only that, I got to see a lot of unrelated but very interesting cars I wouldn't have seen otherwise (like a disassembled 1923 Durant Star phaeton, or a matched pair of Buick Flxible [*sic*] Roadmaster hearses, or a KB Lincoln engine that had been rigged to run a sawmill). What I didn't fully appreciate at the time was the opportunity it provided to do something with my father.

Today there's eBay, and several entrepreneurs who have wondrously undertaken the not inconsiderable tasks of making used old Cadillac parts available commercially, refurbishing faded and dilapidated parts and selling them, and even remanufacturing precious needed parts. The most amazing parts show up for auction on eBay—no telling how much you'll pay or what you'll get, though. Years ago I used to despair at the thought of replacing the aged and hardened rubber parts: grommets around vent windows, pedal pads, door and trunk weatherstrip and so on. Now those things are a phone call away. One fellow rebuilds vacuum wiper motors. Another rebuilds vacuum radio antennae. Several firms recast old plastic parts like steering wheel rims. Cleaned and repainted badges, nametags and emblems are also available. Even fenders and other body parts can be had by calling a nationally-known vendor. The prices are generally higher than they were in the old do-it-yourself-shopping days, but things are much easier to find and obtain (even if, in a certain sense, the hunt was part of the fun).

4. Comings and Goings

Farewell to the Ford

The arrival of the Cadillac in our home completely distracted me from the 1952 Ford Mainline. Like a forsaken lover, it languished in the garage. My father noticed this and hatched an idea. He had as a patient the grown son of one of our old neighbors from when we first moved to Albuquerque, and he believed that this fellow and his wife could readily fix up and make good use of the car I no longer seemed to care for. So one Sunday morning, he helped Don Rood hitch a tow bar to the Ford and haul it away.

When next I saw it, the '52 Ford had been given a new transmission (well, a recycled one, retrieved from a salvage yard), and it was running fine as a daily driver. Don's wife even gave me a ride in it. For an experienced mechanic like Don, the transmission swap had been a piece of cake. I was impressed and a little disappointed that I'd given up so quickly. As it happened, I never saw that car again. Don and his wife divorced. She kept the Ford and left for parts unknown.

The Limousine Goes to School

Of course, I began telling my high school classmates about the amazing old Cadillac I'd just purchased. When my principal Father Eggert heard about it, he asked me to bring the car to school so he could see it. To my surprise he disclosed that he was a fancier of veteran autos, with a Model A Ford and a 1941 Ford sedan that I recall. I said that I'd really like to show him my limousine, but I was worried about parking it with the other students' cars in the main gravel parking lot, what with carelessly thrown-open doors and sprays of gravel from young men spinning their rear wheels. Without missing a beat, Fr. Eggert told me to park my car in the faculty and visitor spaces in front of the school.

So on the appointed day, my brother and I climbed into the limousine, I started the engine and we drove to school. When I parked the car, I felt like I was getting away with something outrageous. Father Eggert was enormously impressed with the old Cadillac and he promised to bring his 1941 Ford sedan for me to see. Throughout the day, I stole glances at the black beast that dwarfed all the faculty cars, and during lunch, I treated myself to a brief spell of reading in the back seat. I showed the car to some of my friends who displayed varying degrees of interest. That afternoon, I drove home very pleased with my car.

The next time I drove to school, I didn't use the VIP spaces, but I did trade on the precedent that had been established to the extent of parking in an auxiliary faculty parking lot that was removed from the maelstrom of the student lot. I continued to park there until I graduated, and when an uninformed teacher decided to reprimand me for parking where he believed I had no business, I persuaded the new principal to confirm officially the concession that Fr. Eggert had made to me.

Of course, the car was a conversation piece throughout my time in high school. One sunny afternoon, I took most of my third-year Latin class downtown to the Federal Court on a field trip that had been gloriously concocted on the strained logic that Cicero had been a lawyer by trade. And then there was the home movie that some of my classmates were making for one of their classes dealing with the "Roaring Twenties." Never mind the anachronism, my limousine was cast as the getaway vehicle for the St. Valentine's Day Massacre, and it played its part without a fuss.

A New Addition

About a year after I bought the limousine, my father showed me a classified ad in the local paper for a 1941 Cadillac coupe. Now, shopping for another 1941 Cadillac was not *the* farthest thing from my mind, but it certainly wasn't on my urgent "to-do" list, either. So, reluctant as I was to discourage any sign of parental interest in my admittedly extravagant hobby, I agreed we should go look at the car, and off we set.

The car in question was a 1941 Series 61 coupe. It was a new design for 1941 and the roofline swept from the windshield header all the way to the rear bumper in a long unbroken curve. An early example of the then-fashionable "fastback" style, it was the most popular choice in 1941, in addition to being the entry-level Cadillac that year. This was the car that Cadillac was extensively advertising at $1345, and at that price it was the reason why General Motors had ceased producing the LaSalle, Cadillac's

The 1941 Cadillac Series 61 Fastback Coupe. This car was what is currently known as an "entry-level luxury" car. It replaced the LaSalle, discontinued after the 1940 year.

lower-priced "companion car." With a Cadillac at nearly the same price, how could you find enough buyers for the less-prestigious LaSalle brand?

This particular Series 61 was unrestored but almost entirely complete (a rubber stoneguard was missing from a fender, the headlight switch was non-standard, and the dome light cover and cigar lighter were missing). The fact that the ID plate behind the hood of this car did not have a "D" after the series number meant that the car arrived at the dealer with a plain black three-spoke steering wheel and no fender skirts. Nevertheless, although it was the "bottom-of-the-line" model for 1941, it had the Hydramatic transmission that first showed up on the Cadillac options list that year.

The owner was a true eccentric named Eddy Horton. An organist by profession (I saw his name on the marquee at the local Holiday Inn once) he drove the car regularly. He had painted the body himself a type of pearlescent blue-grey, and he told proudly of pulling a boat trailer with the car on trips through the Colorado mountains. When my father took the car for a spin around the block, I was amazed at the way the early-model automatic transmission would shift gears. It was like the boost to the backside I received when my kindergarten teacher gave me a push on the playground swing. The engine had a fair amount of valve lifter noise, but it ran smoothly and had plenty of power.

Well, I thought it was all very interesting, both to see up close another variety of 1941 Cadillac, and to experience the difference between my car's standard transmission and the other car's Hydramatic. But for some reason, my father kept talking about the fastback coupe and speculating about ways I could afford the owner's $450 asking price. Although I remained somewhat puzzled, I let myself be persuaded that it would be a good idea to have a pair of 1941 Cadillacs. I sold my brother some silver coins I'd been buying out of the change drawer at my motel job (and saving as silver dimes and quarters and halves started to disappear from circulation). I emptied my savings account and I accepted my father's generous offer to loan me the rest of the price. We drove the car home and it became a part of the family.

Only years later did I come to understand why my father was so keen on my purchase of the '41 coupe. Before I was born, before my mother had met my father, she worked for the US Army mapmaking service in Washington, D.C. One afternoon, her father came to see her at her job and handed her the keys to a new 1949 Chevrolet Deluxe coupe. It was a beautiful white fastback, and my mother was delighted. Not long after that, my parents met and were married. Her white Chevy was the family car, since my father the earnest medical student was a pedestrian (or user of public transportation). When I was about two years old, my father forgot to put antifreeze in the Chevy's cooling system, and the engine froze. That was the end of what I knew as "the White Car," and I'm afraid my mother never let him forget that mistake. Many years later, when he saw a Cadillac in the forties fastback shape, he imagined we would get it fixed up and prettied, and my mother might identify it with that long-lost Chevy and he might somehow make up for that lapse in car care. But it quickly became apparent that my mother was no longer the robust twenty-something who thought nothing of wheeling around a full-sized car with manual steering, and this would not be a car she would eagerly drive. In fact she had become a confirmed believer in power steering, and was perfectly happy to watch others drive the pre-war Cadillacs that now graced our home.

Eddy Horton had included with the '41 fastback several cardboard boxes filled with parts. By the time I figured out what was there, I had a idea of the variety of cars he had owned. There were sun visor brackets for a 1941 Cadillac convertible, a complete taillight assembly for 1942–1947 Cadillacs, assorted thermostats, nuts and bolts, stray 1941 fender spears, and so on.

So, now I had two 1941 Cadillacs. A collection. A spare, in case the limousine was out of service for repairs. A less fancy car I could take places that might pose a risk for a shiny elaborate auto. A source of temporary spare parts while a starter or a fuel pump or whatever was sent away for rebuilding. And even more project material to keep me out of trouble in my spare time. (I quickly found out that surprisingly little of the exterior body or trim items were interchangeable from the limousine to the coupe. For example, the limousine's rear bumper is about 4 inches longer than the fastback's. I found that out after I had laboriously removed both!)

In later years the fastback had opportunities to distinguish itself. During the winter of 1971–1972 (while I was away at college), the overnight temperature in Albuquerque plunged to 8° below zero. The next morning, the only car in the family that would start (not the Dodge station wagon, not the Chevrolet Impala sedan, and not my Uncle's VW bug) was the 1941 fastback coupe. That tale was told and retold as long as my parents lived.

A Ghostly Apparition

One dark evening, my father picked me up from my job at the motel, and as we drove out the back entrance, we turned in front of a car that had two very wide round headlights placed next to an exposed, upright radiator with a pointed emblem midway between the headlights. Even in the instant I was able to see the front of this car, I was sure that I recognized it as a Cadillac from the early 1930s. I asked my father to follow it, but there was no way to turn around quickly enough and the car vanished in the night.

My rash conclusion that there were no early '30s Cadillacs left in the Albuquerque area had just been shattered. I told anyone who would listen that there was one right here in town. When I mentioned it to my boss, the manager of the De Anza Motor Lodge, he said "Oh, yes. That's Jack Hueter, an old friend of mine." I said I'd really like to get in touch with him and see the car. Secretly, I fantasized that there might be some way I could persuade him to sell it to me.

A few weeks after the brief encounter, I came from school to work, and there sitting in the covered drive in front of the office was a green 1932 Cadillac V-8 seven-passenger sedan. My jaw hit the pavement.

1932 Cadillac V-8 Sedan. This is the car I saw in the dark on that evening in 1968, when it was owned by Mr. Jack Hueter. This photograph was taken some 36 years later. Mr. Robert Maher acquired the car from Mr. Hueter and restored it. Mr. Maher's widow was kind enough to permit me to use the photograph.

I introduced myself to Mr. Hueter, and he graciously showed me the car, inside and out. I was like a kid in a candy shop. At that moment I thought that car was the most beautiful thing I'd ever seen. No, it wasn't a V-16, but it was tall, long, stately and elegant. The paint was shiny and spotless. Even in the shade, the chrome caught the New Mexico sun. The upholstery was a soft green broadcloth and the wood trim had a warm glow to it. I thought that having it to drive around in would be like going to heaven.

Mr. Hueter said that he'd restored the car himself. When I asked if he'd consider selling it, he laughed. "You can have the wife and kids, but not the '32!" That was a pretty definitive "No." Well, I'd just have to keep looking. But I decided to keep track of Jack Hueter, just in case he ever did decide to sell his Cadillac. As he drove off, I hoped I'd get to see the car from time to time.

As it happened, the next time I saw that 1932 sedan was in the Summer of 2003, when I saw it on eBay. Knowing what I knew, I suspected that Mr. Hueter had passed away and the car was being sold out of his estate. I contacted the seller and found out that some years ago (after I had left New Mexico) the car had been sold to Robert Maher (one of the first fellow old Cadillac enthusiasts I'd met after buying the limousine), whose family had gotten a great deal of enjoyment out of it. Now it was being sold out of Bob's estate, I sadly learned.

5. Some '41 Cadillac Adventures

A Star-Crossed Club Tour

The importance of proper maintenance (and certainly of knowing what constitutes proper maintenance) cannot be overlooked, no matter how old or new a car may be. Over the years, the number of things that the owner must keep track of and the frequency with which various maintenance functions must be performed, have been greatly reduced. Those of us who dare to keep and drive older cars must not be lulled into forgetfulness by the light maintenance requirements of our modern autos. Aging parts are more prone to leak lubricants, and older designs just required more frequent replenishment of grease, oil or other products. To let the lube schedule slide can be disastrous.

One Spring Saturday, the limousine and I rendezvoused with a group of fellow enthusiasts from the local Veteran Motor Car Club of America (VMCCA) chapter for an outing to some of the nearby retired mining towns. A picnic lunch was to be had in the old town of Galisteo, NM, and then everyone would drive home. The trip there was delightfully scenic and we must have given the passing motorists much entertainment. Our cars spanned at least four decades in a concentration of ancient iron not often seen on the road together. We enjoyed the winding mountain roads and the little ghostly mining towns that we drove through. Lunch was pleasant and refreshing. The bright idea that someone had for another Cadillac limousine owner and me to race our cars in a large fenced field was mercifully short-lived. It was on the trip back that I learned a valuable lesson.

The most expeditious way back home was not the way we had come, but a direct highway route. I pulled onto the road and drove back at a respectable clip. Traffic was very light and I enjoyed sailing down the road in the long shiny Cadillac. It wasn't until I was back in Albuquerque and nearing home that I realized that there was something very different about how my car was running. Whenever I was accelerating, there was an audible and distinctly out of place whining whir that hadn't been there before, rising in pitch as the speed increased. What's more, when I backed off on the gas pedal, as long as the engine and the drive train were spinning at the same speed (or if I disengaged the clutch) there was a metallic clattering sound from underneath the car that was jarringly incongruous with Cadillac ambiance. Uh-oh.

When I took the car to the Cadillac dealer's service department, and they put it on the hoist, with the engine running and the transmission in gear, the technician concluded right away that the differential gears had been worn badly enough to make these new noises (and to warrant replacement). The ring gear is riveted to a case that holds six intermeshed gears. The unit could not be repaired, only replaced, and needless to say, the replacement part was no longer available from the factory. Lesson: Don't go for an extended trip, involving travel at highway speeds, without checking all the lubricant levels (including the differential!). Needless to say, finding a replacement would require some shopping, asking around and even detective work. So I chatted with other old car enthusiasts, who consulted interchange manuals and parts books and yet other enthusiasts. The accepted wisdom seemed to be that if I could not find another limousine from which I could remove a usable set of differential gears, if I could find a hearse from the early-to mid–1940s, the chances were pretty good that the gears from that car would be an acceptable replacement for my noisy worn set.

As it turned out, I heard about a 1946 Cadillac hearse in a wrecking yard off of Route 66 (now Interstate 40) on the way through Tijeras Canyon from Albuquerque. I took a trip to the wrecking yard and verified that such a car was in fact there, and that it had an intact rear end. The owner offered to remove the rear end for me for a small additional charge if I would come back in a couple of days to pick it up. As it is no mean feat to hoist up the back of one of those cars and extract the heavy hunk of metal I was buying, I readily agreed. I returned with my brother and the parents' station wagon, and drove back to town with my prize. I brought the limousine and the hearse's rear end to my friendly service station mechanic, who swapped out the gear sets and left me with a much quieter car. Fortunately, as you will see, I saved the hearse axle shafts.

A Toot in Time

1941 Cadillacs are often inclined to speak out of turn. Bear with me a bit as I explain that statement. The standard steering wheel on a 1941

Cadillac was a simple three-spoke wheel made from black bakelite plastic. The horn button in the middle was a 3-inch bronze-colored plastic disk with a gold Cadillac crest. Buyers who wanted more ordered the deluxe wheel, with a cream-colored plastic rim and two wide flat chrome spokes. The same horn button graced the deluxe wheel as the standard unit. The tricky part of the deluxe wheel was the horn ring, a delicate chrome semicircle supported by three slender spokes. When the driver pressed the ring to sound the horn, the middle spoke took a great deal of twisting and bending stress. Invariably this caused it to break away from the ring, to dangle from the steering wheel hub and to provide an unpredictable intermittent activation of the horn.

Soon after I purchased my 1941 limousine with its deluxe steering wheel, I found out about the tendency for random horn blasts. It could happen almost any time—in the middle of a turn at an intersection—while driving down a quiet residential street—or at 2:00 in the morning when everyone, including the driver, was in pajamas in bed and sleeping. Always the remedy was the same, jiggle the horn ring and the noise would stop. Matters were aggravated by the clarity and volume of the horn. This was not a discreet Euro-beep such as most modern luxury cars emit. No, the limousine gave out with a two-note clarion trumpet call BLAAAARRP! that could continue until you did something or the battery ran down.

After putting up with the unruly horn tricks for some time, I just decided to do without the horn and disconnected it. I rationalized that, generally, by the time I decided to sound the horn it amounted to more of a comment after the fact on someone's driving, rather than a timely warning of impending danger. One morning I needed a safety inspection sticker, so I hooked the horn back up, drove to the gas station, got the inspection done and went to school (absent-mindedly leaving the horn connected). On the way home from the university that evening, I was driving north on a busy four-lane street with no median. It was heavy rush-hour traffic, and I was in the lane next to the double yellow line. I suddenly became aware that a driver on the other side of the double yellow line was veering over into my lane, setting up an imminent head-on collision (we were both doing 35 mph, so it would have been like hitting a wall at 70). Just as I understood the situation, and well before I could begin to react to it, the horn went off. Just a single short "beep!" and at just the right moment. The other driver lurched back into his lane, and I drove home with my jaw hanging open.

I never reached a firm conclusion about what actually happened that day. Did the car decide to preserve itself? Its driver? Or did my guardian angel decide to tap the horn button because it wasn't my time to go? All I know is that an accident that appeared inevitable didn't happen.

A Forbidden Intersection

Whenever I hear about the Bermuda Triangle or other supposedly paranormal places, I think of an intersection in Albuquerque, New Mexico (Indian School Road and Juan Tabo, N.E.). The last three times I drove the limousine through that intersection traveling north, a major breakage occurred. One time is happenstance. Two times is coincidence. But three times is a lesson—don't go this way again in this car!

The first time the limousine and I experienced this phenomenon, we started up after stopping for the light, and the clutch linkage snapped. At first, I didn't know what happened—only that the clutch pedal was back on the floor and the car was running in first gear. I was able to slip the shifter into neutral and pull over to the curb, and there was a piece of steel, pointing down from where the pedals do their business, that moved if I worked the clutch pedal. After a tow and a welding job by my favorite service station mechanic, we were back in business.

Some time after that incident, I found myself passing through the same intersection, only to become aware that one of my rear tires was rapidly going flat. Again I pulled over. I changed the tire, and when I brought the flat to my mechanic, he informed me that the tire was fine, but the wheel was split at the rim. He showed me a 3½ inch fissure in the steel to illustrate his point.

The third time this intersection caused trouble, the car just lost power and coasted to a stop. The transmission was in gear, the clutch was engaged and the engine was running. The engine would roar if I pressed the gas, but nothing I did would make the car move forward or backward. I got out of the car and looked underneath to see the driveshaft spinning merrily, a sight that is impossible if the car is in good working order. Well, I turned the engine off and called for another tow. It turned out that one of the axle shafts had sheared clean through. The one-inch diameter steel shaft had simply separated into two pieces, like a carrot sliced with a knife. This problem was a real "parts" problem. Even back in the mid–1970s, 1941 Cadillac axle shafts were not available through the local dealer, or from the local auto parts store. And because the limousine series had many parts that do not interchange with other 1941 Cadillacs, I would have to find either another 1941 Series 75 in a local wrecking yard, or someone somewhere who was selling parts from one, in order to get a replacement axle shaft that was the right length and construction. I might have to buy an entire "rear end" (the piece that contains the axle shafts and differential gears, and to which the rear brake mechanisms are bolted). So I began my search, already somewhat daunted.

Although I didn't think much of it at the time, I did have something that might be made to work. I still had the 1946 hearse rear axle housing and axle shafts that were left over when I replaced the limousine's differential gears. But when held next to the broken shaft from the limousine, the hearse axle shaft was noticeably longer and the tapered portion that fits into the brake drum was thicker. Oh, well. Better look around for the actual replacement part.

By way of short-cutting some of the suspense and tedium, let us just say that I couldn't find a limousine axle shaft. So I took the broken original and the 1946 hearse shaft to a machine shop recommended to me by several other car buffs whose judgment I trusted. They proceeded to recontour the tapered portion of the hearse shaft so that it mimicked that of the limousine. They remachined the spot where the grease seal has to fit and there it was—a usable replacement. Then it was off to my service station where the car was still up on the lift, and an anxious period of watching and praying while the mechanic inserted the jerry-built part. After the operation, only the presence of three large washers and a larger-diameter nut holding the brake drum on gives away the fact that everything isn't exactly original.

So after that final adventure, I never again drove the limousine through that intersection. I may be slow to learn, but once I've got the concept, I try to hold on to it.

6. 1931 Cadillac Series 355A Fleetwood Cabriolet

Before I bought the limousine, my dream had been to locate and acquire a Cadillac from the early 1930s, preferably a V-16, but the unlikely prospects of finding one that I could afford had become apparent even to me. Nevertheless, those thick chrome radiator shells holding up long hoods between graceful clamshell fenders and huge shiny headlights were hard to resist. I had decided that no such animal could be found in or near Albuquerque, New Mexico when a fellow passing through town proved me quite wrong.

I was driving the limousine to school and to work on a daily basis, and at work it would be parked in the front of the motel and clearly visible from Central Avenue, old US Route 66. Even with the I-40 freeway that bypassed the old highway, Central Avenue was still a "main drag" in Albuquerque and many travelers still used it. One evening a gentleman passing through from Gallup, New Mexico saw my limousine and stopped to chat. In the course of our conversation, he told me about a 1930 LaSalle roadster belonging to a farmer who lived just south of town. He told me that the farmer had told him he'd take $400 for it and he offered to take me to see the car. I jumped at the chance, and the next Saturday, off we went.

The car was located on a farm in Los Lunas that had an incredible collection of cars from the thirties and forties parked in long rows and covered with tarps. We were greeted by a three-legged dog who barked that much louder to make up for the missing limb. My guide introduced me to the farm's owner, Mr. Sam Blaylock, who invited us to look around as much as we liked. We walked up and down the rows like officers inspecting a regiment. There were Dodges, Chevrolets, Hudsons, Plymouths, Fords, and on and on. Nearly all of the makes represented were the workaday, mid- to lower-priced brands, but their remarkable state of completeness and preservation made each a point of interest. Trying to get a better look inside a 1933 Dodge, I managed to shake hands with a hornet who left a lasting impression.

The car I was there to see was the only really fancy vehicle, though. The 1930 LaSalle roadster I'd been told about, hiding demurely under a large olive-drab tarp, turned out to be a Cadillac Fleetwood convertible coupe ("cabriolet") with a V-8 engine (only an eight—rats!), a rumble seat and a golf bag compartment. The car had an uncommon rear-mounted spare tire, instead of the usual fender-mounted spares that one expects to see on these models. The car was almost entirely complete (even had the original crank! and the hub cap wrench) though the right fenders had been sloppily repaired following a fairly serious collision during the 1940s. I saw almost no rust at all (one of the benefits of Albuquerque's inhumanly dry climate), and I thought the car was absolutely beautiful.

Mr. Blaylock had bought the car used in the mid–1930s from the local Cadillac dealer, and he said the original owner had been a doctor. The car had been driven regularly until relatively recently, and even though it had not been started for some time he did not know any reason it couldn't be run. During the only period of time that the car had been garaged, chickens had nested in it and had destroyed the cloth upholstery on the seats and the convertible top. Fastened to the steering column was the dial unit for a Stewart-Warner radio (this was the first year Cadillacs were wired to accept radios). Mr. Blaylock told me about the accident. A 1940 Chrysler had run a stop sign and broad-sided the Cadillac on North Second Street in Albuquerque, damaging the passenger side fenders and running board. One of the Chrysler's headlights had wound up in the Cadillac's top well. The damage to the Cadillac had been coarsely hammered out to approximate the correct shape of the front and rear fenders, and the stainless steel trim piece along the outboard edge of the running board was now held in place with baling wire, an authentic period repair.

During the Second World War, when 18 inch tires were unavailable, Mr. Blaylock had hired a blacksmith to weld 20-inch truck rims onto the Cadillac's wire wheels so he could use truck tires. He had never removed the truck rims, even though they made balancing the wheels next to impossible. Mercifully, he had held onto the 18-inch locking rings for the wheels, and I was not going to have to look for a set of those. It looked as though someone who was handy with a cutting torch could remove the 20-inch rims, and clean out the grooves so that the locking rings could once again hold 18-inch tires on the wheels.

The original flying goddess radiator ornament had been stolen when car and owner had attended a local fiesta years ago. Since my friend had

last spoken with Mr. Blaylock, the price for the car had increased somewhat. Now, he wanted $1,000.

I quickly realized that I was smitten. Stopping at a restaurant on the
way back, I phoned my parents to tell them about this find. When I got
home, I began seriously to work on my father to get him to go look at the
car. I was sure he would be just as eager to have this classic in our garage
as I was, once he saw it. It took some doing, but I got him to drive out to
that farm. Sure enough, he was quite impressed. But I found him consid-
erably more hesitant about finding a way to purchase the car than I had
hoped. This was going to take a lot of work, but I was up for it and I set
about it in earnest. Of course, we did acquire the car, and the trip to pick
it up was a memorable expedition. My father's friend Don Rood brought
his Ford pickup and a sturdy towing rig. I drove my limousine with my
father and two of my brothers rounding out the company.

The weather was chilly but clear (later I would find out it was colder
than I thought). When we arrived, Sam Blaylock had uncovered the Cadil-

Posing for the Camera. My father Dr. Donald Cummings strikes a pensive pose on
the running board. The car's lines are still elegant on this, its undamaged side.

Rear Quarter View of the Cabriolet. The S-shaped landau iron that holds the top up has been put on upside-down. Note the 20-inch truck rims that have been spot-welded to the original 18-inch wire wheels.

lac and pulled it into position so we could hook up the tow vehicle. We had taken care of the paperwork the night before, so there was just the hook-up and removal left to do. Mr. Blaylock took one look at the limousine and asked my father what on earth I wanted his old Cadillac for. We took some photos, one or two posed with an enormous adjustable wrench Don had in his truck. Then we attached the tow rig to the Cadillac's bumper. I got into the driver's seat, and one of my brothers rode next to me. My father drove the limousine back with my other brother.

Our caravan set off on the journey back. Don Rood and his truck towed the Cadillac professionally and safely. I sat behind the wheel of the new prize, trying to make the most of the experience of looking down the hood as the car moved through traffic. The missing convertible top had been replaced, after a fashion, by a tarp tucked and tacked into the top bows and fittings. Against all of the laws of physics, the ancient, cracked tires held air and made the long trip back to our house without leaking or exploding. Ah! The looks we got! I exercised my imagination to the utmost, pretending that the windows and windshield were crystal clear, that the body and trim were glistening like new, that the big V-8 engine was purring

Hitched Up and Ready to Roll. The 1931 Cadillac cabriolet, rigged for towing, shows the damaged right fenders and running board. Sam Blaylock's three-legged dog can be seen standing to the far right of the photograph.

powerfully, and that I was driving the most beautiful classic car in Albuquerque.

By the time we got back to the house, my feet were almost numb from the cold, and I was glad to get warmed up. I spent the next few days cleaning the accumulated dust, nutshells, bug nests and so forth from the cabriolet, exploring and discovering with just as much enthusiasm as I had exercised when the limousine first arrived. Even after I got the car home, I wasn't certain whether it was a 1930 or a 1931. Ultimately, I determined that it was a 1931. When Cadillac introduced the V-16s in 1930, they used the styling cues and features that would not spread to the rest of the product line until the next year. So, 1930 and 1931 V-16s are indistinguishable, while 1930 and 1931 V-8s are noticeably different. The folks at Cadillac's public relations department helped me out by sending me photocopies from the 1930 sales brochure and production photographs from 1931. Unlike the 1930 models, 1931 V-8s had five hinged vent doors on each side of the hood (as my car did) instead of louvres. And where the 1930 V-8s had battery and toolbox doors in the valance panel between the doors and the running boards, the 1931 models had a plain valance. (The 1931 V-12s had a chrome spear and a courtesy light. The V-16s had the courtesy light and the doors.) For the 1931 V-8, the chrome mesh radiator stone guard was standard. By the time I had the difference straight in my mind, I had already purchased a new hood for a 1930 Fleetwood. I knew it was wrong for my car when I saw it had louvres instead of vent doors and the graceful curved bead line across the top panel characteristic of what became known as a "LeBaron hood." That piece is still in storage somewhere.

I became quite the topic of conversation with the local old car club chapter, and several of the members made a special trip to see this car. Some of them had heard about it but had never followed through on the leads. One would spend the next few years trying to find a car he could trade me for it. In my brashness, I began taking the car apart with the goal of a complete restoration. At the time (the end of the 1960s) it was still

Cleaned Off and Parked in the Driveway. The original top boot was still usable, at least for a pattern. Much of the original paint was still shiny, and only mild surface rust spotted the body parts. Very few trim pieces were missing.

The 1931 Cabriolet's Dashboard. All of the instruments were present and in good shape, including the Jaeger 8-day wind-up clock. Notice the dial unit for the Stewart-Warner radio, mounted on the steering column just in front of the wheel. Also note the original broadcloth door panel, unusual for an open car of this era.

possible for an individual of modest means to perform a pretty good restoration of one of the big classic-era cars. The prices of the things that you really can't do yourself as a practical matter (chrome plating, painting, upholstery) had not begun their mad upward spiral, and the old car price inflation that took place in the seventies and the eighties was still in the future.

Between paying my father back chunks of the money he had fronted to purchase the '31 (and the fastback) I would buy paint for some of the parts I was removing, cleaning and setting aside. I got the rear bumper sections and the hub cap for the spare tire chrome plated. I had my mechanic friend cut the 20-inch truck rim off the car's spare tire wheel just to make sure it could be done. And I did a lot of taking things apart and making sure that the nuts and bolts were properly segregated and labeled. I met a service technician at the local Cadillac dealer who had two brand-new sets of ignition points for the car in his tool box that he sold me for fifty cents, which he represented as the price that would have been

The Cabriolet's Engine. This view shows the 353 cu. in. V-8. The engine was entirely complete, including the intake muffler and the sheet-metal valley cover immediately behind it. The conduit for the spark plug wires is unusual for 1931. The wires are the old fashioned fabric-covered type.

charged when they were new. And I found and spoke to Mr. Boyd Ward, the elderly salesman at the dealership who had sold the car *new!* He remembered it and said that there were three doctors in Albuquerque in those days who would buy cars like this one, and he gave me the names. Subsequently, by contacting family members of Dr. Rice and Dr. Cornish, I was able to narrow the original owner down to Dr. William R. Lovelace. That's the man my father went to work for when we first moved to Albuquerque.

There were so many interesting details and touches on this car. There were three chrome-plated step pads leading to the crest of the right rear fender to assist the rumble seat passengers, and the rumble seat itself had little padded armrests and a foot rail for some added security in those days before anyone thought about seat belts. The fuel gauge was calibrated in gallons, with a warning not to expect great accuracy as the level got really low. The dashboard clock was an eight-day windup model that worked quite well. The oil level was monitored with a charming device. Attached to a cork float in the crankcase was a stiff wire that extended vertically out of a hole in the crankcase. Atop the end of the wire was a little red ball, next to which was a small rectangular plate. Levels were indicated on the metal plate, with "Full" at the top, "Fill" about midway down, and "MT" at the bottom. Check the oil at a glance!

The evidence of hand labor in the original assembly of the 1931 was very impressive. Each of the trim parts involved in the convertible top mechanism as well as the cowl vents and many other parts were stamped with the body serial number, as well as the style number. And this was the era when steel bodies still had a basic framework of hardwood, on which the metal panels were mounted and attached. The wood on this car's body was very well preserved, though the tack strip for the base of the convertible top needed to be reassembled. The number of parts that were missing was very small—one rumble seat step, an outside door handle, the radiator cap and ornament and the correct fuel filler cap. This was, in all, a very complete car for its age and history, and it was a fascinating machine to work on.

Still Stately After All the Years. The regal dignity of the radiator and headlights of a 1931 Cadillac V-8 remain, even after a long hard life outdoors. The lettering around the rim of the crossbar badge is the only place on the exterior of these cars where the name "Cadillac" appeared.

Beginning the New Project

When we brought the cabriolet home, I had every intention of completely restoring it. There was really too much serious work to do on this car to permit a cosmetic or "just-make-it-look-nice" restoration. On a car such as this, large portions of the frame are quite visible, and they must be cleaned and painted just as nicely as the body of the car. There was a substantial amount of required body work and chrome plating, and by the time you got involved in all of that, and the upholstery and carpeting, you would be doing quite a lot of disassembly work. After a certain point, it would just be much more efficient to take the entire automobile apart and rebuild it from the frame. The engine had not been run in a long time, but it turned over freely. The water jacket was full of rust scale, however, and there appeared to be some cracks in the jacket, though I never put water in the system to test it.

The mechanical brakes only worked on three of the four wheels. The activating shaft for the right front wheel hung limply from the frame, the universal joint connection to attach it to the wheel's backing plate having been broken years ago (perhaps a casualty of the collision with the 1940 Chrysler?). Cadillac didn't switch to hydraulic brakes until 1936. It and many other distinguished manufacturers were reluctant at first to abandon the direct physical connection between the pedal and the brake shoe in favor of the novel concept of pumping hydraulic fluid with the pedal through pipes and hoses to expansion devices in the wheels. Yes, Duesenberg had pioneered the use of hydraulic brakes in 1921. But by 1931 only eight other manufacturers had followed suit. The rest, including Cadillac, used systems of levers, rods and cables to transmit the motion of the brake pedal to the brake shoes at the wheels. Interestingly, some manufacturers introduced power assisted brakes (either by a vacuum assist or a servo device) before they switched from mechanical to hydraulic. The Cadillac V-16 and V-12 were both introduced with vacuum-assisted mechanical braking systems. When and if I got this 1931 Cadillac V-8 ready for the road, it would require a rebuilding of the brake-actuating mechanism for the right front wheel.

I started taking things off, one at a time, cleaning and painting and making sure that the proper nuts and bolts stayed with their respective parts. Pieces of the engine, the original tools, the battery box cover, and on and on were refurbished, wrapped in newspaper and safely stashed away. Each piston was surprisingly clean, with a single dollar-sized patch of carbon on the top surface. They were stashed together in a drawer. The service manual came in handy more than once. It let me know to expect a left-handed nut holding the drive gear for the water pump and generator. When I got to that part, I saw that some long-ago technician had dramatically gouged the nut with a chisel, trying enthusiastically to remove it by turning it in the wrong direction. It came off very easily for me when I turned it clockwise.

Soon the entire engine was apart. When I took the crankcase screen out, there were some interesting items resting on it, including a large dead centipede, a broken segment of an oil ring and a piece of aluminum alloy casting the origin of which I never figured out. And none of the pistons sported a broken oil ring to explain the piece I found on the screen. Before I took the crankshaft to have the bearing journals turned, it had a walk-on role in a local community theater production of *South Pacific*, as the sailors bustled about their wartime business.

When I began sanding the body parts, it became apparent that the car's forest green main color with pale green accents and pinstripes concealed an earlier paint scheme involving medium and light blue shades. I began to see the extent to which lead had been used to join body panels and to smooth out the contours of the car. The top had been a black leatherette material, a few shreds of which could still be found along the tack strip, and the chrome landau irons were fully functional and still looked sharp. With my interest monopolized by the '31 cabriolet, both of the 1941s took something of a back seat.

A Lucky Bet

My father had lent me part of the purchase price for the 1941 fastback, and the entire cost of the 1931 cabriolet. I started repaying those loans immediately from the money I was earning at the motel. As I moved through junior and senior years in high school, the question of college became more urgent. My first choice was the U.S. Air Force Academy. I don't know why he did it, but my father made a bet that I would not get an appointment to the Academy, and he wagered the remaining balance of what I'd borrowed to buy the cars. To his great surprise (and not a little, to my own surprise) I did get the appointment and for the next two years I was a cadet wearing Air Force Blue. I made the dean's list, became a rated military parachutist and survived the Air Force's survival, evasion, resistance and escape course (including its simulated P.O.W. camp). But there was a Major in charge of my little squadron of cadets, and I managed to get on his bad side. So before he could get me dismissed on his terms (and with a commitment to serve in the enlisted troops before continuing my college education) I left on my own. Three Cadillacs and my family welcomed me home.

Moving Day

In the summer of 1972, my parents' new house in the foothills of the Sandia Mountains was completed, and among the things we had to move from the old house was a partially disassembled 1931 Cadillac convertible. At this point the main section of the body was still mounted to the frame, and the wheels, drivetrain and suspension had not been disassembled. Most of the engine except the cast aluminum crankcase had been removed. But the fenders, engine, radiator and hood were all off of the car. I enlisted the help of a fellow VMCCA member (who still lusted for the car in hopes of using it as trading stock for a fine Rolls Royce or Bentley or such). On the appointed day, he showed up with his truck and a towing strap, and we rolled the chassis down the driveway and attached the strap. I sat in the driver's seat for the second time as the car rolled through Albuquerque streets, trying to imagine driving the car in a refurbished state. Almost halfway to the new house, I noticed an increase in the road noise and realized that the ancient and well-worn right front tire had given up and was no longer inflated. I signaled my friend, but there was nothing to do but proceed cautiously and hope for the best. By the time we arrived, the tire was quite sad to behold, but it was still there, and the car was no worse for the experience. With the help of a group of friends, we backed the car up a relatively steep driveway and into the new garage.

I continued to work on the '31, and the day my brother Phillip and I removed the engine crankcase from the chassis was an example of true fraternal cooperation. I had rigged a support for the clutch and transmission and another for the crankcase (crankshaft still attached) while I removed the engine mounting bolts. There was also a wooden cradle waiting for the crankcase. I looped some rope though the cylinder holes in the crankcase and around a couple of two-by-fours. Phillip and I each placed an end of the beam on a shoulder, slid the crankcase off its positioning studs and lifted out of the chassis. We positioned our load on its new cradle and congratulated ourselves on a job well done.

Second Sighting of a V-16

In the Summer of 1972, I opened the latest issue of *The Self-Starter*, and there was a classified ad that jumped right out at me. It was for a 1934

The Cabriolet in Pieces. This is one of the rare pictures I took during the restoration process. The cylinder blocks, heads, carburetors, manifolds and other parts have been removed from the engine, and the front fenders and hood can be seen in the background. The right front tire is shredded from its failure on the way to our new house, and the light switch can be seen dangling from the left-hand frame rail.

Cadillac V-16 convertible victoria, with an Albuquerque phone number. I knew that car was a magnificent vehicle and quite rare. (Cadillac only sold 41 V-16s in the 1934 model year, and a convertible victoria was not a common style in any year.) I simply had to see it, even if there was no way I could buy it. So I dialed the number, spoke with the seller and drove to his home.

The car had been sold, but the buyer had not yet picked it up. It was indeed a work of art and well worth the trip to see it, but Mr. Bob Friggens,

Robert Friggens's 1934 Cadillac V-16 Victoria. This is the car that brought about my acquaintance with Bob Friggens (the main character in a *Reader's Digest* article that had powerfully moved me years before). It is an extremely rare car. Only one was made in 1934 (courtesy Robert Friggens).

the seller, had other automotive treasures he cheerfully showed me. The one I remember was an SS-100 Jaguar, one of the first cars made after the Swallow Sidecar Company began producing automobiles and adopted the Jaguar name. I left with an authentic 1941 Cadillac porcelained tailpipe extension that Mr. Friggens had given me. It would be some thirty years before I would realize that Bob Friggens had been the young man about whom the *Reader's Digest* article I mentioned at the beginning of this tale was written. Just one of those funny things that happen in life.

The Cabriolet Departs

Not long after I finished law school, I got a phone call from a gentleman inquiring whether I was willing to sell the 1931. For some time now, I had been aware that there were some "big nut" items on the way to restoring this car that would be hard to get past. One was the bodywork. The front and rear fenders on the passenger side had been pretty roughly pounded out to approximate their original shape, following the accident the car had suffered in the 1940s. The running board also showed the effects of the crash, but not nearly so clearly, and there were some minor dings in the body from the same event. These body parts were *really* heavy gauge steel. Even by 1941, the auto companies had begun to use thinner sheet metal to save weight (also to benefit from improved metallurgy and stamping technology). To get the body work done properly I would have to find someone with the savvy and skill to work this tough stuff and to make it look like new. That would be a two-part task—finding the artist and paying what would surely be a not-inconsequential price.

Another hurdle was posed by the necessary paint job. One would be foolish indeed to take a premium classic auto such as a '31 Cadillac Fleetwood cabriolet to any old paint and body shop (let alone a discount enterprise!). These cars had (and are expected to have when shown) mirror-smooth finishes. Anyone who pays attention knows that these days the standard for automotive finishes (even on luxury cars) is significantly lower than that. There is a certain amount of ripply unevenness that is tacitly accepted, so long as the surface is shiny and the color is pretty. Moreover, the old classics were painted with lacquer paint, whereas enamel is now the rule in automotive painting. Getting a quality lacquer paint job today is both difficult and extremely expensive. As originally finished, this 1931 Cadillac sported a two-tone blue finish with decorative pinstriping. The chassis (at the very least, the visible parts) and the undersides of the fenders would have been included in the overall paint scheme. So even the amount of paint consumed in the process, and the time involved in getting into tight places would have been greater than for a more modern car.

Then there was the upholstery. The craft of automotive upholstery as practiced before the advent of plastics is to a great extent a lost art. It requires access to quality material in widths for which there is little market nowadays. It requires skill with an industrial sewing machine and the ability to fit and assemble the padding and covers in the same elegant fashion as the factory effected years ago. It is basically fine furniture upholstery performed in tight quarters, and it is not cheap. There is a well-known company in North Carolina that upholsters classic automobiles and advertises in the major collector publications. They told me recently that they typically charge $12,000 to $15,000 to replace the upholstery in a limousine. The 1931 cabriolet had cloth upholstery in the passenger compartment (fairly unusual for open cars of that time), and leather upholstery for the rumble seat. One could either go with leather all around, or stick with the original scheme. In any event, it would not be inexpensive. (Moreover, leather is purchased by the hide, and there is a lot of unusable scrap left with each hide.) Of course, the convertible top and its protective boot are a separate expense related to upholstery and requiring care and quality.

Not the least of the hills to be surmounted would be chrome plating. As a New Mexico car, the '31 had almost no pitting to speak of on the major chrome parts (there was some minor pitting on pot metal detail parts and some surface rust in places on the top mechanism, but nothing significant). But, of course, for a worthy restoration of this type of car, the chrome must be "like new." And there was a lot of it, from those bumpers to the massive radiator shell and screen, glorious headlights, windshield and window frames, door handles, and so forth. Although the effects of the EPA's heavy hand had yet to be seen, the price of chrome was already being pushed up dramatically by economic boycotts of South Africa and what was then known as Rhodesia. (In later years, environmental concerns about the by-products of metal plating operations of all sorts would bring a great deal of extinction pressure on the American tradition of flashy chrome trim.)

With all of that as a backdrop, I heard from a fellow that he would like to know what I wanted for the '31 Cadillac. Without really researching the issue, I named a price that was seven times what I had paid for the car, not really thinking I would be taken up. As it happened my offer was accepted right away. In a few days, this fellow had shown up with an enclosed trailer and winch and a cashier's check. He winched the chassis up into the trailer and stacked all of the fenders, engine parts, hood, accessories, trim, nuts, bolts, jack, crank and the rest inside the trailer and drove off. I admit that I had some "seller's remorse" over the next few weeks, but I had to recognize that the process of properly restoring one of those beasts had changed (from when I bought the car to the time I sold it) into a rich man's hobby. What was once possible to accomplish on a limited budget was quite simply beyond the means of most people.

As a postscript to this parting, some years later, my father was watching on cable TV a vintage car auction being held in California when he saw a fully restored 1931 Cadillac Fleetwood cabriolet, billed as having been sold originally to an Albuquerque doctor, put on the block. As the auction progressed, all of the bidders dropped out except for two men, one of whom my father recognized as a member of a well-to-do Albuquerque family. These two conducted a bidding war until the price reached twelve times what I had sold the car for.

7. The '41s, Neglected and Recovered

Body Work and Paint for the Limousine

With money in the bank from the sale of the '31, I decided to do something about the limousine's finish. The paint job I had paid for several years earlier had been a terrific disappointment. The shop had underbid the job and when I held them to their estimate, they retaliated by skimping mercilessly on the amount of paint they used. Their workmanship left something to be desired, as well. By this point, the paint was peeling alarmingly in several places.

A new coat of black paint was in order, at the very least. And as long as that was being done, there were some minor bodywork items to attend to (such as the welting that frequently fills the seam between the fenders and the body on older car bodies). My parents' neighbor had a body shop downtown, and he had approached me (and my parents) on several occasions to tell me what a wonderful improvement I'd see in the car's appearance if I would take it to his shop and let him use a wonderful new paint he had. So once again I turned the limousine over to the tender mercies of a body shop and hoped for the best.

When I heard that the car was ready to be picked up, I asked my brother Mark for a ride down to the shop. An old family friend, Monsignor Albert Chavez, was visiting Mark and he came along for the ride. The limousine was gloriously shiny, especially so since I had asked the body shop to have the bumpers chromed as part of the deal. The rear bumper was no longer split, and the car really did look nice.

I paid for the work, and Msgr. Chavez and I got into the car. When I started the engine and drove off, I heard a familiar but ominous sound. The way the engine sits in the frame of the limousine, the lower part of the engine (and particularly the flywheel and the metal cover that protects it) is exposed and vulnerable. This vulnerability is amplified in the case of

58

my car by a previous owner's switch from 16-inch to 15-inch wheels. If the car is driven on severely rutted roads, or if it is driven off a curb, it is very easy to bring the underside of the engine into contact with the street or the curb or some other hard, unforgiving object. It quickly became apparent that the body shop folks had either miscalculated when approaching a driveway, or had done something else to cause the flywheel housing to be smashed into the spinning flywheel itself. The gear teeth on the rim of the flywheel were now making contact from time to time with the edges of the hole that the flywheel had dug in the collapsed housing, and that was the source of the noise I was hearing. I shrugged my shoulders and continued on my way, certain that I'd be better off getting the problem fixed myself than trying to get a body shop to perform a mechanical repair.

But that was not to be the only difficulty we encountered on this trip. I noticed with some alarm that the oil pressure was plunging whenever I braked the car. Once I stopped and blipped the accelerator it would come back up, so I was pretty sure I knew what was wrong. Once years ago I had run over a rock that dented the oil pan, adversely affecting the oil pump's ability to draw oil from the pan and send it into the moving parts of the engine. The remedy was to have the pan removed and hammered out to its correct shape. The body shop people must have really high-centered the car in a big way, to get both the flywheel housing and the oil pan. Well, that second realization added to my disappointment, which now threatened to overshadow completely the pleasure of seeing the car painted and new-looking. So I drove the rest of the way home praying that the oil pump would succeed in its efforts to keep the engine properly lubricated. In retrospect, it was a very good thing to have had a man of God in the car with me for that trip.

For a very long time I didn't get around to tackling the repairs I now knew would be required. I brought the limousine home from the body shop, parked it and didn't drive it again for almost twenty-five years. (Only then did I find out that I had driven the half-hour trip from the body shop to my parents' house with no brake lights, another piece of mischief worked by the body shop folks.)

The Long Sleep

In August 1978 I took a trip to New York City to try my hand at making a living in show business. My principal interest was in classical dance, but over the course of my stay in New York, I stage managed an off-off-Broadway show, sang with the St. Patrick's Cathedral Choir and the Paulist

Choristers, and once with the New York Philharmonic, and I took thousands of dance classes and performed with several regional ballet companies. I even had some walk-on roles as an extra or "supernumerary" at the Metropolitan Opera. I only planned to spend a year or so in New York, but time passed and life stayed interesting, and I met a lovely lady and married her. All the while, I let myself get pulled deeper and deeper into the legal profession, ultimately taking the New York Bar examination and working as an associate attorney in a 90-lawyer firm in the Chrysler Building.

So here is the embarrassing disclosure section. I never did for either of the 1941 Cadillacs the things a careful car enthusiast is supposed to do to put a car in storage. I never thought I would be away as long as I was, and on the occasional brief trips I would make back to Albuquerque, there was not enough time (and prudent reflection) to organize a remedial mothballing process for one or both of the cars.

Shortly after I decamped for New York, my parents moved to a different house in Albuquerque. In my absence they towed the Cadillacs to the new house, placing the limousine in the garage and parking the fastback in the driveway. These would be their parking places for the next 25 years or so. The limousine would be protected from the weather (more or less, given a garage roof that leaked a bit for many years). But the poor fastback sat in the shade of a mulberry tree, counting on the generally dry climate to preserve it.

At various times I responded to stirrings of the old car enthusiasm. Something always seemed to get in the way, though. In the early 1980s, I answered an ad offering reproductions of the red plastic decorative inserts meant to grace the chrome taillight fins of 1941 Cadillacs (the originals invariably faded and crumbled over the years). I sent in my check and no matter how many letters the seller and I exchanged, I never received my taillight inserts. That was discouraging. In 1985 I sent one of the steering wheels off to be recast. The plastic that Cadillac used for the deluxe 1941 steering wheel inevitably shrank and cracked when exposed to sunlight. I have seen a very few original deluxe steering wheels on very well kept '41s that didn't look bad, but none of them seem to have survived in genuine mint condition. When the wheel came back, although it was seamless and nicely molded, the color was appreciably darker than I expected, despite the merchant's insistence that it was true to the original hue. That disappointment was enough to curb my little flash of renewed enthusiasm for car restoration, though I had ordered a catalogue from a company that reproduces all of the rubber parts (weatherstripping, wiring grommets, etc.) that an old Cadillac needs to be truly drivable.

One day in the mid–80s I encountered an old Cadillac very much like mine, still working for a living. I lived in the mid–50s on the west side of Manhattan, and on the weekend there were a number of places I'd walk to. Often I would cut through the parking garage under Lincoln Center to get between Broadway and Amsterdam Avenue. As I was doing so on a Saturday afternoon, I spotted a 1948 Cadillac series 75 limousine parked just inside the garage entrance. Behind the wheel sat a venerable gentleman in a dark suit and peaked cap—just the outfit you'd expect a chauffeur to wear.

The 75 series cars for the years 1941 through 1949 used the same body. Only a few styling details distinguished each model year's cars from the others, visually—size and number of chrome bars in the grille, decorations on the sides of hood and fenders, running board trim, badges and hubcaps. The profile and basic look of Cadillac's high-end cars remained the same for those years, with no real change until 1950. This car in the Lincoln Center parking deck was a very close relation to the '41 I'd left behind in Albuquerque.

Of course, I stopped to chat with the driver. He told me that the car belonged to two elderly sisters who lived on Park Avenue. They liked to attend the matinee performances of the Metropolitan Opera. They would ask him to bring the car around and off they'd go. This man had been driving the car since it was new, and he'd done a wonderful job of maintaining it. The black lacquer finish and the tan wool upholstery were as lovely as the day the car was delivered. The driver was happy to let me lift the hood and admire the clean flathead V-8. We shared tales of our experiences keeping those old Cadillacs running. I think he had switched to an 8-volt battery, one of the remedies that people have tried over the years when starting difficulties were encountered. (In fairness, when the electrical components are in good order, the wiring and connections are sound, and the engine is tuned, flathead Cadillac engines start quite dependably, hot or cold.)

I saw that '48 limousine again on a couple of occasions, but I didn't get another chance to speak with the driver. It was fun to see a car like mine still honestly employed in the role it was built for.

Around 1990, I actually called the one mechanic in Albuquerque whom I knew I could trust to work on a 1941 Cadillac engine. I was going to spend some of the savings that the legal profession had permitted me to accumulate to have him rejuvenate the engine of the fastback, since that was the noisy one up to the time I stopped driving the cars. My father urged me to save my money for the family expenses he was sure were soon to face me. I deferred to his judgment and the fastback slept on.

In January 1993 our daughter Emilyann was born and in 1994, I took a job with the federal government and my wife Barbara, Emilyann and I moved from New York to the Washington, D.C. area. In 1996 we built a house in Manassas, Virginia, where we live today. Through all this time, the 1941 Cadillacs slept patiently at my parents' house. Occasionally a passerby would ask my father how much he wanted for the fastback, but it was usually an impoverished would-be hot rodder or low-rider, hoping for a bargain on a unique old clunker to work on. My mother passed away in 1998 and I began to think seriously about selling the cars.

The Fork in the Road

At the end of the year 2000, my father died and I was left with the job of distributing the assets of my parents' estate. Owing to misguided efforts to minimize insurance costs, and just plain sloppiness, the '41 Cadillacs were still titled in my parents' names. Not only that, when they moved to their final home, they'd filed away the titles to the cars so carefully that I didn't find them until a year after I'd gone and paid the New Mexico DMV to issue new titles. Over the years, I had finally come to the decision to sell the cars and to kick the old car hobby cold turkey. I had convinced myself that project cars were space, time and money hogs that would be an enormous imposition on our life here in Virginia. The cars would have to be garaged or at least covered, or they would rapidly rust away in the humid East Coast climate. The amount of money that could be spent on them was potentially limitless, and with an acre of property to take care of, who has time for afternoons and evenings in the garage wrestling with the innards of one (let alone two) ancient mechanical contraptions? It seemed only logical and prudent to let the cars go to someone with the resources to do them justice. Then some interesting things happened.

On September 15, 2001, I took Barbara and Emilyann out in our family car to pick up a friend of Emilyann's and bring her back to our house to play. As I turned onto Dumfries Road, the car I saw in my rear view mirror caught my eye, with its pre-war General Motors shape. I slowed a little to let it get closer and it started to dawn on me that it *just might* be a Cadillac. And as the distance between us shrank, it became clear that it was a 1941 Cadillac that I had behind me. I kept stealing glances in the mirror at the (very shiny and new-looking) car, which I was beginning to decide was a Fleetwood Sixty Special Sedan.

Barbara suggested I watch and see where the driver turned off and follow him. Sure enough, just past the Prince William county fair grounds, the Cadillac turned into a parking lot, and I did the same. I got out and introduced myself, and the owner and I had a delightful time, looking at his car and talking about 1941 Cadillacs. (My wife and daughter drove off to get my daughter's friend, planning to pick me up on the return leg.) He told me his name was Carl Pohler and he lived in nearby Springfield, Virginia. I told him about my high school cars, then dormant in my parents' garage in New Mexico, and my decision to sell them, now that my parents had passed away and their house would have to be sold. My new friend was aghast. "No! You can't sell them. Bring them out here!" he said.

He told me that he was looking for the fair grounds, where the Bull Run chapter of the Antique Automobile Club of America was having a show that day. He said that another 1941 owner (whose car was a convertible) would also likely be in attendance, and he graciously invited me to come. Unfortunately, our family's day was already planned, and I couldn't break away to attend the show. But after the shiny black Sixty Special drove off and as I waited for my wife to pick me up, a green 1941 Cadillac convertible breezed down Dumfries Road from the other direction, heading for the show. Two 1941 Cadillacs in one day were two more than I'd seen since I'd moved to the D.C. area 8 years ago.

Because my '41 Cadillacs were left in my parents' names, they had to be valued as part of the inventory of the estate assets. So my uncle contacted Bill Sullivan, the president of the Albuquerque chapter of the VMCCA and asked him to come out and look at the cars. Mr. Sullivan examined the cars, and told me that, being a "fellow Cadillac lover," he was quite impressed with both of them. He wasn't able to turn the fastback's engine over by hand, but in spite of its exposure to the weather, it was very complete with little rust. He was most impressed by the limousine, and thought that it would not take much to get it running again. Though the upholstery needed replacement, he said the interior wood trim was in excellent shape and he marveled at the preservation of all the small interior parts unique to the limousine series. He said that if he'd had room, he would have made me an offer for the cars.

Bill Sullivan turned out to be a wonderfully enthusiastic and friendly fellow, in addition to really knowing his way around old automobiles. He gave me useful value estimates for both of the cars and said wonderful things about them. More significantly, he joined the growing chorus of voices telling me not to sell the cars. (My daughter looked at me with saucer-sized eyes and said "You have a LIMO!?!?!") Bill told me how wonderful he thought these specimens of the 1941 model year were. He liked the fastback better than the limousine for its rakish styling, even though the limousine was the fancier of the two (and potentially the more valuable).

I was still trying to hold to my decision to sell when my family and I traveled to Albuquerque to work on organizing the personal property for distribution and the house for selling. At one point I opened the garage door and when Barbara looked at the limousine sitting under a coat of dust, she said "You CAN'T sell that car!" Well, that did set me back a bit. At least I could sell the fastback, couldn't I? So I called Bill Sullivan and asked him how I would go about preparing the limousine for shipment to Virginia. We discussed it and he recommended trying to get the engine running, if only to make it easier to get the car on and off a trailer and into my garage at home. He estimated how much it would take and he steered me to Larry Bergstrom, a local old car enthusiast who also ran a car shipping business. In the meantime, Bill would put the fastback on the market and take a commission when it sold. There in the driveway of my parents' house, we struck a deal and I believed that at last I had settled the matter.

Then Barbara talked me out of selling the '41 fastback. Now I really felt mind-boggled. I was going to have to clean out the garage and I was going to have to figure out ways to get all of my chores and work done expeditiously enough to permit time to work on these temperamental beasts, once they arrived. And then there was that scary thought—Do they still make garages big enough to hold a car the size of a 1941 Cadillac limousine? I did not know the answer to that question, but it turned out that the limousine is 2½ inches short of the entire length of the garage!

After Barbara and I returned to Virginia, I called Carl Pohler to tell him the news, and he was delighted. He gave me names and phone numbers for a number of fellow old Cadillac enthusiasts in the area, including Harry Scott, a fellow living very close to my house who had a six-car(!) garage with a service pit (for working under a car without having to crawl about on your back). He also told me about the cancer for which he was being treated. I regret I didn't have a chance to show the 1941s to Carl or to get to know him better, because he passed away shortly after they made their way to my home.

8. Getting the Limousine Running

Brought Back to Life

Bill Sullivan set to work with real determination. The internal parts of the engine moved freely, so there was no need to figure out how to free up a stuck engine. The recipe of fuel, spark and compression should produce a running engine with the right encouragement.

On November 28, after a long afternoon of frustration, Bill and my uncle David were able to start the limousine. The spark plugs, points, distributor cap and rotor had been replaced, but the engine refused repeated attempts to get it to run. Bill thought that the compression was just too low to get it going, though the engine would fire feebly now and then. It was one of those "Let's try just one more thing" occasions. Bill injected oil into each of the cylinders to help the rings seal against the cylinder walls, and he jumped the starter from a twelve-volt battery. Finally, the engine caught and ran, and after that, Bill was able to start it again from its own six-volt battery. According to Bill, the engine sounded quite good. That the engine was running again after 25 years was completely astonishing to me, not because I doubted that Bill was a capable mechanic, but because I had become so accustomed to thinking of it as a non-running car.

The next day Bill and my uncle topped up the anti-freeze (1 gallon low, not bad for 25 years) and ran the engine for about an hour. It sounded very good and stayed cool. Oil pressure was well over 30 psi and very steady. The generator worked properly and charged well.

Bill initially ran the engine with new gasoline from a separate can, as the car's fuel tank had never been drained and gasoline does not age well over the decades. Bill hooked up the fuel pump and took a sample from the tank. He told me it looked pretty good, though quite red (from the lead, he suggested). Bill and my uncle found that the engine would run satisfactorily on the fuel in the tank, so they reconnected all the fuel lines

In the Sunshine Again. The limousine and the fastback pose on the driveway of my parents' home before leaving for Virginia. The limousine had been garaged since 1978 (but not dusted or washed!). The fastback had waited patiently in the New Mexico sun.

and decided to add a few gallons of new fuel to the tank because Bill felt uncomfortable feeding the engine that 25-year-old gas.

The next agenda item was to restore the car's ability to stop. Bill had planned to bleed the brakes and make sure that the system would hold pressure without leaking, but things did not go as planned. The master cylinder outlet was plugged and it simply would not pump brake fluid. Bill and my uncle even applied vacuum at the wheel cylinders, but with no success. So Bill removed the master cylinder (an ugly job, by his account) and he ordered a rebuild kit for it (amazingly still available from a local NAPA store).

As it turned out, the master cylinder piston was thoroughly stuck. Bill was able to drive it out at his workbench, rebuild the master cylinder with new parts and replace it in its snug little nest in the chassis. After struggling with the brakes for a couple of days (including freeing and cleaning each of the wheel cylinders) the dynamic duo managed to get them working respectably.

Finally, the car was ready for a test drive. On the 8th of December, Bill and my uncle started the car, climbed in and drove around the block. Bill reported that they really did enjoy their limousine ride, especially after having spent some frustrating hours wondering if it would ever run at all. It was an incredible concept to me, after all the years, that the limousine was once again in "running condition."

The Trip East

Bill had recommended that I work with Larry Bergstrom to take care of transporting the '41 Cadillacs from Albuquerque to my home in Virginia. Larry was another Albuquerque VMCCA member. When I called Larry to discuss the arrangements, he told me that he had owned a num-

Leaving Albuquerque. The limousine climbs the ramp onto the tow vehicle under its own power. My late parents' house in the background had been its home since 1979 (courtesy Bill Sullivan).

"Don't Forget Me." The fastback waits to be pushed onto the tow vehicle to join the limousine for the long trip to Virginia (courtesy Bill Sullivan).

ber of old cars, including a 1939 Buick sedan that he drove in his own livery service, using it for weddings, proms and other special occasions. With some surprise, I recalled having spoken to him at an air show in Albuquerque in the summer of 1989, where he had set up a table next to his Buick, handing out fliers promoting his limousine service. This realization was quite reassuring—I would be entrusting my cars to someone who understood that these were not junkyard derelicts he would be hauling. We agreed on a very reasonable price, and I sat back to wait.

Barbara suggested that I persuade Bill to work his amazing magic on the fastback, but he was not able to get that revival underway before the time came to hoist the cars onto Larry's trailer. At the last minute, there was an unexpected glitch. After all the work Bill and my uncle had done on the limousine's brakes, when they prepared to load the car onto the trailer, the brakes were gone! The master cylinder was empty, but there was no easily visible leak. Bill filled the master cylinder and did a quick job of bleeding the brakes. He was reasonably sure that I'd have brakes when I took the car off of the trailer in Virginia, but I'd have to figure out why the system was losing fluid before I could do any significant amount of driving.

The vagaries of Larry's business meant that the cars would not arrive until after New Years Day, so I had some waiting and anticipating to do. When the day came that Larry called to ask for final directions, I really wasn't sure what to expect. The feeling was not unlike waiting to greet a friend with whom you hadn't spoken in years, after an awkward or uncertain parting. I talked Paul Bjarnason, a fellow car buff from the office, into showing up to lend a hand with ushering the beasts into their new stable.

Arrival

On the afternoon of the third of January, 2002, a mild and sunny day, there it was. A three-car trailer fully laden with a Volkswagen beetle and two 1941 Cadillacs. I looked at the rig and shuddered to think what it must be like pulling that load through mountain passes and crosswinds and the myriad nutty drivers one encounters on the road. While we began unloading the cars, neighbors began dutifully gawking. The limousine was the first off the trailer, and when Larry couldn't budge the gear shift lever, I knew just what to do—I unlatched the hood and returned the shift linkage arm to the proper position, just as I had when the car occasionally got its linkage hung up decades ago. It took some assistance from my friend Paul Bjarnason working the choke, but I got the car started and drove it up our (150-foot) driveway and into the garage. Barbara helped me inch it right up to the wall, and to our great relief, the car fit! There was even a smidgen of room left over (about 2½ inches). I ran the engine for a while just to give the generator a chance to charge the battery, and incidentally to give me a chance to listen to the deep roar when I pushed the accelerator, and to fully absorb the fact that I had a running, working 1941 Cadillac limousine again.

The next task was to get the fastback up the driveway. The nonworking engine and the slight incline of the driveway meant that some concerted effort would be required to coax the almost 4000 pound car to the garage. Getting it past the slight lip at the entrance to the garage would be another challenge, but first things first. The car's service brakes had not been restored, and the hand brake was only feebly effective. The vehicle could be immobilized pretty securely though, by putting the automatic transmission in reverse gear. Once we got the fastback off of the trailer, Barbara got in to steer and Paul and I got ready to push. Larry couldn't give us much help due to a pulled muscle. We got the car moving and soon found we had a unique way to get a really good aerobic workout! The driveway seemed interminable, but we did get to the garage, and we actually

Top: The '41 Cadillacs Arrive. Paul Bjarnason and I look on while the fastback is freed from its restraints. *Bottom:* Home Again. The '41 limousine after I drove it up the driveway and into the garage. In the lower right of the picture is the hood ornament of the fastback.

Waiting at the Threshold. The fastback before we convinced it to roll past the slight lip at the edge of the garage floor.

got the front wheels over the lip. That was as far as we got though, and we decided that would have to do for now.

I paid and thanked Larry, and he went off to deliver his remaining cargo. A couple of neighbors and Harry Scott came by to examine the new arrivals. I just kept looking at the limousine and the fastback, marveling that they were both here. The next day, a promised rain began, and I watched with anxiety as the drops began to hit the bare-metal spots where the fastback's paint had receded. I recruited a neighbor and Barbara (God bless her!) and we finally got the fastback into the garage and closed the door.

The next weekend after the cars arrived, I went out into the garage to start the limousine, but it would not cooperate. That was odd, because the car had taken only minor coaxing to start when we removed it from the trailer and again few nights later. But now it wouldn't start at all. It wouldn't even try to catch. No tentative cough or momentary speed-up in the starter's drone. Nothing. I tried holding the accelerator to the floor for a timed minute (the old remedy for a flooded engine). I tried changing the choke plate angle. I tried spraying starter fluid down the carburetor throat. Nothing made the slightest difference. Now worried *and* frustrated, I phoned Bill Sullivan in Albuquerque. He was hugely sympathetic and supportive (having been through this experience many times) and he offered a range of helpful suggestions, including the fall-back option of using a twelve-volt battery to jump the engine (always a bit chancy, as the '41's electrical system isn't designed for it). I went back out to the garage and kept trying to start the car the standard way, but still to no avail.

All this spinning of the starter motor was beginning to drain the battery. After a while, it was clear that continued cranking would be pointless, as there might not be enough current to run the starter and fire the cylinders simultaneously. The question now arose where I was going to take the battery to get it recharged, or how I was going to get the front end of the limousine (now deep in the corner of the garage) close enough to another car to stretch jumper cables between the batteries. Things were getting very complicated (and discouraging!) very quickly. But with characteristic efficient thinking, Bill suggested I get a trickle charger that I could hook up to the battery overnight. Then I wouldn't have to worry about finding 30-foot jumper cables or backing the limousine out by hand and positioning it for a jump-start. Meanwhile, Barbara reminded me that this whole project was supposed to be fun!

I found a battery charger that would actually accommodate a 6-volt battery (many don't). Relieved, now that running down the battery had been rendered an inconvenience instead of a calamity, I could proceed with getting this car to start.

I asked Emilyann to sit in the driver's seat and push the starter button while I held the end of one of the spark plug wires near the engine cylinder head. There should have been a nice blue spark jumping between the wire and the engine, but there was nothing. Aha, Dr. Watson! The problem is probably electrical! So, even though the engine compartment had smelled of fresh gasoline, how much gas I gave the engine when I was trying to start it was not important. The answer would be somewhere in the ignition circuit. The battery is connected securely or the starter wouldn't be turning. Check the coil wire to the distributor and the spark plug wires, too. Check the other smaller wires from the coil to the side of the distributor. A loose connection? Maybe we're on to something! Let's look inside the distributor. (It was at this point that I went to two local auto parts stores looking for a set of small wrenches, such as were once packaged as "ignition wrenches" and intended precisely for what I was now doing. I was told "Not many people work in distributors anymore." Yep. Cars have changed.)

Now, make sure the wire from the breaker points is solidly connected. What's that? Another questionable connection? Good going! Make sure that the breaker points are opening to the right gap and make sure that the little condenser is securely in place. Now put everything back together.

Before I tried to crank the engine again, I took the spark plugs out and by pulling on the belts, I turned the engine through a couple of revolutions just to ventilate the cylinders in case the engine really was flooded. As it turned, I noticed that a loose plug wire sparked against the cylinder head. Eureka! There's hope. Sure enough, this time the engine fired up and ran happily. Oh, those little wires and nuts and connections. As my wife pointed out to me, each time I run into difficulties, I learn more about the inner workings of the car and how things play off of each other.

Getting Down to Work

The cars had arrived with a ready-made collection of projects, large and small, that could keep me busy for hours (not to mention the tasks that would have to be farmed out to businesses that specialize in upholstery, paint, body work, and so on). Bill Sullivan had advised me that several things would need to be done before the limousine could be driven regularly. When he revived the brakes, he replaced the rubber parts in the rear wheel brake cylinders with new parts. He wasn't sure which of two possible sizes to order for the front wheels, so he simply cleaned and put back the existing parts. The rubber dust covers, however, were dried out and crumbling, so it would be good for me to replace those parts sooner rather than later. And there was that mysterious brake fluid leak that had taken Bill by surprise the day the cars were shipped. Maybe that would sort itself out when I rebuilt the front brake cylinders?

Speaking of rubber, the various hoses in the engine cooling system and the heater and defroster circuit would need replacement. I had replaced the radiator hoses in my youth, but the hoses to and from the heater and the defroster pre-date my ownership of the car and a break or leak in one of them would not fairly come as a surprise. Although the fanbelt and the belt that runs the generator and the water pump seemed healthy, their replacement due to age alone would be prudent.

At some point the antique wiring was going to have to be replaced with a new wiring harness. The yards of wire that form the car's "nervous system" are by modern standards a marvel of simplicity, but the wrapped bundles are threaded through some pretty close quarters, and both the rubber insulation and the woven wrapping had become quite brittle with age. There were places where bare wire was exposed, raising the ugly prospect of short circuits or even fire. Bill strongly recommended disconnecting the battery whenever the car would be left alone. A new wiring harness would not be hard to obtain, as several companies manufacture them with mod-

Top: Washed Up. The hubcaps have been replaced and the grime of the cross-country trip washed off. The old elegance begins to show through. *Bottom:* Rear Quarter View. The car's lines are particularly pleasing and elegant from this angle.

ern insulation material and a very believable reproduction of the woven covering originally used. But the price is substantial (the main harness costs about $800) and the process of installing it is tedious and tricky, requiring one to work in fairly tight spaces and make dozens of connections correctly. In the meantime, electrical tape would be very useful and I determined to heed Bill's advice about unhooking the battery.

Another priority would be to figure out why only the instrument panel lights worked. No headlights, turn signals, brake lights, fog lights—nothing. Even during the day, relying on old-fashioned hand signals would be enormously chancy. The windshield wipers would be a worthy project at some point. I had all but given up on the vacuum-powered mechanism back in my younger days. Fortunately, precipitation of any form was relatively infrequent in Albuquerque, and I had gotten to be pretty good at peering around the raindrops on the windshield when caught on the road by an unexpected downpour.

One item, while not a critical safety factor, nevertheless generated annoyance and distraction. The speedometer had developed a nasty growling vibration that had already shaken the tip off of the indicator needle (which lay wedged between the instrument face and the glass). The cable would not be difficult to lubricate, but if the problem were in the instrument itself, removing and dissecting it would be a bother, not least because it would involve snaking one's hand and a screwdriver through the wiring behind the dash and trying to avoid causing mischief in the process.

As I examined the limousine, I became aware of more things that needed attention. The first time I opened the hood when the cars arrived, I noticed that the chrome-plated casting on the front lip was precariously loose, held on by only one or two of its attaching screws. As I had time to look further, there were more and more misplaced or missing screws, nuts and fasteners. My friends at the body shop had dutifully removed the chrome trim from the car before spraying the paint on, but they hadn't really kept track of which fasteners went with which piece of trim. So when they went to put the car back together, they could only guess how things were supposed to go. As it happened, they got it partly right, but there was a fair amount of remedial work required (and quite a few extra nuts and bolts left in the trunk and lurking in places like the battery box).

The Lights

Why all of the exterior lights would be non-functional was a real puzzler. But when I looked carefully, I found that they were all disconnected from the wiring harness. The good old body shop folks had disconnected and removed the lights before painting, but when they put them back, the wires were never reconnected. Ah, progress! So one by one I hooked the lights back up. The headlights required the additional step of replacing a broken lamp and a burnt-out mate. The front parking/turn signal lamps required work to reestablish a good electrical ground, replacement of the missing wingnuts that held them in place, as well as cleaning paint over-spray from the contacts and taping the exposed wires where brittle insulation had fallen off. The taillights had three connectors each (tail, signal and brake) that had to be sorted out without benefit of the once-clear, but now faded color coding on the insulation. How nice to pull the light switch knob out and have the correct lights shine obediently!

Harry Scott had advised me that after a car is repainted, it's not at all uncommon for some of the lights to lose their grounding connection to the chassis. This information came in handy a number of times during the struggle to get the lights to work, especially while I was agonizing over the front turn signals and parking lights. I had a photocopy of the car's wiring diagram, and with each restored circuit I would trace that part of the diagram with a yellow highlighter, just for the positive reinforcement that the activity provided.

The Brakes

Going to work on the brakes meant really getting my hands dirty, literally and figuratively, for the first time since the cars had arrived. In the old days I had never pulled off a brake drum, always leaving that to the mechanic at the service station or the technician at the Cadillac dealership. Certain jobs had always intimidated me, and that was true about going into the brake system. Whether it was not trusting myself to put it back together correctly, or whether I just thought it was too difficult to get right, I'm not sure. In any event, I had lots of incentive now. There was an identified need pointed out by Bill to replace the dust covers (and preferably the rubber cups as well) for the front brake cylinders, and there was also concern about the recurring loss of brake fluid. That the two might be the same problem offered the enticing proposition that one procedure might remedy everything.

Before starting the job, I sent Bill an e-mail message in which I laid out in step-by-step fashion the operation of removing the wheel, bearing, brake drum, brake shoe retainers and springs, loosening the brake cylinder, removing and replacing the rubber parts, and reassembling the whole structure. When he replied that I had written a set of instructions worthy of a good technical manual, I felt sufficiently confident to go ahead.

I started with the right front wheel in the corner of the garage. This would be the first try-out of my new floor jack, a luxury I had desired but never had in the days I was driving the car around regularly. The way this big car is sprung, lifting it high enough with a bumper jack to pull a wheel off the ground (especially one of the rear wheels) results in a very precarious arrangement. The jack is nearly at the top of its range, and a 5,000-pound auto is in a terribly ungainly position. Even on level ground it's not a safe way to work. Moreover, in the rear, the spring is so long that it can flip its shackle if the weight of the car is removed from it. The manufacturer was not unaware of this situation, but their solution was eccentric, to put a nice face on things. The jack that came with the car was designed to hook under the lip of the wheel rim. That's right, the thin, sometimes dented flange where the wheel meets the tire. It was supposed to lift the car by that narrow strip of metal, after which the owner was supposed to place a thoughtfully-supplied jack stand underneath the front suspension arm or the rear spring, depending on which end of the car was being raised. The car was to be lowered onto the jack stand and the flat tire replaced or what have you. When the repairs were done, the car would be jacked up again as before, the jack stand removed, and the car lowered back to the ground. It is a mark of how ill-considered this idea was that very few original 1941 Cadillac jacks are to be found still with the cars they came in. A floor jack (especially with a jack stand as a backup) is the perfect solution. It lifts the car just enough, without risking spring dislocation or a disastrous collapse. And this compact model I bought shortly after the cars arrived was just what the doctor ordered.

The tire came off, followed by the cotter pin and nut securing the outer wheel bearing. A tug on the brake drum and it came off, exposing the mechanism. Bill had recommended not actually removing the brake shoes, and that was excellent advice, saving significant work. I simply removed the return springs so they were loose enough to pull the cylinder out and work on it. With a small gush of spilled fluid, I removed the metal pistons that Bill had freed up back in Albuquerque, and the rubber cups that allow the fluid to push the pistons (and thereby the brake shoes to stop the car) without letting the fluid escape past the pistons. The local parts store had readily furnished me with repair kits for these cylinders (the NAPA part number was "15"), and I quickly swapped the new parts for the old and reassembled the cylinder, adding the new dust covers with some chassis grease inside to prevent moisture from getting in. Everything went back together pretty smoothly, and I enlisted the aid of my daughter to push the brake pedal while I bled the air out of the line to that wheel.

I repeated the operation on the driver's side front wheel and this time Barbara helped me with the line-bleeding. Now for the moment of truth. I asked Barbara to push the pedal and hold it down, hoping fervently that it would give firm and steady resistance. Instead, she reported that it sank slowly as she pushed it. Though the replacement of the front wheel brake parts had been a necessary thing, it did not turn out to be the solution to the leakage problem. I looked under the car for a tell-tale puddle of brake fluid, hoping that I could find a leak and then decide how to fix it. But there was no unambiguous evidence. Several of the wheels had stains on the inside surfaces, but that could easily have come from the spillage that inevitably results when the wheel cylinders are opened to replace the cups, springs and dust caps. There was some puddling where the engine was dripping oil, and where I'd spilled some brake fluid topping up the master cylinder for the line-bleeding procedure.

I took a chance that one puddle under the front suspension arm was not coolant from the water pump, but was in fact brake fluid that had dripped from the rubber hose segment that connects the wheel cylinder to the metal brake line (permitting the wheels to steer and the suspension to work without breaking the brake line). I replaced the flexible hoses on both sides (again the part was available at the local parts store). Once again I bled the lines, hoping that the system would now hold fluid and keep the pedal firm. But the problem persisted.

The only remaining possibilities I could think of to explain the loss of fluid were a leaking master brake cylinder or a problem with the mysterious vacuum-operated brake booster that had been installed on the car as an after-market option (perhaps by the dealer who sold it new in Chicago). I leaned away from the master cylinder option, because Bill Sullivan had removed and rebuilt this item, and if it were sufficiently unserviceable to permit this kind of fluid leakage after a conscientious rebuild, he would not have reinstalled it with any confidence. Moreover, if the bore of the master cylinder were pitted (and that was the most likely reason it could be leaking) I would expect the freed fluid to come out the back end where the pushrod from the pedal enters. But the little rubber boot that covered that end of the master cylinder had nothing but air inside, and no evidence of noticeable fluid flow.

The vacuum brake booster was an early form of power brakes, using the sucking force generated by the engine to augment the pressure of the driver's foot on the pedal. Unlike modern power brake systems, where the unit helps the driver actually push the pedal, this system increased the hydraulic pressure and helped push the brake fluid though the lines. The device itself is tucked up in the angled crook between two frame rails. A thick vacuum hose runs from the engine past the steering column and under the driver's feet to the booster unit. And when the brakes are applied, the brake fluid passes from the master cylinder through the booster unit and into the lines that go to the wheels. If there were a leak inside the booster unit, it could easily fill with brake fluid without leaving any evidence. When the car was still in Albuquerque, Bill Sullivan had recommended taking the booster out of the braking system, as the car stopped quite adequately and manageably without it. He simply didn't get around to performing the necessary surgery. I was coming to the conclusion that it was worth doing, if only to see if that cleared up the leak mystery (and made the car safe to drive!).

Silencing the Speedometer

Back in high school, one of the challenges the car threw at me was a speedometer vibration that started as an occasional buzz on cold mornings. Sometimes a firm tap on the face of the speedometer would eliminate the noise, but only until the next time it started up. The problem progressed to involve more frequent occurrences, more noise, and increasingly wild gyrations of the speedometer needle. Eventually the speedometer needle would fling itself at the maximum limit of its range with enough force to break off the tip and then the counterweight. The "firm tap" technique became ineffective and only resulted in a broken glass cover. At the time I had taken the speedometer out and tried to lubricate it (probably with WD-40). I'd sent away for a used speedometer for the glass and the needle. The repaired instrument worked fine for a while, but soon enough the noise came back, together with the destructive side effects (except for the broken glass!). This time, I reassembled the needle (gluing a wire behind to hold the parts in place) and I left the cable unhooked for years.

By the time the car was parked for its long hibernation, I had reattached the speedometer cable, so one of the first things Bill Sullivan noticed when he and my uncle took the limousine for its first round-the-block spin was an impressive grinding noise from the speedometer. After all the years, and with the winter temperatures, it was not surprising to me that this noise was back. When I got the car back, the tip of the speedometer needle was lying sadly at the bottom of the circular dial. When I took Barbara and Emilyann for a first ride in the car, the noise was quite obnoxious. One Saturday afternoon I took out the speedometer cable, wiped it and squirted some powdered graphite down its housing. When I replaced the cable and took the car out to see if that had solved the problem, not only was the noise still there, but the rest of the needle shook itself free of the shaft and joined the tip at the bottom of the dial. There was no way around the removal and disassembly of the instrument itself.

The 1941 Cadillac dash has a large squarish chrome radio grille in the center, flanked by two six-inch chrome rings encircling a speedometer on the driver's side and a clock on the passenger's side. The speedometer is held in place by a circular bracket that presses against the dashboard from behind. To free it from this bracket, one must unscrew three nuts from behind the dash. That means snaking one's hand (together with a nut driver or socket wrench) around the ignition switch and starter button wiring, the bracket and lever for the cowl vent, the wires to the instrument panel lights and the turn signal and headlight indicator lights, and the hose for the defroster. Oh, yes, I know how vastly more intricate and cramped the space behind the dash of a modern car is. But this is still a small space, and the wires are fragile (what with the brittleness of the aged insulation). I got the three nuts off (without losing them) and I detached the speedometer cable from the instrument. Then I pulled the instrument out from the dash far enough to remove the four lamp sockets that attach to it. I unhooked the cable for the trip reset knob and took the speedometer out of the car.

Dissecting the speedometer was a trip down memory lane, complete with the difficulties posed by the odometer and trip odometer number dials and the little plates and gears that let them advance as the preceding dial passes from 9 to 10. When I had the instrument in pieces on the kitchen counter, I pieced the needle back together and put a drop of Duco cement at the break with the optimistic hope that it would hold as long as I stopped the mad vibration.

Now that I had it apart again, I was reminded that the shaft (approx. ¼ inch in diameter and 2" long) that the cable turns is permanently mounted in place, with a press-fit ring binding it in its tube. Spinning the shaft while applying various pulling and pushing forces produced the same vibrating that translated (when the instrument was mounted in the car) into that familiar yet hideous growling grinding sound. There is no lube fitting or easy way to get a lubricating powder or fluid unambiguously inserted between the shaft and the wall of the tube it turns in. (There is a brass plug about midway down the length of the tube that might permit a generous application of grease or whatever, but that would involve a drilling and reproduction adventure that I didn't feel up to.) So I did my best to work some motor oil into the seemingly inaccessible reaches of that little shaft and housing, and I spread some lithium grease around the spot where the shaft emerges into the heart of the instrument. Then the shaft turned freely and no longer produced that vibration when I twirled it, so I put some lithium grease on the worm gears in the odometer drive system, cleaned the odometer number discs and the speedometer face and glass, and put everything back together. I put the instrument back in the car. (The greased parts are sufficiently isolated from the face of the speedometer so that I didn't anticipate any unsightly stains.) The next time I took the car for a spin, it looked as though I'd succeeded at silencing the dashboard monster!

The only kicker, at this point, was that in removing and replacing the speedometer, I seemed to have disturbed the ground connection for the light that illuminates the little strip of four instruments (temperature, oil pressure, fuel and ammeter) that extends from the speedometer to the side edge of the dashboard. Isn't it always that way? You go to fix something and wind up knocking something else out of whack. I think that must be one of the secondary corollaries to Murphy's Law.

Murphy's Law, Did You Say?

When I set out to take the limousine around the block to see if the speedometer noise was truly gone, there was a problem. Normally, when the ignition key is turned, there's a quiet "clunk" sound as the temperature and fuel level instruments spring to life. Then the button marked "Start" is pressed and the engine starts. This time, there was no little "clunk" sound and the gauges remained quiet. Nothing happened when I pressed the "Start" button, either. The lights worked, but the part of the system that starts and runs the car was not working at all. I was certain that in the wrestling to remove and replace the speedometer I had jostled loose a connection or shorted a wire somewhere in the labyrinth behind the dash. Once again, I stuck my head down where the floor meets the firewall and set my droplight to light up the wires, levers, tubes, hoses, etc. behind the dash. I couldn't for the life of me find any likely causes for this new problem.

In deep despair, I thought I had irreparably wrecked the behind-the-dash wiring nest, and the car would have to be left idle until I could afford a new wiring harness and spend the time (and potentially, the tedium and frustration) of inserting and hooking up the many connections.

Later that night in bed, as I mentally pored over the wiring and the wiring diagram, I remembered that there was a rather thick-gauge wire to the ignition switch that carried a lot of current. In my high school days I had once let that wire touch the dash ever so briefly, producing a very impressive spark. So, I got up early the next morning and crawled back under the dash. I checked to see if that fat wire was live, and there was no evidence that it bore any current at all. So I traced it back to the starter solenoid connection it shares with the battery cable. (This wire from the solenoid to the ignition switch is a non-standard bypass of the ordinary wiring scheme. Sometime before I got the car, someone had installed this wire to fix a problem I never heard about.) I unscrewed the nut holding the wires in place on the solenoid terminal, wire-brushed the connectors and the terminal parts and reassembled the whole arrangement. Sure enough, the car started twice. So I washed up and left for the office, planning to take my postponed test drive (to verify that the speedometer had been silenced) when I got home that evening.

After work, I got into the car, turned the key and nothing happened. I pulled the headlight switch out to see if the lights were working, and suddenly the instruments sprang to life and I could start the car. I backed the car into the driveway, only to realize that the brakes were very low. I changed my mind about going for a spin, needless to say, and decided just to run the engine for a while to recharge the battery. I thought of turning on the radio, just to make sure that it still operated after my romping around in the wiring. As soon as I hit the on-off switch, the engine died, along with the instruments. And no amount of turning the key would let me restart the car. Since it was late, I went back inside, fearing that I would have to recruit neighbors to coax the car back into the garage, there to sleep until the wiring could be redone.

Another night to sleep on the wiring diagram. (Can you believe I was lying in bed reviewing the car's wiring in my mind, while my wife peacefully slept?) Slowly the fog cleared and I realized that the connections at the solenoid terminal, even cleaned, must still be a problem. So the next morning, I got up earlier than usual and went out to the limousine (which had spent its first night outdoors in the several months that had elapsed since it arrived). I repeated my cleaning of the connectors and the terminal, and on a hunch, I wiggled the connector on the wire that runs to the ignition switch. Sure enough, I felt a little bit of looseness. So I peeled the electrician's tape off and pulled the crimp-fastened connector off the wire. The end of the wire that had been inserted into the connector was coarsely twisted and not at all shiny. So I snipped that end off, uncovered a half-inch length of bright copper wire and reattached the connector. I got out my soldering iron and made sure that that connector was what they call "a good electrical connection."

After I buttoned the solenoid terminal back up, I went and turned the key and voila! The instruments leapt to life and the radio came on. Meanwhile, I had filled the nearly empty master brake cylinder. Because we were planning to go out shortly, my wife discouraged a test run around the block, lest by any chance the car might not be able to return right away under its own steam. So I contented myself with a run down the driveway to the street and back. Brakes worked. No speedometer noise. I forgot to look at the speedometer needle to see if it moved smoothly, but that could happen another time.

So, I didn't break the car, as I had feared. The starting problem was not something I had caused reaching around in the wiring. No, it was simple coincidence that an iffy connector attachment decided to disconnect at the same time I was doing my speedometer operation. But, if the problem had not manifested itself when it did, I might have gone off to test-drive the speedometer without first checking the brake fluid level, and there might have been a larger problem altogether. This would not be the first time that this car had evidenced a self-preservation capability that might be explained away as coincidence, but not entirely convincingly.

Bypassing the Booster

On a Sunday towards the end of March, I rolled up my sleeves and tackled the job of bypassing the vacuum powered brake booster and returning the brakes to the original fully-manual setup. I had been "eyeballing" the job for some time, knowing it would be messy and somewhat difficult, but seeing how it could be done. I confirmed what Bill Sullivan had told me (that whoever installed the booster had not reworked the original plumbing of the brake lines, but had simply inserted the lines for the booster between the existing brake line fittings and the master cylinder. I'm not sure I would have attacked this project alone if new lines or fittings had been required.

The first thing I did was to remove the brass plug from the hole on the master cylinder where the rear-wheel brake line had originally attached (that line, and the line to the front wheels, now fed off of the booster unit's output). Disconnecting the brake lines from the "tee" junction with the booster output, and removing the booster input line from the master cylinder went pretty easily, give or take the tight quarters and plentiful grease. There wasn't even much brake fluid spillage when the lines were pulled free (and even better, none in my face!). The tricky part was convincing the lines from the front and back wheels to let me reattach them to the master brake cylinder. The fitting at the end of the line has to be lined up just right with its hole on the front end of the master cylinder or it won't screw in. Or it will screw in crooked, crossing the threads and making a leaky connection. The installation of the booster unit years ago had involved bending the existing lines minutely, but just enough to make aligning them with their original holes problematic.

First, the line from the front, which was bent so that it would meet the master cylinder from below. (This curve formed sort of a "p-trap" and seems to have prevented significant fluid loss from the front end of the system.) I spent a fair amount of time under the car reaching up and trying to start this fitting. I did an awful lot of hopeful twisting of the fitting, trying to change the angle a bit, massaging the tubing to try to perfect the alignment. I even asked my daughter to say a prayer (which she dutifully did, enlisting her mother as well!). Finally, it caught, and I was pretty sure it was properly threaded, because it was pretty easy to turn. I tightened it and turned my attention to the line for the rear brakes.

The rear wheel brake line passes the master cylinder and does a relatively sharp 180° turn to approach the master cylinder fitting from the front. I had to pull on the line to get the end over the lip of the hole into the master cylinder. Then the fun began. The slight amount of bending involved in removing this line to hook up the booster unit, plus the slight amount of bending involved in trying to replace it on the master cylinder meant that the threaded fitting was just not meeting the threaded hole in the master cylinder at an angle that would let the threads mesh. So no matter how much I turned the fitting with my thumb and forefinger, it just wouldn't catch. I gently bent the end of the tube first one way, then back, then another way, all to no avail. I was becoming intensely frustrated, what with the small space to work in, the by-now solid coating of black grease on my hands, the repeated "get out and get under" gymnastics, and my sore fingertips.

My wife wisely invited me to take a break and sit with her in the sun for a few moments. I (also wisely) refrained from sitting where my greasy decorations could contact the new cushions on the lawn furniture. We talked for a while, and she reminded me that there was no need to complete the job today. But I knew there were good reasons not to interrupt the process, once begun. Open brake lines can easily invite the moisture that brake fluid loves, but that wreaks havoc with the pistons, cylinders and lines. And now that I was thoroughly dirty and involved in the operation, why not stick it out to the end? Moreover, I would not be able to relax until I knew that the integrity of the limousine's brakes had been restored. There's just something personal about knowing that the car is in running condition and I can open the garage and take it for a spin. (I don't know why that didn't matter for 25 years, but it seems to now.)

Back in the trenches, it turned out that only a bit more fidgeting was necessary before the recalcitrant fitting let me tighten it down securely. Finally, the brake system was back to its original configuration. I attached the loose end of the booster's input line to the "tee" fitting on its output line, and I plugged the remaining hole with the brass plug I had removed from the master cylinder at the start of the adventure. This entire assembly I wired to the frame to prevent a new mysterious rattle on the road.

With great joy and relief, I set about removing at least the majority of the black gunk from my hands. I knew I had an extensive brake-bleeding job ahead of me, and I gently invited Barbara to perform the pedal-pusher function. She gamely accepted. I set up shop with my wrench, tube and container at the right rear wheel and we pumped quite a bit of brake fluid through those lines before the bubbles stopped coming out. I topped up the master cylinder after the last round of pumping and when I tried the brake pedal it was gloriously firm. Ah, the satisfaction when things go right! The tips of my index fingers and thumbs were numb from twisting and twisting the little brass fittings, but the job was complete and the car had been put back together. On to the next project!

I recall from the "old days" (it's hilarious to be speaking like that!) that the booster actually did make a difference in the effort required to apply the brakes. I remember once noticing that it was significantly harder to stop the car when the engine was not running (and the fastback always required a heavy foot to stop it). For the time being, I'll trade braking security for the luxury of 1941 power brakes. Maybe as I get older and more mechanically adept I'll reinstall the booster and treat my aging frame to the convenience of power brakes!

What About That Fastback?

Well you might ask! The fastback arrived with a stuck engine. After years of sitting still, with oil and combustion by-products aging and becoming less slippery, the crankshaft could no longer be turned by hand. Before the engine could be started again, the crankshaft (and the pistons) would have to be freed to move freely in the bearings (and the pistons in their cylinders). The quick way to do this is simply to remove the cylinder heads, essentially taking the tops off the cylinders. A block of wood applied to the exposed pistons and rapped with a hammer would readily dislodge whichever of them was adhering to the cylinder walls. The drawback of this method is that the engine is opened up (potentially allowing dirt to enter and cause mischief) and one must be ready with replacement head gaskets and gaskets for the water outlet pipes.

Ever appreciative of a simpler alternative, I went for the option of inserting penetrating oil into the cylinders through the spark plug holes. After letting the penetrating oil sit for a while, the idea was to apply a turning force to the crankshaft pulley (for example, by pulling on the water pump drive belt, by grasping the fan by a blade and trying to turn it, or by applying a socket wrench to the bolt that attaches the pulley to the crankshaft). Eventually, the penetrating oil would do its job, and the parts would begin to move. I started the process as soon as the cars arrived, and I kept it up regularly. On February 7 (a red-letter day!) for the first time, there was just the faintest bit of movement. I could only tell because one of the spider web-bound leaves was amplifying the motion of the pulley it was adhering to. I was overjoyed and I told Bill right away. Encouraged by the first tiny signs of progress, I kept up a near-daily campaign to leverage that little bit of movement into success.

9. The Interconnectedness of Things

Here's another example of how one thing leads to another (and sometimes how disparate things converge). For as long as I could remember, the limousine's windshield wiper transmissions, those little chrome fixtures the wipers attach to and pivot from, had been loose where they sit on the cowl. The unfortunate effect of this was that water (rain water, car wash water, snow melt, etc.) could enter and drip over the dashboard wiring, the carpet and the driver's feet. Fixing that looseness had been one of my "to do list" tasks.

The problem (for years) had been to figure out how to reach and tighten the mounting hardware from underneath the dashboard of the car. Some of the optional accessories with which the '41 limousine had been equipped (automatic heating and defrosting system, radio, fog lights) complicated things somewhat under the dash. While this complexity was nowhere near the tightly-packed nightmare behind the dash of the average modern car, it was enough to make some structures (like the wiper transmissions) inaccessible to the casual owner/repairman.

Now, having a second, less elaborate version of the car you're working on is often an enormous help in figuring out how something comes apart, how it goes together (or how it originally went together) or what you can expect to find when you finally dig down to the item you need to work on. In the case of the wiper transmissions, on the limousine the bolts attaching them are neatly blocked from view (and from ready wrench access) by the fan-shaped outlets for the defroster. On the fastback (with no defroster) the mountings are exposed and quite accessible from underneath the dash.

Another, more recently-bestowed blessing not to be minimized is the Internet and the willingness of people who want to sell old car parts to post pictures of those parts in full color and from different angles. It was

87

from just such a selling effort that I was able to see which bolt one would turn to remove a '41 Cadillac wiper transmission (or, as the case may be, tighten it securely in place!).

Armed with new knowledge of the structure of the gizmos, I felt around up under the dash of the fastback, behind the glove compartment for the bolt that would let me remove the passenger-side wiper transmission. I slipped a nut driver up there, twisted out the bolt, removed the retainer and from outside the car I could lift out the transmission (the operating strut was wired to the transmission, in a jerry-rigged repair of a broken swivel joint). Now I could see how everything should fit together and how it worked. A little chain looped over two sprockets, like a bicycle chain. One sprocket was turned by the operating strut from the wiper motor, and the other sprocket rotated the wiper arm. A drop or two of oil on the chain made it operate more smoothly, and moving the adjusting nut took out the play in the mechanism.

I thought I'd see if I could slip a wrench up behind the limousine's defroster outlet and tighten at least the passenger-side wiper transmission. I felt the bolt (there was no way to *see* it) and I guided the wrench up to it. But no matter how persistently I tried, I could not get the bolt to turn. It seemed to be stuck, and the tight quarters did not permit or encourage applying more force. With regret I realized that the defroster outlet would have to be removed. As I explored that option, it became apparent that the outlet was secured to the windshield frame by two screws, one on either end of its long, thin opening. The first screw I could see—the second must be behind the fiberboard box of the glove compartment. The obvious thing to do was to remove the glove box, and no sooner had I removed the five screws just inside the glove box opening when I discovered that there was no way to remove the box without first removing the motor and blower unit for the defroster.

At this point we come to a convergence point. One of the other items on my "to-do" list had been to establish the integrity of the engine cooling system. The main perishable parts of that system (aside from the seals in the water pump, a perennial old car problem) are the rubber hoses. Heat, physical stress and age take a toll on rubber, and I knew for a fact that the heater hoses had not been replaced since at least before I bought the car in 1967. And in a couple of places, those hoses looked positively decrepit (cracks, deposits, congealed rubber).

The water that provides heat for the defroster and the limousine's under-the-seat heaters begins its journey from the rear of the left-hand cylinder bank through a short length of hose into a pipe that passes over the engine between the distributor and the carburetor. A second length of hose connects this pipe to the inlet for the defroster on the firewall. On the other side of the firewall, the water flows through the defroster (including a 1½-inch section of rubber hose). Through the defroster's outlet fitting, the water passes back into the engine compartment and into a long piece of hose that goes down the firewall and under the floorboards to the first of two heater units located directly under the front seat, and through a connecting hose, into the other heater. From that point, a final long section of hose carries the water back to the water pump inlet at the front of the engine. It's a long trip rife with opportunities for leaks.

That little segment of hose I mentioned in the defroster unit was one of the most untrustworthy-looking pieces of rubber I had ever seen. It was quite likely untouched from the day the car was built. Deposits around the ends spoke eloquently about leakage, and I had known for some time that I'd have to replace it. Two of the other hose segments were particularly scary. The point where the hose from the defroster turned downward to head for the heaters featured cracks and gooey, gluey drips of something that was neither water nor antifreeze. And at the point where the final length of hose was clamped to the water pump inlet, the rubber was split and crushed by the hose clamp.

The reason I had not yet replaced all of these hoses was the potential for a large, slimy mess, from the escape of coolant during the removal and replacement steps. There was also the bother of working underneath the car while dealing with the hoses to and between the heaters (with the potential for a surprise facial rinse of antifreeze, water and iron oxide). Ideally there would have been a petcock or valve at each end of the circuit, so that one could isolate the water in the heater hoses from the rest of the cooling system, minimizing the dripping and spraying. But as there was no such convenience, the choice was to drain the system or try to be quick (and lucky) in switching new hoses for old. I'd been putting this off, but now my hand was being forced.

Since I was going to have to remove the defroster, in order to remove the glove box, in order to remove the defroster outlet, in order to tighten up the wiper motor transmission, there was no avoiding the heater hose situation. For in order to pull the defroster unit from the firewall, the hoses that attach to it from the engine compartment side would have to be removed (and either plugged, joined, or allowed to drain a lot of coolant). I opted for connecting them together with a short piece of PVC pipe left over from the underground dog fence project, and with a Pyrex bowl (purloined from the kitchen and thoroughly washed afterwards!) to keep most of the spillage off the battery and starter, that's what I did. I left things at that stage for a few days while I worked up the courage to tackle more of the project.

One evening after work, I started to remove the defroster. I had thought that I could simply detach a single wire, uncouple the flexible air hoses, unscrew the mounting bolts and remove the defroster from the car. I discovered that there were two additional wires (all three led over to the crowded plexus behind the driver's side of the dash). And a control cable from the heater levers beside the steering column attached firmly to the defroster mechanism as well. There was also a thermocouple of some sort that was attached at one end to the defroster, and that was wound at the other end around a bracket screwed to the firewall (apparently intended to regulate the heater output based on the ambient temperature in the passenger compartment). The actual removal would be a bit more complicated than I had first estimated.

The defroster and the under-the-seat heaters were part of an integrated system of which Cadillac was rightly proud in 1941. It was an extra-cost option called the "Automatic Heating System," and it featured a two-speed blower for the defroster, thermostatic regulation of the valve that let engine coolant circulate through the system, and thermostatic control of the fans in the under-the-seat heater units. For its day, it was, as Cadillac billed it "THE *ULTIMATE* IN HEATING COMFORT." Plumbing and wiring connected each of the units, and the driver controlled the system with a unit to the left of the steering column.

Once I got everything unhooked from the defroster unit, the gentle and awkward process of moving the entire assembly out of the car followed. Just moving the defroster enough to provide room for removal of the glove box would not do. In order to get that pesky little bit of old rubber hose out of the defroster and replaced, I would have to perform additional surgery on the defroster unit itself. That would require some maneuvering room that was not available on the floor of the front seat. Gently removing the defroster from the passenger compartment, I still managed to spill some remaining coolant from its innards. Good thing I hadn't reupholstered the car yet!

Out on the floor of the garage, replacement of the troublesome little piece of hose went smoothly and I even put new hose clamps on. Being able to look at the defroster mechanism out in the open and unobstructed, it was easy to see how it was meant to work. With the fresh air intake closed, the defroster would pull air from inside the car past a ring of finned tubes through which heated engine coolant flowed. That heated air would then be directed to the right and left sides of the bottom of the windshield. If the fresh air intake were opened, the air directed at the windshield would be cooler. On my car, errant front seat passenger toes over the years had mashed many of the copper fins for the ring-shaped radiator flat against each other, significantly blocking the air flow. So I took the opportunity to use one end of a "5-in-one" tool to straighten and realign the fins as best I could.

Back in the passenger compartment, the glove box only required a moderate amount of manipulation to remove it (I remembered to unhook the glove box light in the middle of that process). Now I discovered that the defroster outlet used only one mounting screw—the other end hooked into the end of the long thin opening under the windshield. The irony of discovering that the defroster outlet could have been removed without taking out the glove box and defroster was balanced by the satisfaction of having replaced the worrisome hose in the defroster, and having straightened the radiator fins.

Out came the defroster outlet, and the exposed wiper transmission was wonderfully accessible. I completed the removal of the retaining bracket and pulled the transmission up and out of the car as far as the still-attached operating strut would permit. Thus exposed, I could remove the hardened remains of the old gasket that sealed it to the cowl sheet metal when the car was new. I took the new gasket I had made out of an old rubber floor mat and worked it down over the wiper arm and the transmission itself until it fit where it was meant to go. From there, it was a simple matter to replace the transmission, put the retaining bracket in position and tighten the bolt. There. Something I had wanted to do since the late 1960s was accomplished.

The car came with a lighted glove box (with a mercury switch in the glove box door). I'd been unable to get it to work for years, and now that I had things apart, I took the opportunity to take the lamp unit inside and test it with a lantern battery to make sure it really worked. Sure enough it lit up, so I knew that part of the circuit was not the problem. Next trick was to see if the switch worked and if the unit had been getting current in the first place. Sadly, the mercury switch had either lost its mercury or otherwise become defective. And in the brave new world of the EPA, one cannot just go ask an electrical supply house for a mercury switch(!)

The defroster outlet went back in with no trouble. The glove box was a different story. Lining up the screw holes in the box with the matching holes in the dashboard brackets was proving to be a challenge, with the fabric lining getting in the way. By this point it was really past quitting time, so I called it a night. I actually persuaded myself to rise early the next morning, and I resumed working on reinserting the glove box. I used some Duco cement to tame the fabric lining at the edges of the box, and I was able to get it back in without much trouble. Just enough time to wash up and head off to work.

A couple of days later, I had an opportunity to put the defroster back in the car, a somewhat pressing matter, as it was fairly vulnerable on the floor of the garage. First thing was to thread the wires behind the vacuum line and the radio bracket, then ease the water inlet and outlet pipes through the firewall and the unit into position. I refastened the mounting bolts, reconnected the wires, reattached the control cable, and reconnected the air hoses. Gratifyingly, the unit worked when I tried the switch.

It was about a week before I tackled the driver's side wiper transmission. The intimidating factor there was the nest of wires, cables, brackets and such behind the driver's side dashboard instruments and controls. To see what one is doing there requires crawling in to position one's head between the pedals and the steering column in an uncomfortably contorted position. To actually *do* anything up there requires careful snaking of the hand between and around wires fragile with age and other items that can be dislodged or damaged if one is not careful. Using a tool in those quarters is a delicate process indeed.

Well, I could see the screw I'd need to remove to take out the other defroster outlet, but I couldn't see it and connect a screwdriver to it at the same time. So I was spending a lot of time trying to get the screwdriver into position by feel, when I had a wonderful idea. Buy a really long, thin screwdriver and let the tool do all the snaking. I'd be able to watch what I was doing and keep my clunky hands out of the wire nest, minimizing the potential for damage. So I took my idea, got out from under the dash and just started the car and ran the engine for a while to keep the battery charged. Having a 62-year-old car that starts when you want it to is a pleasing thing.

The next day, I stopped by the hardware store on the way home from work and bought the longest, thinnest Philips head screwdriver they had. After dinner, I went to work and the proper tool made all the difference. The job went wonderfully fast. The defroster outlet came out easily and I only made one impressive spark when I accidentally touched the ammeter terminal with the screwdriver. The wiper transmission was easily loosened, stripped of its old, hardened gasket, oiled and seated on the new (homemade) gasket. Tightening it back was also a simple matter, and the defroster outlet only took a modest amount of trial and error before the screw (taped cleverly to the new long thin screwdriver) went home and the air hose could be replaced. Best of all, I didn't knock anything loose or break anything behind the dash in the process.

Now that the reassembly process was complete, it was only natural to wonder whether the wiper motor worked after all these years. I'd tried turning the switch on once when I was running the engine, and the wipers tried to move, but seemed to stick. I should mention that the last time I had replaced the wiper blades, I had allowed the parts store to sell me wiper arms, as well. These items fit the car and looked sharp, but the springs that held the blades in contact with the windshield were quite strong (more so than the wiper arms that came with the car). I began to wonder if the added friction was preventing the wipers from moving.

I removed the wiper arms and blades, and started the car. When I turned the wiper switch to the "on" position, the hubs dutifully began to rotate, then switch back the other direction, and so forth, just the way they were designed to turn. Although they turned with only moderate speed, they did so with a fair amount of force. Evidently, the motor worked, and if I reinstalled stock wiper arms (with their lighter springs) the wipers would likely function well enough at least for a mild-to-moderate level of rainfall. This was great news to me, as I had thought the wiper motor was basically non-functional and in need of a complete rebuild (or replacement).

So, a seemingly isolated and simple task had become very much more involved than I expected. On the other hand, the original job did get done, and some other useful things were accomplished along the way. But it is impressive how often one thing leads to another and you wind up doing much more than you anticipated.

10. Getting Serious About the Fastback

Meanwhile Back at the Fastback...

Both of the 1941 Cadillacs had shown up at my house in January 2002. It was now mid–September and I had not been able to get the fastback's engine to turn more than the slightest wiggle—maybe a degree, but probably less. I had been trying all along to avoid Bill Sullivan's prescription, which was to remove the cylinder heads and knock a block of wood against the pistons to break free whichever of them was stuck. Opening up the engine requires replacement of head gaskets and water outlet gaskets as a given. And there is all the care you must take to keep dirt and grit from getting into the cylinders (and subsequently scraping up the smooth surface of the cylinder wall, reducing the piston's ability to compress the fuel/air mixture, and the latter's ability when burned to drive the piston and turn the crank). Not the least obstacle would be the firmly-attached, stout bolts that held the heads to the block. As time passed without progress, I lost patience with the closed-engine approach.

So, I had gradually begun trying to loosen the 21 bolts that hold the right-hand cylinder head to the block. I knew that none of these bolts had been loosened for at least the 35 years since I'd bought the car. How long they'd been untouched before that I couldn't say. I tried several bolts before I found a couple that would yield to my efforts. I would place a box wrench over the bolt head and rap the other end of the wrench with a hammer, as hard as I dared under the circumstances. A misplaced blow could mean injury to me or to some part of the engine or fender. Some of these bolts were very solidly anchored indeed.

When I first got a bolt to turn and permit me to remove it, I was quite surprised that coolant followed the bolt it out of its hole! Then I remembered that at least some of the bolt holes are open to the water jacket, and I put the bolt back to stop the flow of liquid down the side of the engine.

Two things were clear. First, the engine had coolant in it, which meant that I probably wasn't responsible for a frozen and cracked block due to failure to leave antifreeze in the engine when I moved to New York. The second thing was that before I removed a cylinder head I was going to have to drain at least a substantial amount of the coolant.

So, after a bit I hooked a length of tubing to the petcock on the water pump inlet, and I filled that same Pyrex bowl repeatedly underneath the car, emptying the full bowl into a bucket. It took some time, but I removed enough coolant (surprisingly clean and bright green) to permit me to remove the head bolts without making a large antifreeze puddle. I began working on the driver's-side cylinder head, in the hope that the bolts on that side would come out more easily than the several very obstinate bolts I'd encountered on the passenger side. To some extent, my hopes were fulfilled. However, the second-to-last bolt had the bad manners to shear right where the threads start (about an inch down the length of the bolt from the head). This bit of luck meant that after I got the engine to turn over I'd have an extra bit of creative mechanical work to perform (namely finding a way to remove the bit of bolt that remained stuck in the engine, and finding a replacement cylinder head bolt) before I could reassemble it and try to get it to run.

By the time the last bolt was out, the hose to the radiator was removed and the wire to the temperature gauge was disconnected and the head was loose, with the gasket adhering slightly to the block at one end and the head at the other. Coaxed free, the head found a nice resting place on the box that our DVD player came in. The head gasket came free without being damaged, and there, revealed in the light of day (or at least the light of my drop light) were four of the cylinders.

A First Look Inside the Engine

According to the system used by the 1941 Cadillac service manual, the four cylinders on the driver's side of the engine are numbered 1, 3, 5 and 7. Numbers 3, 5 and 7 appeared to be normal, with a modest amount of carbon deposited on the piston heads. But Number 1, with the piston poised about ¾" below the rim of the cylinder opening, was a different story. It was as if the engine had decided that this cylinder would be dedicated to storage of orange-yellow gummy debris. Perhaps during the last months of the engine's operation there had been none of the normal combustion of gasoline mixed with air in this part of the engine. Just a slow accumulation of chemical trash within the spatial limits imposed by the up and down cycle of the piston. And here was a likely cause for the tenacious sticking of the crankshaft, fending off my earnest efforts to turn it.

I carefully wiped the carbon and other debris from the exposed cylinders and placing a block of wood on each piston in turn, rapped the block with a hammer, trying to move the pistons in their cylinders and thus get the crankshaft moving. Alas, I succeeded only in making noise and eliminating the "budge" I had laboriously persuaded the crankshaft to yield over the months. Now the crankshaft and pistons were quite immobile, indeed. So I spent some time applying penetrating oil to the junction of each piston and cylinder, and I devoted some serious extra attention to Number 1.

I cut some triangular pieces of clear plastic from one of those annoying packages that so many small objects come in these days (the kind that can't be opened without sturdy scissors and a strong hand). With these hand-fashioned tools I set to work on the deposits that filled the space between the top of the Number 1 piston and the cylinder wall, down as far as the top compression ring. Progress was slow, and when I tried using Gum Cutter, it softened and ate away at the plastic. But it also began to soften the deposit, so I tried to find another tool to help remove the softened material. I remembered that I had a ribbon-type feeler gauge in my toolbox. swinging out the thinnest band of the feeler gauge, I used its rounded end to work the deposit and scoop it out of the narrow cavity. Eventually I was able to feel the gauge click against the compression ring at each point on the circumference of the piston.

I did some more oiling and cleaning of the other exposed cylinders and then tried to move the crank. Pressing the fanbelt so it wouldn't slip in the pulley, I pulled and pushed the fan, but I couldn't get the crankshaft to turn in response. Always before, I'd been able to see movement of the generator pulley (attached by a separate belt to the crankshaft pulley) as an indicator that I was getting the crankshaft to turn. Alas, the crankshaft was not moving. Removal of the other cylinder block was unavoidable.

Time Out for a Taillight Lens

At this time, I purchased from Harry Scott a replacement taillight lens for the fastback. For a good 26 years or so, the passenger-side taillight bulbs had been naked and exposed, the red glass lens having been shattered when I carelessly knocked it with a wrench I was carrying. Now at last I could look at the back end of the car without that familiar pang of guilt over that long-ago careless accident. Also, the car was another small step closer to legal operation. Progress is progress, after all.

That Pesky Broken Bolt

That broken piece of bolt that now protruded from the engine block would have to be dealt with before any serious effort was made to start the engine. Engines are designed with careful attention to the placement of the bolts that hold the heads to the block. A missing or improperly tightened bolt can mean that gasses escape from one or more cylinders, sapping power and posing dangers of fire or explosion. Or coolant can enter and fill a cylinder, jamming the engine (as liquids won't compress). Or the uneven stress can simply crack the cylinder head. Removing such a stuck and broken fastener is something of an art, and it is easy to make the situation much worse.

One approach is to drill a hole through the remaining piece of the bolt. Then an extractor tool can be inserted and used to unscrew the remnant. This procedure requires much care to ensure that the drill does not veer out of the bolt and into the cylinder block, ruining the threaded hole for future use. Another method is to cut a slot in the bolt that can accommodate a screwdriver, permitting a careful operator to unscrew the broken piece that way. If, as was the case here, the broken bit of bolt protrudes from the block sufficiently, a stud puller tool or even a pair of vise-grip pliers can be used to turn it, unscrewing it from the hole. Before this is attempted, though, one is well advised to make thorough efforts to loosen the threads with a penetrant (Harry Scott strongly recommended a product called "PB Blaster"). So I did my best with a sharp drywall screw to scrape clean the place where the bolt shaft disappeared into the block, and I periodically sprayed it with PB Blaster. To help things along, I tapped the broken end with a hammer, both to loosen it and to encourage the penetrant to infiltrate the hole. I was prepared for a leisurely siege with this process.

Two Heads Are Better Than One

On a subsequent weekend I pulled the other cylinder head from the fastback's engine. Thankfully none of the bolts snapped off on this side (the casualty on the driver's side was still being subjected to the solvent-plus-hammer treatment). There were a couple of truly recalcitrant bolts, though, and the idea of borrowing an impact wrench and air compressor had been under serious consideration.

When the second head came off, three of the cylinders looked fairly normal—smooth bores, a bit of carbon on the piston faces and small piles of powdered carbon at the lower arc of the piston heads. But the cylinder

Passenger-Side of the Fastback's Engine. You are looking into cylinders 1, 3, 5 and 7, by Cadillac's numbering system.

closest to the firewall was a different story. The piston rested near the low point of its travel and there was a 2-inch deep pool of the stuff I had squirted through the spark plug holes over the months of trying to get the crank to turn without opening up the engine (that would have included generous helpings of penetrating oil, Gum Cutter and PB Blaster).

But the most perturbing difference from the others was a coating on the cylinder wall with a clay-like consistency and a color that varied from reddish brown to off-white or bright orange if you scraped it with a finger-nail or brushed it with the edge of a feeler gauge. It was hard to imagine a piston with four rings sliding up and down repeatedly past this plaque deposit, as it was fairly substantial in some places. It also seemed like a clear contributor to the persistent immobility of the crankshaft. But how could this much matter have accumulated after the engine was last shut down in the late 1970s? Where could it have come from? The fastback had been running dependably at that time, without smoking or otherwise hint-ing it had serious internal blockage. There was some valve clicking, but that had been unchanged over the ten years I had owned the car.

I soaked up the pool of dark liquid with several paper towels, and saw that there was no gap at all between the rim of the piston head and the cylinder bore. Normally (and as was the case with the three cylinders in front of this one) there is a slight space between the piston and the wall of the cylinder. It is the compression rings and oil rings (that occupy parallel grooves around the piston head) that contact the cylinder directly. This keeps friction to a minimum while ensuring an airtight seal for good compression. Here, however, the space was filled with a solid accumulation of gunk. If an engine is allowed to sit for months or years, the remaining gas and oil in the cylinders break down into other chemical compounds as the volatile components escape and natural decomposition processes play out. The by-products of all this settle out and follow gravity into the little gutter formed between the round side of the piston and the cylinder wall, extending down as far as the first compression ring. It's not hard to imagine how this could act like a nice effective cement.

But that still didn't explain the origin of the extensive fresco lining the inside of the cylinder. I shrugged and tried out my various solvents on this cylinder wall deposit. The Gum Cutter seemed to be the most effective, especially when aided by careful stroking with the feeler gauge. Gradually I was even able to begin cleaning out the space between the top of the piston and the cylinder. Still, however, the crankshaft stayed stuck. And so did the broken segment of head bolt over on the driver's side. Harumph!

A Sleeper

Back in my high school days I read car magazines voraciously. One article that made a lasting impression on me dealt with buying used cars (including very used cars). It identified a number of distinct types of used cars and went into some detail regarding the characteristics, favorable and un-, of each type. One of the types the article described was the "sleeper." A sleeper was an otherwise unprepossessing machine that was relentlessly dependable notwithstanding neglected maintenance. It was not a stylist's masterpiece and it was not a high-strung thoroughbred. It was not the sort to inspire regular care. But it would start every time the key was turned and it never stalled. It went where it was asked to go whenever the owner wanted, with a bare minimum of fuss. With a sleeper, the article cautioned, one must not disturb the thin but distinct layer of dirt and grease encasing the mechanical innards. Don't do anything to jinx the charm.

It was plain to me that the fastback fit the "sleeper" description nicely. It was an example of the least expensive 1941 Cadillac one could have bought new. The only frills were an aftermarket Firestone heater, an optional Hydramatic transmission and a deluxe steering wheel (crumbling sadly by the time I bought the car). The car needed some minor bodywork on the right rear fender, and the previous owner had repainted it twice by hand. The seats and door panels had been covered with vinyl. The engine ran enthusiastically, although with pronounced valve tappet clicking. Anything but a show car, it was nevertheless a very forgiving and dependable car. It would even let my absolutely non-mechanical brother drive it to work and back on a regular basis.

But the car's finest performance in the "sleeper" category occurred when I was away at college, and the overnight temperature in Albuquerque hit 8 degrees below zero. The next morning, none of other family cars (a five-year-old Dodge station wagon, an eight-year-old Chevrolet sedan, a three-year-old Volkswagen bug and of course, a 1941 Cadillac limousine) would start the next morning, but the fastback did.

That was how it was with the fastback, and I never considered opening up the engine. Now, after sleeping for real from 1977 until coming out to Virginia last January, the car was resting in my garage while I continued to coax its crankshaft into moving. I had removed the heads and found a couple of very interesting cylinders. I wasn't sure how much farther into the engine I'd have to go, but I was determined to get it running again.

The Broken Bolt Comes Free

On the 17th of October, the spray-and-tap method yielded results and I was able to turn the broken piece of cylinder head bolt and remove it from the block. Can I tell you how relieved I was that I would not have to try to drill it out? So nice to leave the block undamaged and only have to worry about obtaining a new $7/16$ inch cylinder head bolt.

Turning back to freeing up the pistons and other moving parts, I resumed cleaning out the spaces between the piston heads and cylinder walls, and gently working on the deposit lining the bore of cylinder Number 8. After a session of this work, I picked up my little block of wood and my hammer, and I began rapping on pistons. Each of the pistons seemed to be free (to the extent that they could be wiggled ever so slightly from side to side, nestled in the embrace of their rings that in turn pressed the cylinder walls). Each, that is, except for my good friends, Number 1 and Number 8. Coincidentally, since Number 1 was sitting almost at "top dead center" (the high point of its up-and-down travel range) and Number 8 was lodged near the bottom of its travel, there would be no point in pounding on either of them to try to loosen them by brute force. That would only stress the piston, wrist pin, connecting rod, crankshaft and bearings. Rather like trying to get a bicycle moving when the pedals are straight up and down by stomping on one or both—not very effective. Bad luck, that.

So the approach would have to be more subtle. Yank back and forth on the fan while tensioning the belt with the other hand to keep it from slipping in the pulley. Keep applying penetrant to encourage the reluctant pistons to let go. Keep debris out of the exposed cylinders. Bang on the pistons poised in the middle of their strokes. Repeat these steps, and hope for the best. Some have tried dropping the oil pan and rapping on the piston connecting rods from below, but Cadillac discourages that in the service manual, and in any event, it would be as useless for me as striking the pistons from above, and for the same reasons.

Bill Sullivan told me he'd heard people swear by automatic transmission fluid as an elixir to free up sticky pistons, and since I had a quart of that lying around (from who knows what forgotten use) I applied it liberally to the cylinders. Come the next evening, I went back to see whether the fluid had dissolved all gunk and disappeared down the sides of the pistons into the oilpan. Four of the cylinders were entirely free of the deep red fluid, two on either side of the engine. Of course, Number 1 and Number 8 still had the fluid I had poured into them. And interestingly enough, two other cylinders still retained fluid, raising the possibility that they also were somewhat stuck.

Another thing Bill told me was that when he would take a hammer and a two-by-four to the pistons of a stubborn engine, it would be a small sledge or maul (as opposed to the standard carpenter's hammer I was using from time to time). And the board he would use would be long enough to extend outside the hood so he could give it a really good whack with the hammer. This was force on a significantly larger order of magnitude than I had envisioned. And I imagined myself cracking pistons or bending connecting rods, all for naught.

The Budge Is Back!

A side effect of the initial hammer work on the pistons was that the slight motion in the crankshaft I had been observing disappeared. Over the last weekend in October, I did some more piston-whacking (still using the carpenter's hammer, not yet having sprung for the recommended small sledge or maul). To my surprise, when I went back to yanking on the fan blade, I saw that the crankshaft pulley was moving again. And it was almost the same amount of movement as before the heads were removed. I knew it was not my imagination (Honest, Bill Sullivan!) because it was enough movement to watch the vanes on the generator pulley move relative to the generator mounting bracket. The crankshaft pulley drives two belts. One turns the water pump and the generator. The other belt turns only the fan. It was this second belt I'd been yanking on, without bumping or touching the belt that turns the generator. So, if the generator pulley turns, it's because the crankshaft pulley is turning.

As I yanked the fan back and forth, there was a quiet noise near the back of the engine, sort of a thin muffled thump, that could have been the Number 8 piston trying to move. And there was a rhythmic disturbance in the pool of transmission fluid sitting in the Number 8 cylinder. Could there be a freed-up engine on the horizon?

11. Freeing Up the Engine

First You Have to Get Their Attention

There's an old Army joke about the veteran sergeant who tells a green PFC to go get a mule and bring the animal over. The sergeant instructs him that he must be very gentle with the animal, speak nicely to it and lead it calmly over to where he would be waiting for it. The private goes off and spends a very long period of time unsuccessfully coaxing, wheedling, cajoling and pleading with the mule, all to no avail. The sergeant finally walks over to the private, picks up a piece of lumber and with a wide swing, brings it down smartly across the mule's face between the eyes. Then he takes the bridle and leads the animal easily away. The bewildered PFC protests "I thought you told me to be gentle." "I did," said the sergeant. "But first you have to get their attention." Freeing up the fastback's engine reminded me of this little tale.

I had spent the better part of a year trying gentle methods to get the engine to turn over. I pulled on the belts. I poured penetrating oil, carburetor cleaner and wonder solvent through the spark plug holes. I yanked back and forth on the fan. The most I could get was a noticeable but small wiggle of rotation in the crankshaft. So, once the cylinder heads were off, and the cylinders more or less cleaned out, I took Bill Sullivan's advice and got a length of 2 × 3 (2 × 4 is just large enough not to fit down the 3½" bore of the '41 Cadillac cylinder) and a small hand sledge. I had begun banging away on piston heads, selecting those that were in mid-stroke, to avoid mashing a piston and rod that had little or no leverage to turn the crank.

I'll say this for the old engine. It stood up to my blows pretty stout-heartedly. As a matter of fact, I couldn't see any effect from my pounding. I would pound a while and then go back to yanking on the fan blade. Over and over, I did this. Then one day I looked at the harmonic balancer and started. Before I took the heads off, I had sprayed carburetor cleaner on the harmonic balancer to clean it and see if I could see the timing mark.

That had left the rim of the balancer clean and shiny, with a triangular "shadow" underneath the timing pointer. Now as I looked down, I saw that the shadow was out from under the pointer and there were two greasy triangles next to each other. The unavoidable conclusion was that the crankshaft had turned enough to move the "shadow" one-half inch away from its starting position. I was getting the engine's attention!

Needless to say, this positive feedback energized and motivated me for lots more hammer-swinging. I soon beat my piece of 2 × 3 into splinters, but I got the crank to continue moving. I seemed to get the best results from working on Number 1 piston. That's the one that had been ½ inch from the top of its stroke with a mass of yellow-orange gelatinous gunch filling the space between it and the head when I opened the engine. I bought some new lumber and over several days, I kept hammering, dripping automatic transmission fluid into the cylinders to loosen and lubricate, and noting progress, until I got the crank to a free spot where I could actually pull it (using the fan) back and forth through about a 45 degree range. At this point, I brought my daughter out to see pistons moving up and down in cylinders. It's not really a "girl thing" but she really did find it more interesting than I expected her to.

I tried just yanking the crank back and forth through this free spot, hoping I could get it to go a little farther in each direction as I pushed and pulled. Perversely though, after a bit of this treatment, everything would tighten up until I could no longer move the crank by hand. Then it was back to the hammering until motion was restored. So after a few cycles of yanking, seizing, hammering and yanking again, I went back to pure hammering to work the crank through more rotation in the original direction (backwards, as it happens, from the direction the engine normally turns). By this point, Number 1 piston was nearly at the bottom of its stroke. Pounding on it would not be useful again for a while. Coincidentally, additional progress had become harder to achieve. So far I had gotten the crank to turn nearly a half revolution, and each additional degree of rotation was requiring greater and greater work.

Of Rings and Things

In the course of working directly with the pistons, I had used a thin feeler gauge to scrape out the gunk as well as I could from the space between each piston head and its cylinder wall, down as far as the top compression ring (about a quarter of an inch from the top of the piston). Even Number 8, where the piston had appeared to merge seamlessly with the cylinder wall, with everything coated with that clay-like deposit, now had clear separation. To my disappointment though, on Number 8, I was able to slip the feeler gauge down substantially farther between the piston and the cylinder wall than for any other piston. That likely meant that the top compression ring (and perhaps the second, as well) was either compressed into its groove and held fast by petrified petroleum by-products, or broken and no longer even trying to press against the cylinder wall. Either situation meant low or non-existent compression from Number 8, and little or no power contribution to the engine. It also explained how the deposit I found when I removed the cylinder head could have built up on the cylinder wall. The prospect of a ring job in the close quarters of my garage did not delight me.

To work on (or even examine) the piston rings on an automobile engine, the piston must be removed from the engine. That means opening up the bottom of the engine (dropping the oil pan and baffles) and removing the bolts that hold the lower end of the connecting rod to the crankshaft. Half of the bearing that encircles the crankshaft comes away and the connecting rod is free. Then the piston is pushed up through the cylinder and out. Because the top compression ring usually doesn't move all the way to the top of the cylinder block during the piston's ordinary up-and-down motion, there is likely to be a slight but abrupt change in the cylinder's diameter just before the opening. Often that ridge has to be ground down before the piston and its rings can slip past in the removal process. In any event, unless the engine can be removed from the car to be worked on in the open, the mechanic is forced to crawl underneath to loosen the connecting rod and push the piston up through the cylinder. It's a dimly-lit, oily, grimy mess down there, and the bolts are likely to be tightly attached. And the fun has just begun.

Once the piston is out, there are four rings, each fitting freely in a slot around the piston head. On the flathead Cadillac V-8 piston there are two compression rings designed to push the fuel-air mixture into a tight mass to be ignited for the power stroke, and two oil rings to keep the engine's oil from getting into the combustion chamber (only to be burned and converted to smoke), while making sure that the cylinder walls are lubricated. Worn or broken rings fail to serve their intended purposes and must be replaced. Frequently, old rings have to be dug out of their grooves, and the grooves have to be scraped clean to allow new rings to fit properly. And because even well-lubricated engine parts wear over time, careful measurement is required to determine what size rings should be ordered to replace the old rings. The cylinder diameter must be measured and examined to determine whether its surface is smooth and true enough for further use, or if it must be bored out to a slightly larger diameter. The piston must be measured to be sure that it is not deformed, and if the cylinder is to be rebored, a slightly larger piston may be required, as well. And the size of the new rings must be appropriate for the final cylinder diameter. All of this requires accurate equipment (such as inside and outside micrometers) correctly used (measurements must be taken at the right spot, and allowance must be made for heat or cold, as iron (cylinders) and aluminum (pistons) expand and contract at different rates).

Assuming your cylinder is usable as is, putting the new rings on requires a special tool (or a wrestling match). Along the way, you have checked the connecting rod bearings to make sure they aren't worn or scored. Then you gently put the piston, connecting rod first, down into the cylinder. You wrap a steel band around the piston to hold the rings close in their grooves so that they can enter the cylinder. Because they are designed to press against the cylinder wall, the rings must be compressed to fit into the bore. Now it's back underneath the engine to catch the lower end of the connecting rod, fit it back over its spot on the crankshaft, replace the bolts holding the end of the connecting rod around the crankshaft, and tighten those bolts with a torque wrench to the specified number of foot-pounds.

If you feel lucky, you'll do that job just for the pistons you figure are problems. (You may be right, or you might be wrong.) If you feel conscientious, or if you want to be sure your engine runs like new, you do it for all eight. Or you spring for the cost of a professional ring job. And did I mention bearings and valves? Oh, we'll get to that later.

Having pounded pistons some more to get the crank as far as it would go in the backwards direction, I dripped some more transmission fluid into the cylinders, grabbed the fan blade and set about pulling it back and forth repeatedly through the limited amount of travel the ancient mechanism would allow. The pistons in mid-stroke were moving about ⅜ inch up and down, and the timing pointer was rubbing a comparable shiny line on the surface of the harmonic balancer. That shiny line was ever so gradually increasing in length, and I was getting some good shoulder and arm exercise.

Another Broken Bolt

Well, on March 28, I broke another bolt on the fastback's engine. I had decided to take the manifolds off the fastback's engine, and open the baffles to try lubricating the valve train directly. As I turned one of the bolts holding the crossover pipe to the passenger-side exhaust manifold it gave up and left part of itself embedded with the manifold. Oh, @#%**! And I was afraid (I didn't know for sure, yet) that this one didn't leave enough exposed to grab on to it with my trusty vise grips. Yikes. It was hard enough to use the available time productively working on this engine, without inventing additional tasks that had to be accomplished. So, I was thinking that maybe I could find a piece of metal tubing that would fit in the hole where the broken-off piece of the bolt was, and that could guide a drill bit and keep it centered while I tried to drill a hole through the stuck piece. But once I got that piece removed, I would still have to find a replacement bolt. Man, I sure do make work for myself! Better repeat Bill Ingler's mantra "I am having fun! I am having fun!"

Sure enough, the bolt had sheared even with the surface of the manifold flange, so there was no hope of fastening a tool around it and twisting it out. The only alternative was to drill a hole through the stub, insert a screwdriver, "E-Z-Out" or other tool that could be used to turn the stub and get it out of the hole. Over a period of weeks, I worked on that stub, using a drill press to guide a bit straight through the center (to avoid chewing up the threads in the hole that I'd have to screw a replacement bolt into). But my efforts to twist out the hollowed-out stub were unsuccessful. Then I tried a Dremel Mototool with a little grinding bit, and with that I was finally able to reduce the stub enough to dig its remains out (with the help of a small screwdriver and needle-nose pliers).

I was left with a part that had three standard holes that could safely hold properly-torqued bolts and one very questionable hole, the threads having been interfered with in the course of my bolt removal efforts. A bolt inserted in the compromised hole would be held, but only when it reached the deep threads. And it did not appear that a stock replacement for the broken bolt would be long enough. I decided not to worry any more about it until I was ready to put the manifolds back on the engine.

Memorial Day

My family celebrated Memorial Day 2003 with some friends by taking a cheerful tour of the neighborhood in a 1941 Cadillac limousine, with both jumpseats deployed. Everyone enjoyed the attention we got and the experience of sailing along in such a conveyance, regardless of the worn upholstery.

And on the other front, it had taken me almost a year and a half, but I had pulled the fastback's crankshaft through two complete revolutions

Memorial Day Tour. Cruising through the neighborhood with friends in the '41 Cadillac limousine.

(and thus, the camshaft through one complete turn). Of course, the rotation was opposite the direction that Cadillac intended it to turn, but that's the way it was willing to turn. It worked out to something like negative 0.00003 r.p.m. by my rusty calculations. The enormity of my accomplishment overwhelmed me!

There were now two spans of the 360 degree circle where the crank would turn freely. In between were stretches where I had to yank back and forth on the fan to coax it through the stickiness. In the second revolution (accomplished the previous night and Memorial Day morning) there was only one spot where it got bogged down enough to require a couple of hammer whacks conveyed via a 2 × 3 to a piston head.

Over the weekend, I had gone back to doing the fan-yanking routine with persistence and determination. By that point I had gotten the crank somewhere past 180 degrees of rotation and I was just trying to plug on. After watching slow but real progress for a while, I started to see some larger chunks of motion, and, encouraged by this, I set about yanking with renewed vigor. Slowly the mechanism freed up and I watched as the part of the harmonic balancer I had cleaned off to look for the "IG/A" mark over a year ago came back into view. Now I could use the fan to spin the crank through a large arc extending in both directions from the little shadow the pointer left when I sprayed carb cleaner on the harmonic balancer (I'd done that about the time I first started seriously trying to move the crank). What fun to watch the four pistons on the passenger side do their dance as I turned the fan back and forth!

I had taken off the intake and exhaust manifolds, intending to expose the valves and the lifters, and to see if I could lubricate or otherwise free up those parts. As of the previous weekend, I had gotten as far as removing the crankcase breather manifold and the rear baffle assembly. I was discouraged to discover that the camshaft was not readily visible, and that uncovering it would require disconnecting the oil feeder tubes from the lifter galleries and removing the long metal plate that covers the camshaft. So I had turned my attention back to yanking the fan.

Though the camshaft was almost entirely hidden, I could see the helical gear at the rear and the bronze idler gear that drives the distributor and oil pump shaft. (Curiously, the bronze idler gear was the only item in that compartment that was not flat black and coated with the meanest and stainingest grease that cars can generate.) I decided to observe the motion of the cam gear and the distributor as I moved the fan (at this point, the crankshaft had not yet freed up, and the range of motion of the crank pulley was about two degrees back and forth). Even though the pistons moved noticeably as I yanked back and forth, the cam and distributor gears remained still. My conclusion was that there is some play in the timing chain, such that the crank can move a bit without moving the cam. Then I reached up and tried turning the distributor rotor, which action demonstrated a fair amount of play in the distributor shaft gear and the bronze idler gear. Hmmmm.

So I put the rear baffle assembly back in place and did the additional fan yanking that brought the crankshaft into the range where it would turn freely through a nice long arc, coming back to where the IG/A mark was adjacent to the pointer. I wiped the cylinder bores to remove any debris and squirted motor oil around piston rims and pushed and pulled the crank back and forth through this free range to explore, and perhaps to expand its limits. And I reopened the valve compartment to watch the effect of this newly extended motion range on the cam and distributor gears. Again, I noted a significant amount of movement by the crankshaft before the camshaft started moving. I'd begun to worry that the timing chain might be worn to the point of requiring replacement. I thought I might be able to replace the chain and gears without removing the engine, though I would have to remove the generator, fuel pump, pulleys, engine front cover and probably radiator. (But I'd have preferred not to.)

Monday night in the course of trying to open up the free movement range for the crank's rotation, I got it stuck again. So I decided to just wrestle it through a second revolution (and the second half of the camshaft's first turn). I got to the place where I'd been stuck, up until that last weekend, and behold! the crank was stuck again. This time there was no back-and-forth smidgin of movement, just stillness. So I turned in for the night, encouraged by earlier events and somewhat stymied by the latest.

The next morning, I went out into the garage and gave the piston in number 2 cylinder a couple of whacks. That freed up the system so I could yank it gradually around to the free range and the completion of a second revolution. One complete cycle of the engine (in reverse) with each piston and valve having gone through its proper range of motion. I came to the conclusion that these machines have a life and a will of their own. Maybe that's why we're so captivated by them.

I sought the advice of my wise friend Bill Sullivan, who suggested that now that the crank could be turned by hand through better than a half revolution, I should hook up a battery and use the starter to continue the work of freeing up the internal engine parts. First, the crankcase should be drained and refilled with clean oil. (The water and fuel pumps would, of course, be inactivated to avoid spurts of ancient degraded gasoline and splashes of coolant from the now-opened water jacket). A live battery would be installed and a jumper wire used to short out the solenoid relay. According to Bill, it's fun to watch the pistons and valves go up and down, and the process pumps oil into the bearings and valve lifters.

I undid the cable clamps on the old dust-caked battery and traded it in on a new one. The battery cables begged for replacement (one clamp bolt disintegrated when I turned the nut) and I complied. When the battery was in place (somewhat precariously suspended in a sheet steel sling the previous owner had rigged on account of a rusted-out battery box) I attached a new cable from the negative post to the starter terminal and bolted the new ground cable to the frame. I brought the clamp of the ground cable slowly up to the positive battery terminal to see if a big spark would disclose a massive short circuit somewhere in the worn wiring. There was no visible or audible spark, but, in true '41 Cadillac fashion—the horn beeped! First time in more than a quarter century (and the first "sign of life" for this car).

Free at Last!

On Saturday, June 21, 2003 (the first day of summer), I applied power to the fastback's starter, causing the crank, cam and distributor shafts to spin rapidly, smoothly and in a coordinated fashion, and letting me see the pistons and valves run up and down. After all the work, it was a delightful sight.

I had started the process by performing the first complete oil change I've ever done. That involved jacking up the front end enough to crawl under (oh, yes I did use a jack stand!). I slid the plastic catch vessel I'd bought from AutoZone under the engine and wrestled the securely fastened drain plug free of the oilpan. The oil first flowed freely and then got gloopy as lumps of partly congealed oil squeezed through the half-inch opening. I let the dripping continue for a couple of hours to give everything a chance to come out. By the time I was ready to continue the process, the flow had stopped and an exploratory poke with a narrow wooden dowel failed to disclose a stoppage with any more oil behind it. So I replaced the drain plug, lowered the car and filled the crankcase with seven quarts of non-detergent 30-weight.

I unhooked the flexible fuel hose from the metal line that runs from the tank, and I caught the liquid that dripped out with an old butter tub. Far from smelling like gasoline, the stuff reeked of some strong variety of varnish. At least I would not be watching that goop spurt from the carburetor line as the engine turned over. Next I loosened the bolts holding the generator tensioned against the belt that drives it and the water pump. Dropping the generator to the loosest belt adjustment meant that the water pump would not be turning and sending coolant flying. With the cylinder heads off, the water jacket passages between the block and the heads were open, and if the pump began churning up the remaining coolant it could be a nice mess.

I wiped the cylinder bores and piston heads again with paper towels and squirted some more motor oil around each piston head, and I disconnected the switch wire from the horn relay. This time when I touched the ground clamp to the positive terminal of the battery, there was just the dull "clump" sound of lead on lead. So I attached the clamp to the terminal and retrieved the little jumper wire that Bill Sullivan had left behind in the limousine when he revived it back in Albuquerque. I fastened one alligator clip to the bolt of the negative battery terminal clamp, and touched the other to the starter relay terminal on the starter. The solenoid did its twin jobs of pushing the starter pinion gear into neatly meshed contact with the flywheel ring gear, and turning on the starter motor. The engine sprang to life with surprising enthusiasm, pistons rushing up and down and each valve waiting its turn to raise its head and close. Above all of the commotion, the distributor rotor turned like a nautical radar scanning the horizon. There was no hesitation or catching as the engine turned rev after

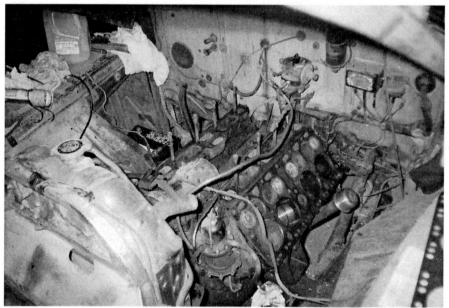

Top: Right-Side Pistons Exposed. The bare cylinder block after I'd got the crankshaft and pistons freed up. Touching the thin white wire in the lower left corner to the solenoid terminal would cause the starter motor to run the pistons and valves through their paces. *Bottom:* Left Side of the Cylinder Block. The dark varnish-like aged gasoline has yet to be removed from the fuel pump. The oil filler cap to the right of the cylinder block is also the handle for the dipstick.

rev, just the slight "ping" of a bent fan blade gently brushing the radiator at the same spot each time it came around.

I showed my wife and daughter, who were suitably impressed by this lively display of mechanical choreography. It had only been a year and a half since the '41 Cadillacs arrived at my driveway. Now I could definitely say that the engine was no longer "stuck." And now I would be able to put the heads, manifolds and carburetor back on, and see if I could rig the engine to start and run (not using the evil stew in the car's gas tank, but fresh gas in a separate container). The shopping list would have to include new plugs, points, distributor cap, rotor and condenser. Maybe new plug wires, but the existing set seemed pliable and intact. I was dying to see if the fuel pump would pump. When and if the engine roared to life, it would be time to replace all the rubber parts in the brake system and get functional stopping power. After that, road test time!

12. I Finally Got Around to...

The Limousine's Gas Pedal

From the time I first bought the limousine, I wanted to replace the accelerator pedal, the rubber covering of which had been worn flat in places, exposing rivets near the bottom end. I had found nearly new brake and clutch pedal pads on a junked 1942 Cadillac sedan, but the only accelerator pedal I had found in my "salvage yarding" resisted my efforts to remove it from the floorboard of its home car. So for all the years I drove the car, I avoided looking at the gas pedal. Today, however, Steele Rubber Company produces a rubber cover that matches the original in texture and ribbing, and that can be slipped over the metal core of the pedal, once the old rubber is removed. One of the items I ordered from Steele in September was one of these nifty pedal covers.

On the 28th of October, I set to work with a putty knife, a razor blade and a screw driver to cut off the old rubber on the limousine's accelerator pedal. The original manufacturing process had involved molding the rubber cover to the front and sides of the metal core. Now that rubber was hardened and securely stuck to the steel. But breaking off the edges that wrapped around the sides, top and bottom of the pedal permitted me to work the razor blade or the putty knife between the rubber and the steel and to gradually peel the old coating away. The razor blade didn't hold up well to the repeated pushing and prying, but the putty knife worked pretty well.

About halfway through the process, however, the pedal suddenly lost its spring tension and "went limp." The significance of this development was that the pedal was now disconnected from the throttle linkage, which was either broken (oh, no!) or simply unhooked. Time out for reconnaissance. I raised the hood and followed the throttle linkage from the carburetor to the firewall. Looking down, I saw the shiny ball of the swivel joint (now disconnected) between the below-the-floor end of the accelerator pedal and the rod that starts the mechanical linkage to the carburetor. Reaching down between the master brake cylinder and the steering column, I could bring these two items together, but I couldn't rejoin them. So I brought my trusty floor jack over, raised the left front corner of the car enough to comfortably slide myself underneath, and then reached up and snapped the little ball back into its socket.

Back in the passenger compartment, I continued the rubber removal process, and I was nearly done when the same sudden limpness overcame the pedal. I decided to finish the refurbishment process before dealing with the linkage again, and after the last shreds of old rubber were shaved off of the metal, I slipped the new cover on, and folded the edges around the steel core and marveled at the nice new pedal. I repeated the linkage reattachment process, cleaned up the crumbs and chips of old rubber from the carpet and admired this long-desired improvement. Sometimes the smallest things warm the heart deliciously.

A Parking Brake at Last

The day before St. Patrick's Day, 2003, I succeeded in replacing both of the parking brake cables on the limousine. I'd been wanting to do that for 35 years. When I got the car in 1967 the parking brake was not working. The diagnostic series I had asked the local Cadillac dealer to perform before I bought the car had pointed this out. I asked the dealer's service department to make the appropriate repair, only to be told that the parts were no longer available. I tried local auto parts outfits, mail order establishments, brake repair businesses and any other remotely likely source, all without success. And I kept trying over the years, hoping I might ask the right person the right question and get lucky.

Meanwhile, I had to learn to live without a parking brake. Fortunately for me, Albuquerque is more spread out than hilly. In any event, starting on hills was never a real problem with that big flathead engine. I had become fairly adept at heel-and-toe technique in the early hard-starting days trying to keep the battery charged. Parking the car, though, could be dicey. Under most circumstances, one could avoid having to park with the car aimed up or down a steep grade. Usually, it was enough to leave the car in gear and rely on engine compression to keep it from rolling. On those occasions when I parked by a curb, the front wheels could be turned appropriately to keep the car from going anywhere. But leaving the car with the engine running was asking for trouble.

One of the nuttiest things I did in my life was born of the difficulty I had starting the car when the engine was warm. Taking a trip in the car in the early days was a pleasant enough experience, as long as it sat long enough to let the engine cool down. Trying to start it again shortly after turning it off could be very chancy (starting problems largely disappeared when the starter was rebuilt by a large truck repair facility). I blush to admit that on more than one occasion I drove somewhere (say, the grocery store) and left the car locked, with the engine running, on the levelest piece of the parking lot I could find. Even allowing that I was gone only a few minutes, it was a hugely foolhardy stunt to leave a 5,000-pound automobile unrestrained with the engine running. But then teenagers are not known for farsighted thinking and prudence. I thank God I got away with that.

When my parents moved in 1972, their new house faced the end of a cul de sac that sloped downward. The grade was steep enough to permit me to start the limousine by letting it roll backwards with the transmission in reverse and quickly letting out the clutch. I usually parked the car pointed at the sidewalk next to, but not blocking, the driveway. One morning an apologetic city trash collector rang our bell to inform us that he had misjudged when backing up, and the steel plate across the front of his truck had caught the front corner of my car, slicing through the headlight trim ring and a good inch or so into the fender next to the headlight. The miracle is that the impact didn't send the car rolling into a neighbor's yard.

Long before I bought the limo, the front parking brake cable had broken right next to the handle. The cable had then slid out of its casing and onto the street, taking the rear cable with it to drag under the car. Eventually, the rear cable broke off at the spots where it entered the casings that lead to each rear wheel. The obvious fix was to get new cables and put them in. Only trouble was that when I was driving the car, nobody, but nobody, could offer me the replacement cables. I never found a junked Series 75 I could take used cables from, and I was well enough informed to know that cables from any other model would almost certainly be the wrong length.

The closest I ever came was to take a front cable from a 1946 hearse in a salvage yard, and replace the empty casing that remained in my car when I bought it. Of course the hearse cable was a different length, but I blithely hoped something could be worked out. Alas, that was not to be. It wasn't until 2002 that a veteran member of the Cadillac-LaSalle Club steered me to a fellow who makes brake cables himself up in Pennsylvania. I ordered the cables from him, but it wasn't until March 16, 2003, that I got the gumption and the tools together to do the job and face the music if the new parts didn't fit (I had gotten several somewhat different length measurements from different people and their parts books while I was ordering the cables). I must say the product appeared to be significantly better quality than the original.

Well, the installation process was pretty straightforward, although I don't remember doing so much work when I replaced the front cable the first time, back in 1968. I didn't even have a floor jack back then to ease the cramped working space. And I had to slide over gravelly street surface, instead of smooth garage-floor concrete. The clamps that secure the rear cable casings to the frame had to be manipulated a bit to accept the fittings on the remanufactured cable, but that went pretty smoothly, and to my shock, the rear cable fit neatly into the sheave, and that item slid nicely onto the threaded end of the front cable. Add a washer, a nut and a lock-nut just for good measure, and a new era begins! What a concept. Pull the handle and the brake is set!

Paul Bjarnason supplied a brake drum puller (marvelous invention!) and his ¾" drive socket set for the rear wheel operation. I used oomph instead of a torque wrench to reattach the axle nuts, put everything back together, and with one wheel up and the transmission in neutral I pulled the parking brake handle—the rear wheel wouldn't turn. Released the handle, and the wheel would turn. I pronounced the job a success, removed the jack stand and lowered the car back to the floor.

Success is a nice feeling, however fleeting it may be!

New Wheels for the Limousine

On July 9, 2003, the new wheels I had ordered for my '41 limousine arrived, and what a difference they made! I had found an ad in *The Self-Starter* for 16" wheels from a 1949 Series 75, and had sent a check to the seller Mr. Bruce Hight. An unexpected extra thrown in by Mr. Hight was the set of four (slightly used) Lester wide whitewall tires he'd removed from the 1949 car along with the 16" wheels. The anticipation I had felt was the accumulation of thirty-some years of frustration about wrong-sized wheels and tires, and the effect they had on the car's appearance.

It doesn't take an automotive historian to know that tires have changed enormously since 1941. Where we once heard about 2-ply and 4-ply (or even 6- and 8-ply) tires, or nylon cord or white sidewalls and had to deal with inner tubes, today there's asymmetrical tread design, steel radial belts and everything is tubeless with hardly a whitewall (or even a white stripe!) in sight. Where a tire's cross-section once was roughly circular, now it's more of an oval. Where once we bought tires based on a simple size measurement (width in inches by wheel size in inches), now tire designations include width (in millimeters), aspect ratio, rim diameter, load index and speed rating. Without disputing the many important safety improvements over the years, modern tires on an older car often produce a contradictory appearance, not unlike the visual contrast of a woman wearing the latest Nike running shoes with a fancy evening gown.

When I bought the limousine, it had wide whitewall tires. These were older tires with a taller profile than most tires being sold at the time (1967). But rubber ages and those tires needed to be replaced if that teenager was to drive this car on a regular basis. I didn't know much about buying tires, and when my uncle took me to Bellas Hess's automotive department to buy a new set, I really didn't know what I was doing and I deferred to the salesman. It was not until I got home that I regretted the results. Instead of the wide whitewalls the car came with, the new tires had a pencil-thin white circle in the middle of the sidewall, but that was not the worst of it. And even though I'd asked the salesman for 8.20 × 15 tires (the size designation of the tires I was surrendering) he'd sold me 8.15 × 15 and I hadn't even noticed. I kicked myself for that oversight as well as for letting the old tires go so easily. The smaller size, the lower modern cross-section of the new tires, and the incorrect 15-inch wheels all worked against the original design of the car. The whole appearance was radically different now, lower and missing much of the lordly bearing a top-of-the-line limousine is expected to effect.

When new, a 1941 Cadillac Series 75 sported 16" wheels, with tires that had that old taller profile. The result was a car that stood quite tall. Over the years, many owners switched to 15" wheels (especially during the war years when tires became scarce and the more common sizes were easier to find), and when I met this particular '41 Series 75 it had 15" wheels. The old wide whitewalls I found it with were tall enough to compensate to some extent for the smaller rims. After the car was fitted with new, modern-design tires, with a flatter cross-section, the effect of the nonstandard wheel size was exacerbated. The result was not just a "low-rider" visual impression, but structural problems, as well. The running board on the passenger side was now low enough to scrape on sidewalk curbs with distressing regularity (and the support brackets were bent backwards as a result). And the engine oilpan and flywheel cover, extending somewhat below the level of the frame rails, were subjected to more frequent contact with sharply-graded driveways and rutted road surfaces.

Thus began a long period of wishing and wondering about getting full-sized wheels and proper tires for this car. I soon discovered that a few companies had staked out a niche market for classic car tires, including the wide whitewalls that hallmarked the classic era. Names like Lester, Denman and Coker meant proper footwear for older cars. But the tires were expensive, and they required inner tubes. Unlike the miniskirt, wide lapels, and suspenders, for some reason, wide whitewalls are a fashion that never came back once it had gone out of style. Instead, whitewall tires of any sort (even the thin stripe variety) seem to have disappeared altogether on new cars and on generally available replacement tires. So for years I dreamed of saving enough money to get a set of authentic tires and I wondered what 16" wheels *and* wide whitewalls would do for my car.

About a week after I sent my check of to Mr. Hight, I got a phone call at work from my wife to tell me "Your wheels are here and they're big! The Fed Ex man thought they were for a truck." Needless to say, I spent the afternoon distracted as I watched the clock. When I arrived home there was a nice stack of four of the most amazing, clean, almost brand new tires mounted on dark green rims, fully inflated and ready for installation. Oh boy! Just wait. After dinner I finally had the opportunity to go to work.

I started with the left rear wheel, putting the floor jack under the spot where the spring passes under the axle. I loosened the lug nuts and started pumping the jack handle. The wheel left the garage floor and I lifted it a couple of inches more, since the new wheel was going to require additional room. I removed the old wheel and set it aside, and I brought over the new one. Right away, I saw I was going to have to raise the car a good deal farther before the wheel would fit into the fender opening. It took several rounds of working the jack and trying to insert the tire before the necessary clearance was achieved. I did worry a bit about the amount of lifting I was doing. Once I got the tire into the wheel well, though, it was a simple matter of slipping the wheel onto the brake drum and twisting the lug nuts on as their studs poked through the holes. I tightened the nuts a bit, *gently* turned the pressure release on the jack and watched the car settle onto a new rear shoe. I stepped back and admired the vast amount of white now visible in the fender opening. Beautiful! I tightened the nuts the rest of the way and moved on.

As I went to work on the other rear wheel, I began to see another reason why people went to 15" wheels. And I began to understand why every late-model car you see on the road today has completely exposed wheels all around—no fenders partially covering wheels, and with the exception of the Honda Insight, no fender skirts. It's just a lot less scary (and dangerous) to change a tire if you don't have to worry about fender clearance as well as getting the wheel off the ground.

I also began to see clearly what the owner of a new 1941 Series 75 was up against if his rear tire went flat. On an earlier page I've described the

Rube Goldberg–type jack and instructions that came with the car. I often thought that Cadillac had devoutly wished that tires would be changed at authorized service centers with the car on a hydraulic lift. But that seemed pretty optimistic, considering the state of tire technology and general road quality before World War II.

With the rear wheels changed, the car had an interesting forward tilt reminiscent of a Chrysler PT Cruiser. I thought the front wheels would be easier and less worrisome to replace, and to an extent I was right. But the size and shape of the fender openings still required significant lifting of the car before the new wheels could be worked into place. By this time (even in the late evening) I had worked up a good sweat. My wife gave me a break when she invited me to come in and help move the dining room table to prepare for an upcoming party.

I returned to the garage to replace the final front wheel and stand back to exult in the amazing difference in the appearance and sheer impressiveness of the car. Not only were the wheels now a visual treat with their size (much more proportional to the rest of the design) and the authentic whitewalls. But the car now stood significantly taller. Gone was that "low-rider" quality, and in its place a stateliness I'd only seen in the 1940 and earlier 75s (or in pictures of new 1941 75s). It was clear that the running board could now hope to clear most curbs, and I was sure that the oilpan and flywheel cover would be much less likely to get into trouble. I brought my wife out to the garage to look at the result, and I think she really was impressed (and not just humoring her husband in his chosen hobby).

The next day I applied Soft Scrub to the whitewalls to coax their maximum pristine glory to the fore. And I took pictures of this new car on a sunny day with a nice scenic backdrop. Another youthful dream had at last come true.

Replacing the Flywheel Cover

On July 14, I finally got around to reattaching the '41 limousine's flywheel cover. It's a stamped sheet-metal piece that bolts onto the lower cut-off edge of the bell housing and completes the enclosure of the flywheel and clutch behind the engine. When it isn't there, the lower ¼ of the flywheel is exposed. Its purpose is to keep water, dirt, vegetation and other foreign matter from interfering with the flywheel and clutch. Bill Sullivan had had to remove mine in the process of getting the car running again.

As I've described before, this part of the engine (like the oilpan) hangs below the level of the frame rails and is vulnerable to curbs or abrupt drive-

Top: **What a Difference the Right Wheels Make.** The 1941 Series 75 after I installed the 16-inch wheels and wide whitewall tires. A substantial improvement in the car's proportions and general appearance can clearly be seen. *Bottom:* Comparison with the Old Wheels. This view of the car with 15-inch wheels and narrow stripe tires shows the contrast between the correct configuration and the wheels I'd made do with for so long.

ways, dirt or gravel roads where the wheel ruts are deep, as well as debris left in the road. The policeman I bought the car from mentioned this clearance problem, and on more than one occasion, I heard the disturbing "clunk" as I passed over a badly-graded driveway or rough road. One of my early repair adventures had been to replace the flywheel cover that came with the car with one I'd removed from a junked Series 61 sedan (the same junked sedan I was to see driving past me on the road some years later). The original had been dented by one or more collisions with foreign objects and a section of metal had been chewed out of it by the spinning flywheel teeth.

When I had the car painted again in 1977, I drove it home listening to the flywheel teeth clattering against the edges of a new hole in the replacement cover I'd installed. I knew what had happened, even if I hadn't been told the particular details. Someone at the body shop had driven the car off a curb, or had run up a sharp driveway too quickly, and the bottom of the engine (oil pan and flywheel cover) had hit the concrete with some force. In addition to the flywheel noise, I was watching the oil pressure drop off repeatedly, as the intake sucked up to the dented oil pan. So my joy at finally having the car shiny and dent-free was severely tempered by the knowledge I'd have to get the damaged parts removed and pounded out (and I'd have to obtain a new oil pan gasket for that part of the process). I parked the car when I got to my parents' house and didn't drive it again for almost 25 years.

When he began working to get the limousine started, Bill Sullivan removed the oil pan and cleaned it, pounded it back into shape, and replaced it. He removed the flywheel cover to eliminate the noise it was causing, and he left the cover and bolts in the trunk, where I found them after the car arrived in Virginia. From time to time I would pick up the flywheel cover and its ⅛" thick steel spacer and scrape off more of the old grease or work at pounding it back into the correct shape. There was now about a 3" by ¾" rectangular space where sheet metal used to be that the flywheel had nibbled out from the cover. Gradually, though, the cover assumed an approximation of its original conformation and I could hold it without blackening my fingers. I put off reattaching it for a number of reasons. The engine's chronic oil leak had left a nice messy spot under the car at just the place where the work would be done. The dozen bolts that hold the cover to the bell housing are inserted from below, which means you're on your back, up close and personal with a very oily contraption. And either I'd grown over the years, or the tires I got for my law school graduation present let the car sit lower than it had when I'd first replaced the flywheel cover—for whatever reason there was too little space to work below the car without jacking it up. So the flywheel cover had lain forlornly on the garage floor, waiting patiently to go back where it belonged.

When the new wheels and tires arrived though, the ground clearance factor changed. One night I got down on the floor to see if it was enough of a difference to permit working under the car without using a jack. Sure enough, there was ample room for me to slide underneath, use both hands, even turn my head from one side to the other. What a luxury! Thus encouraged, I got the cover, spacer and bolts, and equipping myself with a ⁹⁄₁₆" wrench, I went to work. Getting the parts lined up took some work—the holes in the cover have to align with the holes in the spacer and of course, with the threaded holes in the bell housing. And both the neighboring oil pan and the cover itself had been dented and pounded out, so there was some remaining deformation to deal with. But after some struggling I did get all of the bolts in and tightened. I put my finger in the hole the flywheel had cut and there seemed to be plenty of room now between the flywheel and the cover. Only starting the car would tell for sure whether the job was done.

The engine turned over and roared to life with not a hint of trouble from the flywheel cover. I congratulated myself and realized that now chassis lubrication and checking fluids will be much less imposing tasks. And all of this, thanks to the new wheels and those fabulous tires that Bruce Hight threw in!

A Sunday Outing

On Sunday August 17, 2003, I took the limousine on its first road trip (outside the immediate neighborhood) since 1977. The occasion was a picnic for the local regional chapter of the Cadillac-LaSalle club, and the location was something over five miles from my garage. In immediate preparation I had filled the rear axle, transmission and steering gear box, wired the radiator shutters open, topped off the radiator, checked the oil, and done whatever else I could think of to minimize the chances of road grief. After we got back from Mass, I backed the car out of the garage, and my wife and daughter and I set out on our adventure. The car had started easily and was idling smoothly as I made sure everyone was in place and the doors securely shut.

The day had begun with a furious early thunderstorm, but by 2:00 in the afternoon, you would not have known it. The sun was out and the driveway was dry. We backed out onto our street, and when we passed our neighbors in their Toyota hybrid car, we all waved. I chose a winding two-lane road for part of the trip, instead of four-lane divided roads the whole way. The noticeable play in the steering that I had disregarded in high school and college was more noticeable to me, after years of driving newer cars with more precise steering. Mental note: This is why the worn left kingpin should be replaced.

Unlike many of the other guests, who were misled by the published directions, we found the picnic location easily. Bill Sessler, the club director, had parked his Model T Ford by the turnoff from the four-lane road and there was a sign by his driveway. I turned into the driveway and followed it up a hill and to the left, parking behind and beside a number of old Cadillacs and a '49 Mercury. I turned off the engine and set the parking brake, which gave a short groan. So I yanked again on the lever and left the car in gear. We piled out and went inside to meet people, see the other cars members had driven, and have lunch. We could only stay for part of the event, as Emilyann had a "Little Links" golf program we wanted to get to.

Barbara and Emilyann were very good sports, humoring Dad at a car club activity. As we strolled around, we noted that three later arrivals had pulled into the driveway behind my car, and if I was going to get us under way again at 4:30, some reconfiguration would be required. All during the short business meeting, I was regretting that I hadn't parked on the road adjacent to the driveway where a quick escape would be easily accomplished. When the time to leave arrived, I found Barbara and Emilyann out front, with Emilyann and Bill Sessler's daughter halfway up a tall pine tree. Emilyann climbed down and I caught her in my arms, and the three of us said our farewells as I helped my passengers back into the limousine. Meanwhile, Bill had orchestrated the freeing up of the driveway behind me and I turned the key and pressed the starter button.

Through a mysterious combination of my nervousness, the Cadillac flathead engine's propensity towards hard starting when hot, the warm weather and the noise, I didn't get the engine to catch right away, and I heard the starter turning more and more slowly until I knew it wasn't going to be able to get us going. As I thought quickly about how to ask for and get a jump to get going, I suddenly realized I was on a nice grade! Even though there was a significant bend between where I was and the road, I realized that I could put the transmission into reverse, let the car roll backwards, let out the clutch and voila! The engine would be running. I'd have to watch where I was going, but this was an efficient solution. So I shifted to reverse, released the parking brake, turned around to watch through the limousine's distant back window and lifted my foot from the brake pedal. The car started down the hill and when I let out the clutch the engine immediately started. I put the clutch back in with my left foot and with the heel of my right foot I braked while pressing the accelerator with my toe, just to make sure the car was running happily. Now I turned my attention completely to negotiating the curve of the driveway, and as we reached the road, I passed Bill Sessler and Harry Scott, who thanked us for coming, and we were off.

The marvelous good fortune of having been parked on an incline when the car chose not to start in the usual fashion was not lost on me, and I was quite grateful that I was able to get going using "Contingency Plan B." But since Barbara had cheerfully suggested that I take Emilyann from the picnic to the golf course in the limousine, I became quite apprehensive about whether the car would repeat the reluctant starting routine when it was time to come home. This concern was playing on my mind as I drove, taking away some of the pleasure of driving a fine old car on a beautiful late summer day down a wide smooth road, and enjoying the looks from others unaccustomed to the sight. Moreover, Barbara, who is acutely sensitive to insect bites, had forgotten to bring a can of bug spray for the golf outing, where we would be sure to encounter at least a few mosquitoes. So there would have to be an intermediate stop to buy some insect repellant.

We pulled into the first of several grocery stores between the picnic location and the golf course and I chose to wait for Barbara with the engine running. From here I could still head for home without having to double back, so I was struggling with the question of whether to chance the trip to the golf course (and risk a stuck car) or go home and switch to a different car. The temperature gauge was showing a higher temperature than I'd expected, and I was still worried about the difficulty I'd had starting the car back at the picnic. Even the delighted comments of a trio of admirers (a grandmother, mother and daughter) couldn't ease my apprehension. When Barbara returned and I turned down the parking lot aisle to get back on the road, I was intending to "gut it out" and see what happened. But on turning left in the parking lot, the right front tire rubbed the edge of the wheel well and made a nice, loud whirring sound, causing me to wince and express my embarrassment. Barbara told me "You sound like you'd rather switch cars," and dismissed my protests that Emilyann was already late. So we went home. I parked the limousine in the garage, and we took Emilyann to her golfing in the '98 Mercury. In fairness to the '41 Cadillac, it had gotten us to the picnic and it had gotten us back with only that reluctance to start. It ran smoothly and pleased my passengers, as well as the folks who looked and commented. As noted earlier, these Cadillac flathead engines are famous for starting difficulties when hot. A good deal of that can be dealt with by upgrading the battery cables and clamps and by confirming that all of the connections in the starting circuit are solid. Here was a set of tasks to add to the "to-do" list.

Later that evening, I looked under the hood at the (still quite warm) engine and noticed evidence that one of the smaller hoses in the cooling system had leaked a bit of coolant, some of which had been caught by the airflow from the fan and had been sprinkled on the left-hand set of spark plug wires, the inner surface of the hood and the driver's side of the firewall. It wasn't a lot of coolant, but it pointed up a strategic weakness in the cooling system. Such a flaw could get dramatically worse in the near future when once again the engine was run at normal (or high) operating temperatures. I decided that the time had come to replace that hose (and the only other small-diameter hose I hadn't already replaced). As Bill Sullivan is fond of reminding me, one of the benefits of taking these cars out and driving them is that you find out what else needs to be done.

More Hose Work

Shortly after the picnic, I managed to complete the replacement of all of those pesky ⅝-inch rubber hoses in the engine compartment (and under the car and in the defroster unit). There are seven separate lengths of hose (ranging from about an inch-and-a-half to five feet) and fourteen hose clamps. The last one was the messiest (a six-inch piece connecting the driver's side cylinder head with the crossover pipe to the heater). There doesn't seem to be a tidy way to replace those hoses, especially since the lines to the under-the-seat heater units are lower than the petcock at the bottom of the radiator. No matter what you do, there will be spilled coolant. And draining the cooling system first would involve figuring out how to hook a tube to the radiator petcock (to keep it from drooling all over the front cross member of the frame) and putting the other end of the tube in a bucket (that will have to be emptied repeatedly) or in a convenient drain somewhere (none such in my garage).

If the cooling system is not drained, replacement of each hose involves stopping up two openings through which coolant would like to leave, while you put the new hose into place. Unless you have a helper, you have to devise a way to work as though you had three hands. One solution is to squeeze the old hose shut with a clamp. Then you can pull one end of the old hose free while you quickly clamp your thumb over the now-gushing fitting (and the hose will dribble out no more than what was in it up to the location of the clamp). With your free hand you take one end of the new hose (the other end of which is being held at a position higher than the top of the radiator) and swiftly slip it over the fitting as you slide your thumb out of the way. If it isn't possible to keep the other end of the new hose above the water level of the system, you can plug it with a piece of ⅝-inch dowel. Now that one end of the new hose is attached, you can work on the other end of the old hose (thumb to cover the gusher, other end of new hose quickly slipped onto the fitting as thumb slips out of the way). Hopefully, you have remembered to put two hose clamps on the new hose *before* you started this process. If so, you move them into position, tighten them down, and maybe mop up some of the mess. This dance is repeated, with some level of variation, for each of the hoses.

The defroster unit (actually the water valve for the automatic heating system) encloses a 1½-inch section of hose. To replace it you have to remove the heater/defroster unit from the passenger compartment side of the firewall and take it out of the car. That requires first disconnecting the two longer hoses that attach to the heater/defroster unit from the engine compartment side of the firewall. Then you have to take the unit apart to remove the little hose segment, replace it with new hose and clamp the new piece into place. I had replaced this hose not long after the car arrived in Virginia, and I only mention it here to show how involved the hose dance gets.

When, some time ago, I replaced the hoses that run from the radiator outlet to the under-the-seat heater units, between those units, from the units to the control unit and from the control unit to the crossover pipe, I decided to put off doing the remaining two hoses and to trust them not to break for a while. After our family outing to the club picnic on Sunday, I noticed that one of those hoses had leaked enough coolant to stain part of the left-hand cylinder head and spray some droplets that the fan wash distributed onto spark plug wires, the underside of the hood and the firewall. Taking that as fair warning, Monday evening, August 18, I decided to roll up my sleeves and finish the hose job.

The first hose I worked on that night would not be found on a 1941 Cadillac engine, where the engine temperature was regulated by thermostatically opening and closing shutters in front of the radiator. On later flathead engines (mine is a 1947) the thermostat works internally within the cooling system. The hose in question runs from the water pump over the generator to the fitting that feeds coolant from the left-hand side of the engine to a "Y" joint with the right-hand radiator hose and back into the radiator to be cooled. When the radiator thermostat is closed, coolant is blocked from reentering the radiator, but the water pump keeps pumping away. To keep the thermostat from being forced open (defeating its purpose) and the lower radiator hose from being sucked flat, this hose serves as a shunt, allowing the coolant to keep flowing while the engine reaches a proper temperature. I first had to remove the air cleaner and set that aside. I put a length of new hose next to the old one to determine the length I would need, and I cut the new hose to size. I unscrewed the clamp where the old hose joined the water pump, loosened the end of the hose and did the "quickly-put-your-thumb-on-it" trick before too much coolant could escape. I quickly raised the free end of the old hose even with the radiator cap and left it there while I attached an end of the new hose (the free end of this one I also kept up in the air). Going around to the driver's side of the car, I unscrewed the clamp and loosened the other end of the old hose. I threaded the new hose under the fuel line and into position as I worked the old hose off the fitting. Another quick gush of coolant and the new hose was in place. I mopped up some of the mess and debated whether to tackle the last hose.

As long as I'd made a coolant mess in the engine compartment and on the garage floor, I decided to go ahead and finish the small hoses. The last one was a bright red item running from a fitting on the upper rear corner of the left-hand cylinder head to the crossover pipe to which the heater intake hose connected. It was a short piece, so there would not be much maneuvering room, and the need to work as though I had three hands would be even more pronounced. Once I disconnected the hose, I was not going to be able to calm the flow from it by holding one end above the engine coolant level (the hose was too short). The same would be true for the new hose while I was trying to attach it. So my plan was to clamp the old hose and put a plug in the new hose.

Everything went without a hitch as I squeezed the old hose shut and slit the end attached to the crossover pipe, removed it and attached the plugged new hose to the crossover pipe. I had slipped the new hose clamps onto the new hose and tightened them down just enough to make them stay in the middle of the hose and not fall off. I pulled the old hose off the cylinder head fitting and clamped my thumb to stop the fountain. With my other hand I began to remove the plug from the new hose and discovered to my horror that in handling the plugged hose, I had unknowingly pushed the plug in far enough to make it impossible to remove one-handed! Well, I tried a lot of things. I tried pinching the hose to push the dowel out—got a tiny amount of progress that way. I picked up my utility knife and tried to lever the dowel out with the point of the blade, without success. I tried calling Barbara and Emilyann, but by this time of the evening, both had retired to distant corners of the house where they couldn't hear me call. I needed a pair of pliers, and every set was well out of reach.

So I picked up the old hose, still clamped, and put it back on the cylinder head fitting, spraying more coolant in the process, and freed myself to go fetch pliers. I removed the plug, and with the new hose ready to install, I removed the old hose and worked for what seemed like an awfully long time to persuade the hose to go onto the fitting. But, at last everything was in place and I screwed down the clamps and began the cleanup.

Now the cooling system was much more secure. Each of the hoses I replaced (all seven of them) had been on the car when I bought it in 1967. That means that each was at least 36 years old and probably a good deal older. The three large radiator hoses had been replaced on my watch, so I knew their age. While outward appearance is no guarantee that a rubber hose is sound, the radiator hoses looked fine, while the hoses I replaced were in varying degrees scary-looking. The only other weak point in the cooling system was the water pump, and those pumps are famous for leaking.

The next morning, I started the car to test my hose repair job. Surprisingly (after the incident at the picnic when the starter slowed down to nothing) the starter spun gleefully and the engine caught readily. There was no sign of a leak from the new hoses, but I did notice another job for the to-do list—the speedometer needle was stuck at 23 miles per hour, and knuckle-rapping on the bezel of the instrument would not release it. The prospect of removing the speedometer again was not attractive, especially since the last time I removed and replaced it, I lost the light for the gauge cluster next to the speedometer (probably by dislodging the ground connection). I worried about breaking or shorting the aging wiring behind the dash, and I decided to wait until I'd taken the plunge and put in a new (expensive) wiring harness.

Show vs. Go

The limousine was not likely to become a "show car" for a number of reasons. First of all, it was not a pristine, 100 percent original car. Before I acquired it, the engine it came with (number 3340988) had been removed and replaced with the engine from a 1947 Cadillac Series 62 sedan. The differences between a 1941 engine and a 1947 engine are real but relatively insignificant. For example, in 1941 the engine temperature was regulated by thermostatically controlled shutters that could block the flow of air reaching the radiator. By 1947, those shutters had been removed in favor of an internal thermostatically controlled valve that could restrict the return of coolant into the radiator, and there were some plumbing revisions to accommodate that change. But both engines were 346 cubic inch flathead V-8s with the same specifications, and to the untrained eye, they could be identical. I am told that many pre-war Cadillacs had their engines replaced with post-war engines. Sometimes the replacement engine was a U.S. Army surplus item from one of the tanks that were equipped with Cadillac engines during the war. (In that case, there was a substantial amount of adaptation required to reconfigure the engine's accessories in the passenger car format.) But in the context of old car enthusiasts and car shows, having "matching numbers" is considered a good thing. The serial number stamped on the frame of a Cadillac of this era should match the corresponding number stamped on the engine. Of course, on my limousine, these were different numbers.

Related to the first reason is the fact that the 1941 Series 75 touring sedan, even fully restored, would not fetch a price equal to that of a new Cadillac, let alone approach the stratospheric values of the plainest Duesenberg. Although my limousine is a recognized classic (as defined by the car clubs that control the term), it was a factory-made production car, and not a hand-crafted custom-built or special-order original. Whereas a Dietrich-bodied Packard convertible sedan that was built for a famous screen actress may appreciate in price indefinitely, more mundane (though still not plebian) cars such as mine will not begin to keep pace. As a matter of fact, most collector cars reach a certain maximum value and don't rise much further than that. This consideration is the context in which any decision involving money must be made. If you can't justify putting money into the car as an investment, you must weigh the leisure or enjoyment factor against the real-world needs of the family budget. This hobby can easily become an extravagance. I mentioned the North Carolina company that told me they typically charge $15,000 to reupholster a limousine. In today's market, that's 60 to 80 percent of the price I could get for the car in meticulously restored condition. The economics boiled down to a few simple questions, such as "Will the restoration cost me more than the restored car is worth on the open market?" and "If so, is it worth it to me to put that much money into the car on sentiment alone?" and "Would I rather just spend enough money and effort to make the car respectable and enjoyable to drive around?"

Another reason had more to do with me the owner, than the car. Over the second half of the twentieth century, the standards for what constitutes a complete restoration or a "100 point car" at a show were raised to a degree that often exceeds even normal "fresh from the factory" showroom condition. Basically a car must be either miraculously preserved from the day it was new, or entirely reassembled with rebuilding or replacement of all worn or damaged parts. A certain amount of leeway is permitted for a car that was largely unused over the years, and that looks virtually new without ever having been reupholstered or taken apart and rebuilt. The normal situation involves a vehicle that has been taken completely apart, with the body removed from the frame. Each part has been cleaned, and every trace of rust removed. All components have been restored to working order, and every metal item has been plated or painted immaculately. The wooden parts have been inspected and replaced and refinished as needed, and the upholstery and carpeting have been replaced with authentic material in the proper style. Every part down to the smallest nut, bolt, washer, hose clamp electrical connector, etc. must be the exact same size, appearance and type as the factory used, or points will be deducted. The compulsiveness with which much of the judging and appraising is done is astonishing, although understandable in light of the huge amounts of money investors have been willing to spend for sparkling restored rare classics, and the accompanying increased availability of reproduction parts and specialized restoration shops. The bar keeps rising, until in many instances, a car must be better than original to be considered restored. It takes a certain willful personality type to be so consistently compulsive in restoring a car that all of the details come out exactly right in the end.

Yet another reason follows from the one I just mentioned. Apart from the expense and work involved in achieving a high-level restoration, once a car has been brought to the pinnacle of "mint condition" a major practical problem arises. Now that it's perfect, what can you do with the car? The first time you fire the engine up and go out for a drive, it begins deteriorating all over again. The car gets dirty, the upholstery and tires start to wear, gravel and sun damage begin and you risk a collision with another vehicle (or an immovable object). Since you've invested so much money in getting the car to a fine state of perfection, the logical thing to do is to preserve it in that condition. That means you literally can't afford to drive it around. If you take it to a show, logic requires that you trailer it (probably in a trailer you bought for the purpose). The pet name in the hobby for a car that never moves under its own power is "trailer queen." You guard your prize vigilantly to keep careless fingers, belt buckles and other hazards away. And you should probably climate-control and dustproof your garage. In its extreme form, this sickness is quite a severe burden on the patient and (usually) his near and dear.

There is a more moderate approach to these automobiles that stops well short of the pernicious extremes of obsessive-compulsive disorder. Many people satisfy themselves with bringing the car back to the equivalent of a one or two-year-old actively used example of the particular make and model year. It doesn't matter if there is a nick or two in the paint job.

And if the radiator hoses sport clamps that don't exactly match the factory originals, who cares, as long as they do the job? The upholstery doesn't have to stay immaculate and untouched by the human posterior, though it should be intact and clean. (Of course, modifications that substantially change the car, such as a modern engine, custom bodywork or other "hot rod" changes are not what we're talking about.) The recognition here is that the cars were made to be driven and enjoyed. To preserve them in amber, museum-fashion, has something to be said for it. But that prevents anyone from experiencing them in the first person, so to speak.

So, for all of these reasons, I decided to work on the limousine and fix things and renew the car, but I would not go overboard and it would never be a top prize winner at the fancy concours d'elegance. On the other hand, starting the car and backing it out of the driveway to tour the neighborhood would be a decision on a par with going to the grocery store in the family sedan, and not the four-wheeled equivalent of wagering the family savings on a hot stock tip. I would have a beautiful and unique vehicle, redolent of the tastes and standards of another era, and if something happened to it, it would be a shame, but not a tragedy.

A Trip to an Upholsterer

On Columbus Day I took the limousine to a local upholstery outfit for an estimate. It was an interesting drive, a little longer than the trip to the car club picnic and at higher speed. The car ran well, and I thought I'd cured it of the embarrassing habit of rubbing the right front tire against the lower edge of the front end splash apron when I would turn to the left. I took a chance and turned off the engine when I arrived at the shop. I had hedged my bet on being able to restart by parking on a slight upgrade with a clear path behind me to the driveway.

The president of the Cadillac-LaSalle Club, Potomac Region had given me the name of this shop as one he'd used in the past and been pleased with. The fellow who looked the limo over seemed quite confident that they could do the interior, headliner and all for $2,500 labor if I got the material. He said if he got the material, they'd have to tack on a profit margin, so it would make sense for me to get it myself. I'd already talked with a Cadillac-LaSalle Club member who sells a wide variety of restoration products, and he had quoted me about $2,000 for the necessary broadcloth and carpet material. Did that sound like a reasonable estimate? It certainly beat the $12,000 to $15,000 price that a well-known classic car upholstery firm had given me to do the whole job.

So I got back into the car and set about starting the notorious hot flathead engine. And I almost did it, too, but it didn't quite catch. I've got to get reacquainted with the fine art of starting this car after it's been running! While I continued to crank, the office girl came out and cheerfully asked if there was anything they could do to help. And I said that a push backwards would help a lot. The fellow who'd given me the estimate asked "Will it start in reverse?" and I assured him that it would. So two gentlemen gave the car a gentle shove, I let out the clutch and the engine coughed and came to life. I waved and drove home.

I got back home and parked in the garage, I raised the hood to check the oil usage. Before I could get that far, I saw that the forward part of the driver's side cylinder head was wet, as was the outlet pipe that the upper radiator hose attaches to on that side. It appeared the liquid was coming from the hose I had recently replaced that carries water from the cylinder head outlet over the generator to the water pump (relieving the left-hand cylinder head when the thermostat in the radiator top tank is closed). In fact, occasional drops were falling onto the generator from the top of the arch of that hose. I tightened the clamps on that section of hose, wiped up the moisture, and restarted the engine. This time I tried just giving it a half push of the accelerator, and it kept cranking, so I gave it some more gas. It seemed to almost catch so I pumped a little more. The same thing happened and I held the starter button in and the engine caught and roared. I REALLY need to practice starting when the engine has just been turned off.

I ran the engine for a while to refresh the battery, and noticed that the outlet pipe was once again wet, and the wetness was slowly spreading onto the cylinder head. So I stopped the engine and had a closer look. The upper radiator hose that I had boldly postponed replacing, thinking that it looked intact, had some unmistakable small cracks on the side towards the engine that the casual inspector would not see. It became apparent that this hose was the culprit, and that the liquid it was seeping was being blown by the fan (among other places) up the crossover hose and onto the generator and the underside of the air cleaner.

So the search was on again for 1¼" radiator hose, and darned if I could remember which parts shop it was that I finally located that size hose when I was putting the fastback's engine back together. Shops don't like to stock plain bulk radiator hose any more. They prefer to keep racks of molded hoses manufactured for specific applications. I couldn't check my old receipts because they were all at my office and I was at home. So I visited Champ Auto Parts and AutoZone and Advance Auto Parts, none of which would admit to having or even stocking 1¼" bulk hose.

The next morning, from the office, I called the NAPA store nearest my home, with the idea that my wife could pick the hose up (since NAPA keeps hours during the week that conflict with my work schedule). They had two different brands of 1¼" hose (at significantly different prices, of course!), and I arranged for Barbara to pick it up (plus a Gates 20589 that can be used for the lower radiator hose—might as well do that one as well). And while I was speaking with NAPA, I went through my receipts and found the one for the hose I bought recently for the fastback. I had bought it last month at Champ Auto Parts, who only yesterday said they didn't have anything like it. I think a lot of parts locating has to do with the phase of the moon or the positioning of the stars.

I went to work on the hoses when I got home. Starting on the driver's side I got a small plastic bucket and held it under the engine end of the hose while I poked a hole in the rubber and let the coolant drain out into the bucket. When the flow stopped I knew I could remove the hose and make only a minor mess. I cut a 1-foot section of new hose, cleaned off the cylinder head outlet pipe and the radiator inlet, slipped the clamps onto the hose and worked the hose into place. Once the clamps were placed and tightened, it was time to do the other side.

The passenger-side hose came off without difficulty and I cleaned off the mounting surfaces on the engine outlet pipe and the radiator inlet. When I put the hose in place though, it was just short enough to be unusable. Centered between the two pipes, it only covered ½ inch on each end. Although the clamps could be placed and tightened, and the cooling system would probably hold water, it would not be a safe or reliable arrangement. So there was that familiar "stymied again!" feeling.

The hoses on the fastback (a 1941 engine, unlike the limousine's 1947 powerplant) are both 11¾ inches, and it says so in the service manual. But the limousine's hoses are slightly longer, with the passenger side hose being even longer than the driver's side hose. So I would have to get another length of hose and try again.

More Leak Chasing on the Limousine

The next evening I took a second length of 1¼" hose and quickly cut and installed a replacement for the right-hand upper radiator hose. With the cooling system once again closed up, I added enough antifreeze and water to bring the level in the radiator to within an inch or two of the filler neck. Fetching the key from upstairs, I started the engine to check for leaks.

I ran the engine up to operating temperature and examined the hoses.

The passenger side hose showed no sign of leakage, but the driver's side was a sign of contradiction. Once again, there was liquid on the upper corner of the cylinder head and the base of the outlet pipe, and it appeared to have run down the pipe from the newly-installed hose. That didn't make sense. And drops appeared to have been blown by the fan onto the exhaust manifold adjacent to the outlet pipe. After I retightened the hose clamps, I wiped all those spots with a paper towel and the towel came away stained a golden yellow. That wasn't consistent with coolant, which should have a fluorescent green hue, even if it had some rust in it. The liquid on the paper towel was slippery and more so than coolant should be. The increasingly apparent conclusion was that this was largely, if not entirely, motor oil.

The places I'd wiped gradually became wet again as I watched. And as I brought my drop light closer to the action I noticed another funny activity. On the underside of the air cleaner that sits over the generator and occupies the space between the radiator hoses, I noticed a drop of thin clear liquid dripping off onto the side of the generator. I dabbed at the place where the drop fell from the air cleaner with my paper towel and it came away with an unmistakable oil spot. An unexpected explanation for all of this leaking business was beginning to take shape.

The air cleaner for these flathead engines is an oil bath type. That means there is a round bowl with a pool of motor oil in it. Sitting in that pool is a filter through which the engine breathes. Air from outside must come over the side of the bowl and down towards the oil to get to the filter. Solid particles are supposed to fall into the oil and not make it into the engine. What doesn't drop into the oil is supposed to get stuck in the filter. So the air cleaner is a more or less pumpkin-shaped item poised right behind the radiator. A short 3-inch pipe connects the back of the air cleaner to a muffler shaped like a coffee can on its side that dampens the noise of air rushing into the carburetor. The whole apparatus is nearly three feet long and somewhat cumbersome to remove and install.

I unscrewed the wing bolt that holds the air cleaner to its bracket over the generator, unhooked the attachment to the carburetor, and removed it from the car. The bottom of the air cleaner was dripping onto the garage floor, so I quickly moved it outside and took it apart. I found a corrosion hole in the oil chamber and quickly decided to empty the oil out and see what I was dealing with. I poured the oil off into my oil change vessel and saw that below the freely flowing oil on top was a light-brown, thick layer of congealed oil having the consistency of bacon grease at room temperature. It was a tedious process but I ultimately wiped all the old oil and by-products out of the chamber.

The hole in the side of the oil reservoir was about ⅛ inch in size. It was quite similar to the hole I found in the fastback's air cleaner, and I remember a message thread on the Cadillac-LaSalle Club message board involving yet another similar hole. So this phenomenon was not without precedent. And it was consistent with all of the mess I'd been dealing with since the trip to the upholsterer.

The crossover hose from the left-hand water outlet pipe to the water pump passes between the rear surface of the air cleaner and the forward surface of the intake muffler. Oil leaking from the air cleaner (especially with the fan blowing it back) could ride down the crossover hose to the water outlet pipe and appear for all the world to have leaked from the radiator hose. (That's if you didn't carefully determine that this freely-flowing slippery liquid was not antifreeze but oil.) And this would explain what the fan was spraying onto the exhaust manifold and the firewall. And it would explain why replacing the upper radiator hoses did not stop the seepage at the left hand water outlet pipe.

So from the evidence now available, the upper radiator hoses had not, in fact, failed. But the cracks I saw in the left hand hose indicated that replacement was certainly appropriate. The lower hose should also have been done, but it was a bit more involved—the replacement has to have a spring inside so that when the engine is running hard, the water pump suction would not collapse the hose and stifle coolant flow.

What to do with the air cleaner was an interesting question. Option #1 was to fill the hole (welding or brazing is best—some of my friends assure me that soldering is sufficient, or even a product called JB Weld that combines powdered steel with epoxy). Then replace the oil and use as designed. Some owners just forget about the oil altogether and trust the filter. Unless one were driving the car a great deal and/or in dust storms and other dire conditions, omitting the oil would not likely cause a problem. The third option is to leave out the oil and remove the original filter, replacing both with a modern paper cartridge-type filter made by the Fram company that fits (fortuitously) the filter cavity. Ah, choices! Meanwhile, without the oil, the leaking was stopped. The generator wouldn't get fouled, and the engine would stay clean.

13. A Sleepy Engine Wakes Up

Cylinder Heads and Stripped Threads

As the first signs of autumn appeared in Virginia, I decided to put the fastback's engine back together and try to start it. For some time now, the cylinder heads, exhaust and intake manifolds, carburetor, plug wires and various pieces of tubing had been off of the engine while I got the internal moving parts freed up. Now that these parts were once again able to do their intimate dance whenever the starter was engaged, there were two basic options: continue stripping the engine down for a complete (and expensive) rebuild, or put the pieces back and see if it will run. I chose the latter course.

At the time I removed the cylinder heads, I had taken a $^7/_{16}$" tap and cleaned out each of the cylinder head bolt holes, and I had run each of the bolts through a die. I had purchased some new head bolts from Cooper's Vintage Auto Parts to replace not only the bolt that broke between cylinders #5 and #7, but any of the other bolts that looked significantly corroded or eroded. Most, if not all, of the cylinder head bolts communicate directly with the water jacket, and some were more affected by the action of engine coolant on steel than others.

Now I went over the cylinder heads with a wire brush wheel on an electric drill, cleaning out the carbon and rusty bits in the combustion chambers, removing the old bits of gasket adhesive from the surface that mates with the block, and freeing the outer surface of old grease, loose dirt and rust. The previous owner had painted the cylinder heads silver, and some of that paint remained. As long as I had the heads off the engine, I thought I should paint them a more authentic green color. The truly authentic green color is a kind of olive drab tone that is available from specialty houses like Bill Hirsch's company, but I opted for a store-bought can of spray paint that purports to be the same green that Detroit Diesel paints its engines. It was closer to an aqua color than olive drab, but it would do for this car.

In preparation for the reassembly process, I bought my very first torque wrench. In the days since I started paying attention in the late '60s, torque wrenches had undergone significant evolution. Today you can buy torque wrenches that give an audible "click" when the correct degree of torque has been reached, and you can even buy models with a digital readout. I self-consciously admit I had never before used a torque wrench, although I understood the principle and operation. This was largely because I had never put an engine back together.

I started with the passenger side of the engine, cleaning and recleaning the insides of the cylinders and squirting oil around the rims of the pistons to keep things smooth. I took a couple of the sadder-looking head bolts that I'd replaced with new bolts, and I sawed the heads off to convert them into guide pins for placing the head on the block. Those heads are substantial pieces of cast iron, and holding one of them in place, at a 45-degree angle, against the block, with a head gasket in between while you insert and start a couple of head bolts is a daunting proposition. With pins in place at both ends of the block, on the other hand, one can apply gasket compound to the block surface and the matching gasket surface, put the gasket in place, apply compound to the other side of the gasket and to the inside face of the cylinder head, slide the cylinder head correctly into place, and then place and screw down all of the head bolts with much less nuisance and difficulty.

Once the paint dried on the first cylinder head, I prepared and placed the head gasket and put compound on the head. Placing the head onto the guide pins, I slid it into place with a satisfying "clunk." I inserted all of the head bolts and screwed them down finger tight (easy to do, having previously tap-and-died the threads). Each time I placed a bolt I dipped its end in gasket compound to help seal the water jacket and to ease removal of the bolts in the future. I found out that I'd inserted the guide pins farther than I needed to, but not quite too far to unscrew them. Note to myself—on the other side, just put them in far enough to stand up!

Now I took out my shiny new torque wrench. After a brief review of the instructions, I set it for 50 ft/lbs. The manual calls for 70 ft/lbs. torque on the head bolts, but the estimable Walt Brewer in his series of articles in *The Self-Starter* on rebuilding Cadillac flathead engines recommended a graduated tightening process where all of the bolts are first brought to 50 ft/lbs and then, in 5-ft/lb increments, up to 70. Each time the tightening begins at the center of the block, working outward to the edges and to the ends. As I pulled the first bolt around with the wrench, I felt a sudden slight "give" as the wrench clicked. Ah! That's the signal that the desired torque has been reached. I worked through the tightening pattern the first time and stepped back to look at the bright green cylinder head with its bolts in place.

I realized that at this point I'd gotten a little bit ahead of myself. The water outlet pipe to which the upper radiator hose attaches was still drying in its new coat of green paint. Two of the cylinder head bolts hold it to the head, and it would have to be attached in order to complete the reattachment of the head. Those two bolts are slightly longer than the rest of the cylinder head bolts to allow for the added thickness of the outlet's mounting flange. The service manual is emphatic in warning repairmen not to use these longer bolts elsewhere on the head, as they are long enough to collide with structures in the water jacket that the ordinary bolts won't reach (such as the wall of an exhaust or intake port). The cylinder block could be rendered useless relatively easily.

With a pencil I traced the outline of the gasket on the surface of the head where the outlet attaches, and put gasket compound where the gasket would fit. Then I applied compound to the gasket and the flange of the outlet pipe and let everything dry. Curiously, although the outlet pipe on this side of the engine is an inch in inside diameter, the corresponding opening in the cylinder head is only about ⅜ inch. I thought that was curious until I realized that this outlet is basically right above the water pump, and the idea is to have the coolant coming from the radiator circulate to all of the rest of the engine, not just take the shortest route back to the radiator. The corresponding opening in the other head is full-sized, and this favors the long route through the entire water jacket. So, even though the coolant is encouraged to return via the driver's side radiator hose, some is allowed back into the radiator from the passenger side, assuring a regulated flow around all of the cylinders.

I attached the outlet pipe with its longer bolts and brought them up to 50 ft/lbs before continuing with the successive 5-ft/lb increases that finally brought the right hand cylinder head "up to spec." I stepped back once again and admired my work, beginning to think I might just get to see this engine fire up before too long. I cleaned up and called it a night.

The next day, I bought some new heater hose and 1¼ inch hose for the radiator hoses. It was surprising how many stores I had to call before I found one that would sell a two-foot length of straight rubber radiator hose. Most were only set up to sell molded or pre-cut sections of hose for modern automotive applications. When I got the hoses home, I cut a section of heater hose to connect the fixture on the back of the head I had just mounted to the heater inlet, and I attached and clamped it down. The manual calls for 9½" upper radiator hoses, so I cut one that length and worked it onto the cylinder head outlet and the matching pipe on the radiator before I realized I hadn't first put the clamps on. But the 9½" length permitted easy removal of one end of the hose to accept the clamps. Replace that end, put the clamps in place and voila! It's starting to look like a functioning engine again.

I repeated the cleaning and painting process for the driver's side head, masking the water temperature sending unit. I cleaned the block surface and wiped out the cylinders once more and put more oil in them. I put the guide pins in place and slipped the head onto the pins, starting with the one to the back. This time the head got a little hung up in the front, so I took a block of wood and placed it on the bolt hole in which the front guide pin had started. I tapped the wood with a hammer and the head clanked into place. I placed the head bolts and got the other water outlet pipe prepared for attachment. I began tightening down the head bolts from the center working out and everything went smoothly until I reached the bolt on the top row, third from the back. Instead of reaching a point where the torque wrench did its "give a little and make a click" routine, the handle of the wrench just kept going around in its arc. My heart sank, as this could mean only one thing. The bolt was brand new, so that was not the problem. The threads were giving way and allowing the bolt to turn without "biting" and tightening down. The bolt was not spinning freely, mind you, but it was not meeting the usual resistance and becoming progressively harder to turn.

As I have mentioned before, most of the cylinder head bolts on this engine pass through the face of the cylinder block and into the water jacket. Because of this, the bolts and their threaded holes are subject to the same chemical reaction that produces scale and sludge in the water jacket and the radiator. Over the years, depending on the degree of diligence exercised by the owner in maintaining the car (how frequently the cooling system was flushed, what rust inhibitors were used and so on) corrosion takes a greater or lesser toll. I'd seen that with some of the head bolts I'd removed. Some of them were somewhat "cinched in" at the waist. Now I had a trickier problem. Replacing a head bolt is a lot simpler than replacing the threads it screws into. One solution is to replace the engine block, but the arguments against that are self-evident. Thankfully, ingenious people have developed less drastic solutions.

One way to deal with stripped threads is to go to the next size larger bolt. You run the next larger tap through the old threaded hole, and if necessary, drill the hole through the head so a ½ inch bolt can go through.

The joint is restored and the necessary tightness can again be obtained. But there's one bolt on the visible part of the engine that's noticeably larger than all the rest. A second solution is a thread repair kit marketed by the Eastwood Company. It involves drilling out the hole to a diameter large enough to accommodate an insert that has a threaded hole the same size as the original. This method lets you use the correct size bolt, but it requires removing more material from the engine block, a tricky thing when the hole is close to the edge of the face to which the head attaches. Not only that, I found out that The Eastwood Company had cancelled that kit.

The third option is called Heli-Coil. This kit comes with a special tap that expands the stripped hole and taps it to accept a threaded coil of stainless steel wire (with a diamond-shaped cross section) that becomes a replacement for the original damaged threads. At least one fellow on the Cadillac-LaSalle Club Internet message board asserted that he had successfully used Heli-Coil kits on Cadillac engine bolt holes many times.

So I cleaned the gasket compound from the head gasket and the surfaces of the block and the head. This was relatively easy, if messy, using rubbing alcohol and paper towels. The next day, I stopped by a local auto parts store and bought a Heli-Coil kit, size ⁷⁄₁₆", coarse thread. I also bought the requisite drill bit. After dinner I couldn't resist going out to the garage to try it out. I finished cleaning off the surface of the block and held the drill bit to the damaged bolt hole to gauge how easy or difficult it would be to drill the old threads out, keeping the drill bit perpendicular to the block surface. The hole appeared already to be nearly the size of the bit, so keeping the drill centered would not likely be a problem. This began to look like a feasible operation after all.

The Heli-Coil kit instructions call for drilling out the hole with the specified-size bit (which I had had the good sense to ask about and buy when I picked up the kit). Then the special tap included with the kit is used to make the threads in which the Heli-Coil insert will rest. Then a key-shaped tool (also included in the kit) is screwed into the Heli-Coil insert as far as it will go. The end of the coil comes bent inward and the key-tool catches this tang. You then use the tool to screw the insert into the threaded hole you have just prepared so that the top of the coil insert is just below the rim of the hole by about a half turn. Then you back out the tool and you're done—the bolt hole has been restored to the original size with strong, clean threads that will not rust (stainless steel) and that will hold a bolt securely.

I followed the instructions and the swiftness with which the job was accomplished astonished me. I felt that my friends Harry Scott and Bill Sullivan had held out on me. They didn't tell me this was the slickest thing since sliced bread! In no time at all I was looking at a nice clean bolt hole with shiny threads. I tentatively screwed a head bolt in, and it was a perfect fit, smooth and neat. Now, not only could I proceed with replacing the cylinder head, but I could do so with the confidence that if another bolt hole should collapse, there was a practical and efficient solution at hand.

The next night was taken up with choir practice, but the night after that, I just had to go out to the garage and putter. My bottle of gasket compound was kind of low, but I estimated that it had enough for the job of replacing the head. So, before I knew it, I was coating the block surface and then the corresponding side of the gasket, and letting them dry while I cleaned the excess compound from the head bolts I'd removed the previous weekend. I positioned the gasket, using the guide pins I'd made and used for the other cylinder head, and I set about painting the other side of the gasket and the head surface with gasket compound. After a pause to let the stuff dry (and walk the dog) I picked up the head and started it onto the pins. One end slid down the pin easily, but I had to tap the other side down with a block of wood and a hammer. Clunk! It was back in place. I placed the head bolts with some apprehension at the possibility of another setback once I started tightening. But wondrously, the torquing procedure went just the way it's supposed to go, first to 50 ft/lb and then in five ft/lb increments up to 70. Now there are two shiny, light green cylinder heads on the car. Thanks be to God and Heli-Coil! One begins to understand the places in Genesis where it says "and He saw that it was good."

I had dreaded removing the heads in the first place, but there was really no way around it. Even if I had gotten the crank to turn without pulling the heads (not very likely in retrospect) the gunch I found (and cleaned out the best I could) in cylinders 1 and 8 would still be there. I had to believe that the engine would now be more likely to start, and once it did, to run better, because of the cleaning I was able to do with the heads off. It remained to be seen whether I'd get away with not having torn the engine down further (inspecting and/or replacing rings, for example). I'd have been more amenable to that sort of thing if I'd had an empty garage bay next to the car where I could work on the engine (removed from the car and mounted on a stand). As it was, I got to experience two broken bolts (counting the one in the manifold crossover) and a stripped bolt hole (necessary rites of passage, I suppose). I also got the "gee whiz" experience of watching the pistons and valves dance to the starter's lively tune, and show my family and friends that little show.

Heli-Coil also helped me save the passenger-side exhaust manifold. That was the one where the bolt had broken off and I'd had to dig the broken end out, leaving damaged threads. I bought the proper-sized Heli-Coil kit and went to work with my drill press. In a very short while, the hole had been restored to its proper size with sturdy threads, ready for reassembly.

Now I could put the manifolds, carburetor and various tubes back on, put in new plugs, points, cap, rotor, and condenser, see if the fuel pump still pumped, feed the pump from a container of clean gas, make sure my fire extinguisher was close by and see if I could get the engine to fire up. It sounded so simple!

"Contact!"

On Veterans' Day 2003, Harry Scott came over to help me try to start the 1941 fastback. I had extended the invitation the day before, and not having heard back by the end of the day, I had worked up a list of things to do on the limousine (weatherstrip, replacing a vent window and regulator, etc.). I'd gone off to the auto parts store Veterans' Day morning and when I returned, my wife told me that Harry was coming over after lunch. I switched back to "Plan A" and set about getting things ready.

Over the months that the fastback had occupied the near half of the garage, a number of items had found their way into the space between the car and the wall and even underneath the car. I found new homes, permanent or temporary, for a bicycle, three old wheels, a kite, assorted yard tools and so on. I cleared tools and parts off of the fastback's fenders and out of the engine compartment.

The first "uh-oh moment" of the day was when I realized that the amount of coolant in the cooling system was very low. When I removed the cylinder heads, I had to drain enough of the coolant to bring the level down below where the water jacket in the block communicates with its counterpart in the heads. At the time I put the engine back together, I had not refilled the radiator. Now I realized that if (wishful thinking!) we succeeded in getting the engine running, it would heat up rapidly and we would probably not be watching the temperature gauge to avoid overheating. So I found a stray gallon of antifreeze and poured it into the radiator, followed by two gallons of water.

As I replaced the radiator cap, the second "uh-oh moment" came up. I noticed a fine stream of water issuing from the place where the right-hand cylinder head outlet inserts into the radiator hose. I tightened the hose clamp, but the water kept coming. Looking more closely, I saw a nice pinhole in the outlet pipe and slapped a piece of duct tape over it while I thought about what to do. The hole was close to the edge of the hose, and there was in fact enough room on the outlet pipe to attach a longer radiator hose that would cover (and thereby plug) the little pinhole. Fortunately, after all the struggle with the limousine's radiator hoses, I had a length of 1¼ inch hose that was adequate for the purpose with some left to spare. To replace the hose, though, I was going to have to take some of the coolant out of the system, to bring the level below the opening of the outlet pipe. So I got a plastic butter tub and a length of tubing to drain coolant from the radiator stopcock in a way that would involve as little spilling as possible. I removed the hose and worked the new one on, clamped it down and replaced the coolant, finishing just as Harry arrived.

As we chatted, Harry looked over the electric fuel pump installation I had made just for this purpose. I emptied my portable air tank into the tires so they'd roll better than partly flat tires. We removed the blocks from behind the car's wheels, released the parking brake, made sure the transmission was in neutral and put our shoulders to work moving the beast part of the way out of the garage. To my delight, the brakes I'd worked so hard on stopped the car nicely. We replaced the wheel blocks, set the parking brake, put the shift lever into reverse and went to work.

Harry put the intake hose from the electric fuel pump into a portable gas container and I attached the positive lead to the car's battery. This immediately engaged the electric fuel pump for the first time. Ideally it would have started up, run for a bit and stopped after it had filled the fuel compartment in the carburetor and the float valve inside the carburetor had blocked additional fuel from entering. What actually happened was that the fuel pump slowed down noticeably, but did not stop, indicating that the float valve was not shutting off the fuel flow entirely. I also noticed that there was a thin stream of fuel spraying from the series of couplings where the metal fuel line met the carburetor. I quickly disconnected the battery as Harry looked at the problem. He suggested removing the extra couplings and connecting the metal line directly to the carburetor fitting, which we did.

Now when I connected the battery, the fuel line fitting held. I touched a wire from the battery to the starter solenoid terminal and the engine began to crank eagerly. There was, however, no evidence that fuel was burning in the cylinders and that the engine was trying to start. Because we didn't believe that the carburetor needle valve was doing its job, Harry suggested we try pouring gasoline directly down the carburetor throat. Still there was no reaction. Harry pulled a spark plug wire and tested for a spark. When he didn't find one, I started to remember that months ago I had unhooked one of the coil terminals so I could turn the engine over to build up oil pressure. ("Uh-oh moment" number three.)

As Harry was tightening the wire back on the terminal, the rest of what I'd done with the coil came back to me. Because the existing wiring is missing insulation in many places, for purposes of trying to start the engine I had bypassed several wires with new, securely insulated wiring. That was true for the wire from the battery to the voltage regulator and both wires between the voltage regulator and the generator. Onto the wire from the battery to the voltage regulator, I had spliced a wire with an alligator clip on the free end. This wire was intended to replace the wire that goes from the battery to the ammeter on the dash, to the ignition switch and finally to the coil. That's why one coil terminal was disconnected. I had intended that when it was time to start the engine, the alligator clip would be attached to the coil terminal.

So now we had the spark plugs firing, but the engine still wouldn't start. We squirted oil into the cylinders through the spark plug holes to help the rings seal against the cylinder walls. Once while cranking, the engine did give a little cough like it was starting to try to catch, and that gave us hope. Harry suggested that there might not be sufficient compression in the cylinders, and that the timing might be off. We pulled the engine around to where the timing mark was opposite the pointer on the front of the engine and the rotor seemed to be pointing pretty close to the number one plug terminal. Proving himself to be a gallant friend, Harry drove back to his house to retrieve a timing light and a compression gauge, while I vacuumed the part of the floor that was now exposed while the fastback sat partly in and partly out of the garage.

When Harry returned he hooked up the timing light and I spun the engine over. The timing seemed to be correct. Unfortunately, Harry's compression tester didn't have the correct adapter to fit the tiny 10 millimeter plug holes on the Cadillac flathead engine, so he had to drive back and retrieve it before we could accurately gauge the compression in each of the cylinders. Harry had tried holding his thumb over a plug hole while I cranked the engine, and the result wasn't impressive.

When Harry returned the second time, we removed all of the plugs and checked each of the cylinders. From the time I first pulled the cylinder heads off, I had worried that cylinder #1 (forward-most on the driver's side) and #8 (passenger side next to the firewall) would have no compression at all. I'd found a bunch of orange-yellow gelatinous gunk in #1 when the head came off, and I'd had to dig clay-like deposits out from where the piston meets the cylinder wall. In #8, the cylinder wall was coated with a similar substance, and I was able to slip a feeler gauge between the piston and the cylinder wall down past the top compression ring. As it turned out, these cylinders had the lowest readings, but they did compress. As

Harry worked on the driver's side, I felt sharp puffs of gas-scented air from the plug holes over on the passenger side as I operated the starter with my jumper wire. The test results by cylinder were as follows:

1	 40	2	 55
3	 45	4	 90
5	 50	6	 80
7	 50	8	 40

Not very impressive, but at least there was something to work with.

We tried starting again, and we got a little bit of a lurch where the engine almost caught! Hugely encouraged, we continued to try, squirting oil into the cylinders to help the rings seal against the cylinders and using starter fluid. But we couldn't get the engine to "take off." The cranking engine was making asymmetrical sounds ("ah-RAH-ruh-ruh-RAH-ruh-ruh-") as though the stronger cylinders were firing, but couldn't supply enough impulse to compensate for the weaker cylinders. This was where the battery began to weaken.

Our last card to play was to try a 12-volt battery. That was how Bill Sullivan finally jolted the limousine's engine back to life, like a paramedic defibrillating a heart patient. I pulled the family Mercury up close to the fastback's fender and connected jumper cables. When we cranked the engine and added gas and/or starter fluid, the engine caught for couple of revolutions, but it wasn't ready to keep going and really start up. But that was an astonishing moment, and we now knew that the engine really could start. Alas, we couldn't get a repeat of the near-start (or anything better), and the jumper cables were starting to get really warm. So, I unhooked the cables and we called it a day.

As I cleaned up around the car and we prepared to roll it back into the garage, we marveled at how close we had come to resuscitating this 63-year-old car that hadn't run since 1977. I decided to get the original manual fuel pump rebuilt. The carburetor I could probably do myself (at least as far as cleaning it and replacing the various gaskets). And the gas tank required significant work, as well. We had established that the car had a working ignition system, that its timing was properly set, that it at least had *some* compression, and that it would try to start if encouraged. Now I had to get these things done and think about further repairs like a new wiring harness. Ah, progress!

14. A New Wiring Harness—and by the Way, the Dashboard

In late December 2003, I broke down and ordered a new wiring harness for the limousine. The new harness would replace all of the wiring from the dashboard to the headlights, with the exception of the battery cables and the ignition wiring on the engine itself. I also ordered separate replacement wiring sets for the fog lights and the heater/defroster system. Then I sat back and waited for several weeks while the new harness was made up by the manufacturer in Rhode Island.

Over the years, the insulation on the original wiring of the car (rubber covered with braided cotton) had become quite brittle. As various people had disconnected and reconnected the various electrical items to work on them (generator, voltage regulator, starter, turn signal flasher, headlight switch, etc., etc.) and as hands had been pushed through spaces crowded with levers, hoses and wires, the brittle insulation had cracked in many places and in a number of locations, bare wire had been exposed. I had tried to tape over all of the bare wire spots, but some were out of reach. The safety factor was a real concern, and the annoying short circuit in the turn signals was just the weight that tipped the scale and made me order new wiring.

When I opened the box containing the new wiring harness, I pulled out a coiled, branched black snake sprouting bunches of thin, six-inch yellow tendrils flecked with various colors, each ending in a shiny connector or bulb socket. The harness nicely duplicated the original's black woven binding that gathered together the wires that form the car's nervous system, carrying electrical power from the battery to the starter, ignition switch, coil, instruments and lighting. The accompanying chart and diagrams clarified what each wire was supposed to do, identifying it by the presence or absence of colored threads woven into the yellow fabric covering, and by the type of connector at its tip. Some seventy-plus connections in all. There were also separate wiring kits for the heater/defroster, the turn signal switch in the steering column, and the radio feed.

The first thing I did was to get my circuit tester and make sure that each wire would actually carry electricity where the diagram said it would. Was the wire that hooks up to the field terminal on the generator actually connected to the wire that attaches to the "F" terminal on the voltage regulator, for example? And the dashboard lighting wire that attaches to the headlight switch is supposed to feed six bulb sockets, two each for the clock and speedometer, one for the ignition lock and one for the instrument cluster. As far as I could tell, the harness was correctly assembled.

One challenge I encountered was the instruction to reuse the connectors in my original wiring where the harness meets the parking light/turn signal units behind the grill, and the six-pin connector that joins the wiring from the dashboard forward to the wires that run back through the body to the taillights, rear turn signals, interior lighting and gas tank gauge sending unit. Each of the two parking light/turn signal connectors holds the ends of two wires to the corresponding contacts on the base of a two-filament bulb. The same bulb is used for the turn signal (a 21 candlepower filament) and the parking light (a 3 candlepower filament). Each wire end is soldered to a brass spring-loaded tip with the solder forming a little dome that the spring presses against the bulb contact. It's important to get the right wire to the right contact, so I had to do a lot of checking and rechecking of the old and new wiring before I unsoldered the connectors from the old wiring and attached them to the new harness. Afterwards, I took the harness out to the car with a six-volt lantern battery. I hooked the connector to the lamp unit and hooked the battery first to the turn signal feed wire and then to the parking light wire. Sure enough, both filaments lit up, with the turn signal brighter than the parking light. So far so good.

Next I turned my attention to the six-pin connector to the body lighting. That was located high up behind the dashboard on the driver's side, next to the door frame. Lying on my back with my head between the clutch pedal and the cowl kick panel, I could just see the connector. In between me and it was the parking brake mechanism, the headlight switch and fog light switch (with their attached wires). The connector was held in a bracket attached to the side wall of the car at an angle roughly parallel to the windshield pillar. I snaked my hand up through the obstructions and found I could reach the connector. Operating by feel, since there wasn't enough room to work and watch at the same time, I found the male end of the connector and pulled it up and out of the female end, which was still firmly held by the bracket. At the time, it seemed to me that the male end in my hand was the end of the harness I was replacing. And somehow, I got the notion that the other end was part of the body wiring. So I earnestly began to cut the male end of the connector, leaving about an inch of wiring attached, and once it was free I took my prize back into the house to see about attaching the new wiring harness to it.

As I studied the diagram at the kitchen table, a sickening feeling slowly spread through my limbs. I began to realize that I had cut the wiring on the wrong side of the connector! It was the female end of the connector that I should have been holding in my hand. The body wiring bundle had looped down and back up to meet the connector from above. I had mistaken that loop for the end of the harness I was replacing. Now I was going to have to repair the damage I had done to the body wiring, either by reattaching the male end of the connector to the cut ends now hanging naked behind the dash, or by splicing the body wiring directly to the new harness. Either way, I was going to have to figure out which of the six cut wires was which, notwithstanding that their color coding had long since faded to the point of being nearly indecipherable. More ominously, my naïve hope of being able to replace the wiring harness without removing the dashboard was now evaporating. The only way to get enough room and light to work on the cut wires was to remove the dashboard.

So, I set about removing the dashboard from my car. Fortunately, Barry Wheeler's newsletter for the 1941 Cadillac chapter of the Cadillac-LaSalle Club had published the previous year a detailed step-by-step procedure for removing the dashboard, and I set that on the seat beside me as I began. First, remove the screws that hold the windshield garnish moldings in place and put them in a plastic bag. Gently pry the garnish moldings loose and put them in the back seat out of harm's way. Nice thing about the Series 75 is that there's a lot of room in the back seat. Take out the screws along the top edge of the dash that the garnish molding hides, and put them in another plastic bag.

Remove the radio. Two wires disconnected, two control knobs (each with two set screws) removed. Go behind and remove the nuts that hold two chrome escutcheon plates for the knobs. Go underneath and remove the bolt that holds the radio to a brace between the dash and firewall. Go back out front and take off the two nuts that attach to the knob shafts and hold the radio in place. Reach underneath and gently maneuver the radio out from behind the dash. Wince as you realize you forgot to pull out the antenna lead that just popped out on its own. Put the radio in the back seat. Remove the nuts that hold in place the decorative grille that covered the radio and put the grille in the back seat, too.

Disconnect the clock feed wire, pop out the clock light bulb sockets, loosen the reset knob retaining nut and slide it out of its hole in the bottom of the dash. Remove three nuts from behind the clock and pull it out from the front of the dash. Disconnect the cigar lighter feed wire and remove the lighter from the dash.

Remove the six screws that hold the glove box in (after you remove the glove box light) and work the glove box around until you can take it out from behind the dash. Unhook the link between the windshield wiper knob and the wiper motor.

From behind the speedometer, pop out the two light bulb sockets, and the sockets for the high beam indicator and the turn signal indicator. Unscrew the nut holding the odometer reset knob in place under the dash and work it loose. Twist loose the collar nut that holds the speedometer cable in place, and after you take off three mounting nuts, remove the speedometer and put it in the back seat.

Undo the screw on the back of the starter button and remove its mounting bracket. Pull the button assembly out through the front of the dash, disconnect both wires, reattach the mounting bracket and put the assembly aside.

Unscrew the mounting nut from behind the throttle control knob and pull the knob and cable from the engine compartment, out through the dash, and put it—you guessed it!—in the back seat.

Twist off the chrome ring that holds the ignition lock in place, pull the lock back through its dash opening, and replace the ring on the lock cylinder. Leave the lock hanging on its armored cable.

Unscrew the mounting bolts for the fog light switch and remove the switch from the lower edge of the dash. Unscrew and remove the hex-head bolts that hold the heater control levers to the lower edge of the dash and let the unit hang by its cables.

Reach up behind the dash, release the clip that holds the headlight switch knob in place and remove the knob. With an allen wrench remove the escutcheon plate and the headlight switch will hang free behind the dash.

Reach way up behind the far left-hand end of the dash and guide a 7/16-inch socket wrench onto the nut holding the far side of the instrument cluster to the dash. Once this nut is off, the cluster will hang free behind the dash, supported by the attached wiring and the tube to the oil pressure gauge.

Loosen and remove the bolts and nuts that hold the steering column clamp to the dash. Now the only things preventing removal of the dash are two bolts holding each lower corner of the dash to the cowl. Well, almost.

The instruction sheet mentioned as the last step, removing a bolt from each lower corner of the dash. As things turned out, there were two bolts on each side, and once these came out, the lower edge of the dash would move a little bit, but I couldn't take the dash out. It remained solidly attached across the entire top edge. I tugged, and I poked a putty knife between the dashboard edge and the rubber grommet surrounding the windshield. I tugged some more, but to no avail.

So, I did what I frequently do in a quandary—I called Bill Sullivan. He said the dash was probably held in place by the adhesive/sealant the manufacturer had slathered between the dash and windshield grommet *and* between the underside of the dash edge and the cowl. He recommended a thorough and methodical putty knife operation such as I had begun, accompanied by more vigorous tugging. So that's what I did. And sure enough, after I'd forced the putty knife between dash and grommet along the whole joint, my tugging pulled the entire top edge of the dash free. The lower corners, however, would move but would not come free. But once both front doors were opened, some wiggling, manipulating and coaxing finally freed the dashboard from the car.

Once I removed the dashboard from the car, everything behind it was revealed. What before I had only been able to see obscurely or dimly or indirectly, now sat there in broad daylight (or such daylight as entered the garage). I could see the blue plastic insulated wire that a prior owner had used to bypass the taillight feed wire (to correct some long ago conduction problem). I could see the female end of the body wiring connector (the one I *should* have cut off!). And I could examine the cut ends of the body wiring bundle that I was going to have to either resolder to the male connector, or splice directly to the new wiring harness.

The next few days were extremely cold, but one evening I took a lantern battery and a couple of wires with alligator clips, and I asked my daughter to come help me. While Emilyann watched the taillights, I connected one wire from the lantern battery to the car chassis and touched the other end to each of the cut body wiring ends. We were able to identify, with this experiment, the wires for the brake lights, and the right and left turn signals. When the interior dome light glowed, we knew we'd isolated the feed wire for the various courtesy lights. That left two wires— one for the fuel gauge sending unit and the other for the original (now bypassed) taillight feed. With four of the six cut wires positively identified, I felt much better about the state of things.

Rewiring the Turn Signals

On the first of February, I went back into the garage. I'd been wondering how I would replace the wires that run from the turn signal switch, through the steering column, and out through a hole in the column mounting clamp to a Bakelite connector shaped like a three-note pitch pipe and clipped to a brace behind the dash. (The turn signal wires in the main wiring harness attach to the other side of the connector.) From the steering wheel to the lower edge of the dash there is a metal jacket that encloses the shaft that the steering wheel turns, as well as the shaft that the gear shift lever turns. This metal jacket makes for a tidy appearance and holds a bearing in which the steering shaft turns. At the upper end, it contains the mechanism and switch for operation of the turn signals. Three wires, encased in a woven tube, run from the turn signal switch through the metal jacket and out at the mounting clamp. If I pulled the old wires out, it would be practically impossible to simply push the new wires into the space formerly occupied by the old wires, since the end terminals would hang up along the way. While I considered my options, I took a close look at the turn signal switch apparatus, which had long been quite wobbly in its mounting, and which would no longer cancel automatically at the end of a turn.

I had an idea for how to replace the (formerly) rubber-lined bushings that mount the turn signal lever and switch to the inside of the steering column. I cut some very short lengths of rubber tubing and slipped them over the original brass cores. I had to shave the rubber down with a razor blade to fit the holes in the switch plate, but now I could look forward to a less wobbly mechanism. The hooked metal finger that's supposed to catch on a cam on the steering shaft and cancel the signal after a turn has an adjustable spring that I was able to tighten a notch. Adding some lubrication to the pivot point promised to complete the remedy.

With the switch lifted up, I could see how the wires attached—three brass terminals with Philips-head screws holding the wire ends in place. I tried to make out the original color coding on the old wires, just to be doubly careful about replacing each old wire with the correct new wire. But as I'd observed elsewhere, even in very well protected places, and even if you carefully cleaned the dust of years off the insulation, the red indicator threads were almost impossible to make out, while the green threads had completely faded to indifferent beige.

The three wires were bound together in a woven sheath and it occurred to me that I could use the old bound set to pull the new bound set into place. At the dash end I pulled the old wires out of the Bakelite connector and I cut the ends of the old wires off. I took a length of packing tape and wrapped it around the steering wheel end of the new wires, then butted that end up to the cut end of the old wires and continued taping. I was left with a continuous piece now, with the new wires attached to the old. Then, as I drew the old wires out through the switch end of the steering column, the new wires followed until they were perfectly in place. I didn't have to take the steering column apart, after all! I removed the tape from the wires and used my circuit tester to figure out which terminal is connected to the feed when the switch is moved to the "right turn" position and which is activated for a left turn. With that information, I connected the wires as indicated in the diagram (black and green crossed tracer threads for the left turn signals and green crossed with green for the right turn signals). Then I was able to screw the switch plate mounting bolts down and voila! One piece of the new wiring was in place! I put the lower ends of the new wires into the Bakelite connector and counted my blessings.

A couple of evenings later, I freed up the far forward portion of the old wiring harness. That involved disconnecting the headlight leads from the terminal strips on the front fenders, disconnecting the field and armature wires from the generator, and pulling the horn and turn signal wires back through their holes in the fan shroud. I had to unwind about a yard of dried electrical tape to free the fog light wires from the portion of the old harness that passes over the top of the radiator.

On another evening, I carefully chipped out the hardened rubber grommet through which the main harness passes through the firewall. Through other holes in the same grommet pass the wire to the heater and the fog light wires, so it was important to remove the ancient, dried rubber carefully. Next, I detached the wires to the voltage regulator and horn relay on the firewall, and the wires to the stoplight switch on the master brake cylinder, and the horn switch terminal on the steering column. I had just enough time to remove and replace the wire underneath the car that runs from one under-the-seat heater unit up over the transmission to the other heater unit.

A few evenings later, I detached the wires to the starter solenoid terminals, including the separate wire that a prior owner had hooked up to connect the battery directly to the ignition switch (instead of the intended route by way of the ammeter). I disconnected the other end of this bypass wire where it attached to the ignition switch, and pulled it though the firewall (freeing up one of the windshield washer vacuum hose holes that my predecessor owner had used for this wire). I carefully threaded the remaining solenoid terminal wires through the tight space between the rear of the engine and the firewall (no need to damage anything else, like the wire connecting the distributor to the coil). Now the old wiring harness was entirely undone forward of the firewall.

Having built up some momentum, I went to work on the connections inside the car. I unhooked the wires to the ignition switch, the turn signal flasher and the headlight switch. That left the instrument cluster. Of the four gauges in that cluster, three have electrical connections (the oil pressure gauge responds directly to the pressure in a little tube that runs from the engine to the gauge). Now, hooking these gauges up correctly is very important. To this day, a little red tag is attached to one terminal of the gasoline gauge informing whoever can read it that "Touching the hot wire to this contact may burn out the fuel gauge sending unit." For all practical purposes the color coding on the old wiring is gone (except for black tracer threads). There are a couple of safeguards available, though. The first is a photograph in the 1941 Service Manual that shows the backside of the dashboard with all of the instruments and controls in place and the wiring harness installed. Little arrows point to the various wires and indicate their purpose and color coding. The wires to the instrument cluster are shown, and it's pretty easy to make sense of the picture. In addition, the existing wires to the instruments can be identified without the faded red and green threads. And before removing the wires, one can make a drawing of the back of the cluster, noting which existing wire is attached to which terminal. For example, the temperature gauge has a solid black wire and what looks like a plain natural/beige wire (of course the latter used to have red cross-tracers). That tells you which terminal gets the wire from the engine sending unit (solid black) and which gets the other wire (natural with some kind of color). One of the gas gauge wires has lost all of its color (formerly red cross-tracers) and the other still has a black tracer, so it's distinguishable from the other wire, and so forth. When the diagram is complete, the wires can be removed. Then, when the new harness is attached, the diagram provides additional confidence that the instruments are wired right. With the instrument cluster disconnected, only the ignition switch connections remained. Once those were disconnected, the old wiring harness was loose and ready for removal.

Installation of the Heater Wiring and the New Main Harness

Together with the main wiring harness, I had purchased replacement wiring for the automatic heater/defroster system that came with my car. That system has four main parts. There's a control unit mounted to the bottom edge of the dashboard to the left of the steering column, a defroster/thermostat/water valve unit that mounts to the firewall above the passenger's feet, and two heater and fan units that mount underneath the driver's and the passenger's sides of the front seat. The control unit has a switch

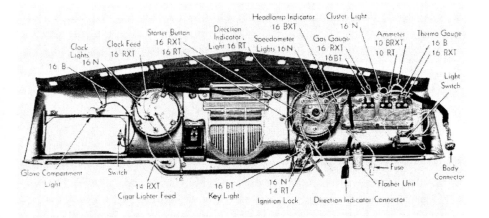

Behind the Dash of the 1941 Cadillac. This illustration from the 1941 Cadillac Service Manual shows the wiring harness and how the various electrical components are connected to it. Not shown are the glove box, the radio, the steering column, the windshield wiper pump and mechanism, the hand brake, the heater controls, the defroster hoses and outlets and the fog light switch, or the way in which all of those components complicate the task of inspecting, repairing or replacing the wiring (courtesy Art Cutler).

for the defroster, a lever to open and close the fresh air vent, and a lever that turns the heaters on (subject to thermostatic control) and varies the amount of hot water the defroster receives. Electric power comes from a short feed wire from the ignition switch to the control unit. From there it gets to the heaters by a wire from the control unit to the thermostat (next to the defroster) and a second wire from the thermostat through the firewall and down to the drivers-side heater and by another wire from that heater to the other. A separate wire takes power from the control unit to the defroster motor.

One thing I noticed when I opened the package was that there was no replacement included for the short wire and socket for the light that illuminates the dash-mounted heater control unit when the heater is turned on. So I called Rhode Island Wiring and at their request I sent them the old item and they sent back a nice neat replacement (using my original socket, cleaned and attached to the new wire).

One evening when I had a small bit of time, I decided to replace the wire that runs from one under-the-seat heater, over the transmission housing to the other heater. It was a discrete project that could be accomplished without mishap or confusion. So I went under the car on the driver's side and unscrewed the bolt holding the wire to the left-hand heater. Then around and under on the other side to disconnect the other end of the wire from the right-hand heater. Then, to escape the need to reach around and over the transmission housing, I taped an end of the replacement wire to the end of the old wire that I had just unhooked from the passenger-side heater. I went back to the other side of the car and pulled the old wire out, drawing the new wire into place. I removed the tape and connected the new wire to each of the heaters. Progress!

Over the St. Valentine's Day weekend, I replaced the rest of the heater wiring. That involved removing the defroster/water valve unit from the passenger side of the firewall, in order to access the posts where the wire from the dash-mounted heater control unit and the wire to the actual heaters attach. That involved pinching off the heater hoses and detaching them from the pipes on the defroster/water valve unit where they emerge into the engine compartment (trying all along to minimize the inevitable coolant mess). Then the nuts and washers had to be removed from the three mounting bolts, the two wires already mentioned had to be unhooked from, respectively, an inline fuse holder and a snap connector, the wire from the defroster had to be unbolted from the control unit, and the bracket for the thermostat tube had to be unscrewed from the firewall.

I lifted the defroster unit out of the car and took it to the kitchen counter to see how I could replace the old wires. On the side of the water valve that normally presses up against the passenger-compartment side of the firewall I saw the two terminals where the wire from the heater control unit and the wire to the under-the-seat heaters are soldered. I guessed (correctly as it happens) that one could hold a soldering iron to the terminal, melt the solder and remove the old wire. The replacement wires had pre-tinned ends that fit easily enough into the newly-vacated slots. Add a little more heat and some solder, and the new wires were in place.

My new wire set from Rhode Island Wiring included replacements for the two wires just mentioned, but not for the wire to the defroster itself. That wire, a 16-gauge lead on which the insulation was brittle and cracked, attaches at one end to the heater control unit by a small bolt that screws into a battered, but apparently still functional, resistor. The other end disappears down a little hole in the side of the defroster motor. I made a half-hearted effort to see if the defroster could be easily opened to expose the point of attachment for that wire. I soon gave up and decided to content myself with cutting the wire two or three inches from the defroster, and splicing on a length of new black-plastic-insulated wire for the rest of its run. I covered the splice with black heat-shrink tubing and called that an adequate repair.

Replacing the defroster/valve unit in the car went smoothly (did that before when I replaced all the heater hoses), and I reconnected two of the new wires. The wire from the defroster to the heaters is one of two segments that join behind the dash with a snap connector. Earlier, I had replaced the lower section of that wire, the one that goes from just inside the firewall through the same rubber grommet that the main wiring harness uses, down under the floorboards to the left-hand heater unit (once again I used the trick of taping the new wire to the old and pulling the old wire out to install the new wire). So now I was able to join the two segments at the snap connector. The wire from the valve to the control unit includes an inline fuse, and when I removed the defroster unit earlier, I had opened the fuse holder and left the far segment of the wire (and half of the fuse holder) connected to the control unit. Now I removed that old piece and attached the entire new wire (fuse holder and all). The defroster wire I left unattached, to save strain on the distressed resistor it screws onto until the control unit was once again mounted under the replaced dash.

After I finished replacing the heater wiring, I started wrestling with myself over which direction to pull the old main wiring harness out through the 2-inch hole in the firewall. On one hand, there were a whole lot more gizmos attached on the section of the harness on the passenger compartment side (light sockets, body harness connector, etc.). On the other hand, the section in front of the firewall was a lot longer, and it had a couple of bulky branching points that might not go through the little hole. I decided to pull from the front, and to cut the body harness connector from the harness so it would not cause the whole thing to hang up in the firewall opening.

I lifted the inside part of the harness free of things it could catch on (like the steering column braces, the instrument cluster and the cowl vent mechanism) and I began pulling from the engine compartment, gently coaxing the wire clusters and bulb sockets through. When the last bit of the harness had come through the hole, I carefully gathered the entire mess out of the space between the engine and the left front fender, carefully making sure that sharp edges didn't scratch the car's paint, and I removed the crumbling bundle from the car. It resembled nothing more than a rotted mass of jungle vines with craggy tendrils dangling in odd directions. The brittle insulation and places where the bare wires were exposed was a sobering confirmation of the reason for doing this project.

On Monday, I laid the new wiring harness out to consider the best approach for putting it in. On balance, I still preferred going in from the front. I had another idea, and I took some Scotch tape and loosely bound each of the bundles of terminal ends along the segment of the harness that had to go through the hole. That way, they would be more likely to slip smoothly through the hole without hanging up. In fact, I was able to pass the behind-the-dash section of the harness easily through the firewall hole up to the point where I could begin positioning the engine compartment wiring.

Seen from the engine compartment, a black tentacle about an inch thick emerges from the firewall and extends downward for about four inches before dividing. One branch extends horizontally along the firewall, behind the engine, ending at the starter solenoid and relay terminals. Along the way, the wires that connect to the horn relay, the voltage regulator and the engine temperature sending unit emerge. A second branch crosses the space between the firewall and the inner panel of the fender on the driver's side to run forward along that panel, jump over to the radiator, run over the top of the radiator and end on the inside of the other fender. Out of this branch come a smaller branch containing the wires to the generator, individual wires to the fender-mounted terminal blocks for the headlight sub-harnesses, and two more smaller branches that feed the right and left horns and turn signal sockets. The third branch goes straight down, splitting into the horn switch wire, the three wires that connect to the headlight dimmer switch, and the two wires that connect to the stoplight switch.

All of these connections went into place reasonably easily. Between the cross-referenced list that came with the wiring harness, and a photograph from the 1941 service manual that indicates the color coding on each of the voltage regulator and horn relay connections, I found a high level of confidence that the job was going correctly. One quirk is that the terminals on the starter relay are unmarked, thwarting efforts to match the color-coded wires to the proper destination. The best advice I could get was to hook them up and hope for the best(!) After the car is put back together, if the starter doesn't engage when I push the button, I can switch those two connections.

A day or two later I started to work on connecting the dashboard wiring. Using the cross-reference list and the diagram I had made before I removed the old harness, I carefully located and attached the instrument cluster wires, starting with the temperature gauge and working my way across the ammeter and the fuel gauge. The behind-the-dash picture from the 1941 service manual provided confirmation that the right wires were in place. Since I'd left in place the little metal tube that connects the oil pressure gauge to the engine, I had used a piece of wire to keep the instrument cluster suspended in roughly its normal position. That way, the stress on that tube would be minimal. Now with the new wiring harness attached (and pulling down on the cluster) that wire was even more important.

The wires that connect to the bakelite connector for the turn signal harness were easy to locate with their little square copper terminal ends.

The three terminals on the turn signal flasher are identified by letters that correlate with the harness chart, so that hookup was easy. Attaching the wires for the headlight switch was also pretty straightforward. Two wires to the ignition switch, and suddenly most of the connections had been made. Connecting the starter button would have to wait until the dash was back in place, since the connections are made with the wires pulled through the hole, and the button is then pushed into the dash from the front and fastened into place.

The Body Harness Connector

That left one remaining cluster of wires to be addressed—the body harness connector. If I'd done things right in the first place, what I'd have to do now would have been to take the old female side of the connector off of the old harness and attach it to the six corresponding wires on the new harness. Then I could rejoin the male and female halves of the connector and call the job done. But since I, in my overabundant zeal, had cut the *male* part of the connector off of the body harness, there was a lot more to do. Bill Sullivan had suggested the short-cut solution to this problem— just splice the body harness wires to the new harness and forget about the six-pin connector. No one would be the wiser, as this connector sits high up behind the dash right at the base of the windshield pillar. Even if I had the car judged at some show in the future, the odds that a judge would (a) look, (b) see that a connector was missing and (c) count points off were low.

But the more I looked at the torn ends of the body harness and the fresh ends of the corresponding wires in the new harness, the more I found myself musing about putting it back together "according to Hoyle." So I cut the female end of the connector off of the old harness and went to work on it with a small screwdriver, gently prying up the tabs that held the outside metal cover to the circular plastic disc with the six sockets in it. When I slid the metal cover back along the attached wires and off, I saw how the wires were attached. Each of the six sockets had a metal tab with a small hole in it. The end of the wire was inserted into the hole in the tab, it was soldered there and the end of the wire was trimmed close to the solder joint. Small pieces of light cardboard were snaked among the sockets to prevent shorts. In the kitchen with my soldering iron I heated and removed each of the wire stubs from the female plug, taking care to open each of the little holes that new wires would have to fit through.

The prongs of the male plug consisted of ½ inch-long metal tubes into which the ends of the body harness wires were inserted. The tubes were then heated, and solder was allowed to flow in to bind wire to tube, and form solid prongs to fit the sockets on the female plug. So I gently pried back the tabs holding the metal cover in place and slid it off over the cut ends of the wires. I applied soldering iron heat to each prong in turn and removed the old wire ends, doing my best to clean out the old solder from each tube. Returning to the front seat of the Cadillac, I trimmed the cut ends of the body harness wires so that they were even, and I carefully stripped the wire ends and tinned each of them with solder. I congratulated myself for remembering to slide the plug cover onto the wires before inserting them into the plug. Using the chart that came with the new harness I took each of the wires that I had labeled during the experiment that Emilyann and I had performed, and I inserted each into its assigned tube (hopefully!). One at a time I heated the tube and allowed solder to flow in through the end. Soon enough all six wires were in place and I could slide the metal cover down over the plug and carefully bend the retaining tabs back over the edge of the plastic disc.

Since I had already placed the wiring harness in the car, I had to work on the female plug in the front seat as I had with the male plug. I stripped a half inch of insulation from each of the six wires. In another burst of unusually rational thinking I remembered to slip the wires through the metal case of the plug *before* attaching the wires to their tabs. (I love averting tragedy.) Carefully double-checking the correct alignment of wires and sockets and working three wires at a time, I inserted the wires into the holes on the respective tabs and soldered each in place. I trimmed the excess wire ends, replaced the paper insulation strips, slid the metal cover into place and carefully folded the metal fastener tabs to grip the plastic disc.

Replacing the Dashboard

My limo sat idle from the time I began replacing the dash and engine wiring harness. At the same time, I had pulled out the dashboard and the windshield glass (one pane was cracked, and why not replace both if I'm doing one?). I had the new windshield glass cut and I ordered the new rubber pieces that seal and hold the glass in place, and I put those aside ready to put back in. I wanted to get the question of the dashboard resolved first. My first preference was to restore the original walnut burl pattern, vs. painting the dash a solid color.

The dashboard's appearance had been an "issue" for the length of time I'd owned the car. The standard dash on a 1941 Cadillac was finished to

The Old Dashboard. Behind the steering wheel the water damage to the dashboard finish can be seen. The rest of the dash was dull and faded.

look like burled walnut. This was accomplished with a decal (trade name "Di-Noc") applied over the metal surface. Generally, the decal did not hold up well to years of sunlight exposure and the inevitable leakage from the lower outside corners of the windshield. So unless the car was extremely well cared for and stored indoors a good deal of the time, odds are that an original dash will be faded, streaked and dull. Over the years, water dripping from the corner of the windshield (a weak point in the weatherstrip seal around the glass) will have eaten away at the decal and left unsightly stains.

The centrality and conspicuousness of this part of the car makes fixing it a high priority. Now, some 1941 Cadillacs came from the factory with dashboards painted solid colors instead of the faux wood finish. Chauffer-driven cars with black leather front compartments would typically have black painted dashes. And Cadillac would paint the dash (and the steering column and cowl vent handle as well) a solid color at the customer's request. So a restorer can legitimately do it either way—woodgrain or painted finish.

With the dashboard out of the car, whatever research I'd done in the past about getting it refinished quickly changed from academic and theoretical, to timely and practical. One old Cadillac parts vendor in California had indicated on its website that a '41 Cadillac dashboard could be refinished for $450. When I called, they told me they could do it in a couple of weeks, but that the $450 price was a misprint, and they would have to contact the contractor they used to determine the actual price. While I waited for the promised callback, I phoned another west coast vintage parts dealer and asked if they knew where I could get my dash regrained. They gave me the name and number of a fellow they enthusiastically recommended. When I called, the fellow said he no longer did that sort of work. When I asked if he knew anyone else, he gave me the name of "the only person in Southern California I'd recommend." When I looked up the second man's phone number and called, he told me I could have the dash done for $375 ($400 if I left stripping it to bare metal to him). But the rub was that it would take 4 or 5 *months*. Aarrgh! To have the car out of commission for that length of time was not what I had in mind at all. Maybe I could get him to put my name in the book for some day this coming May or June, and I could send him the dash then.

At Barry Wheeler's suggestion I contacted a commercial metal refinishing company that had redone a 1941 dash several years ago for several hundred dollars. They asked me to send my dash to their location in Michigan for a price estimate. I nearly fell over when they said it would cost me $1,200. So I asked them to send the dash back to me, and it sat, still packed, in my garage while I pondered other options.

Another query on the Cadillac-LaSalle Club message board elicited a response from Bob Hoffmann in California, who had a refinished dash from a Series 62 that he was planning to strip and repaint in a solid color. He reasoned that it was a shame to strip a refinished dash if someone could use it, and could trade a dash that no one would mind being stripped. Owing to the vagaries of the way 1941 Cadillacs were assembled, dashboards for Series 62 and Series 75 cars interchange, but cannot be used for Series 61, 63, 67 or 60 Special cars. While I waited to hear back from Bob, I called an outfit that advertises in *Hemmings Motor News* and was quoted a price of $1,100. At about the same time, AllCads got back to me with the name of a really conscientious-sounding fellow in New Hampshire who wanted $850.

So, I had this dilemma: On the one hand, I return the dash to its original burled walnut finish, but that would be expensive or long-delayed if I wanted it to look truly authentic. On the other hand, I could get the dash painted a solid color and be within the bounds of authenticity, since Cadillac would do that for any customer who asked them to. The latter course would require some thought as to what would look right with the (real) wood garnish moldings and trim panels. Would a person viewing the car for the first time think it was odd for the dash to be a solid color and the rest of the trim to be finished wood? On yet another hand, to be *really* authentic, the wide wood panels on the doors and behind the front seat would have to be covered with a fake burled walnut treatment with three narrow horizontal strips of a pale color (simulating an inlay). Photos of original 1941 Series 75s that I have seen on the Internet clearly bear this out.

My impression was (and is) that a car like mine would have had a solid-color-painted dash only if it had been built with a divider window and a black leather front compartment, or if the original owner was an eccentric. If I were to paint the dash, I suppose that either black or the bronze color that the steering column is painted would be the two most acceptable choices.

So when Bob Hoffman called me back and proposed a much less painful price than any I'd heard up to that point, I accepted. I shipped my dash to Bob, and he shipped his back to me. When I opened the box that Bob had carefully packed the dash in, I was beside myself with glee. It was lovely and new-looking and I couldn't wait to see how the car looked with it.

Over the next few evenings, I replaced the horizontal chrome trim strips that run from the outboard edge of the speedometer and clock openings out to the edge of the dash. I cleaned and replaced the cigar lighter on the lower edge of the dash, below the clock opening. I cut a paper grommet for the windshield wiper switch, cleaned the knurled knob and replaced the switch on the center of the dash above the radio opening. Some time ago, I had cut new paper grommets for the clock and speedometer bezels, and now I did the same for the radio grille and the instrument cluster.

Then on April 11, a Sunday evening, I put the new dash into my car. I hadn't planned on doing it just then—just wanted to do a dry run and see what was going to have to be done. I had put friction tape on the top lip of the dash and wrapped the body harness connector in foam rubber so it couldn't bang around (since the new length didn't permit anchoring it in its assigned clip). One thing led to another and suddenly I was putting the dash back into place and fastening the instrument cluster to it. I got all the dash mounting bolts into place and tightened them down. I installed the steering column clamp bolts. (Thanks to Harry Scott for the heads-up about the little chromed machine screw that positions the cowl vent brace!) I positioned and fastened the light switch and remounted the heater control unit. The ignition switch went back in easily, though I decided to reroute the wires that attach to it to give them a bit more slack. The starter switch was next. Replacing the fog light switch was trickier than it should have been, because I kept dropping one of the mounting nuts behind the dash as I worked by feel without visual reference. My vestigial throttle cable went back in next. After dinner, I got the glove box manhandled back into position and its mounting screws back in. I attached the cigar lighter feed wire and installed the passenger-side defroster outlet before calling it quits for the night.

The next evening I repainted the clock hands and cleaned the dial glass before replacing the whole assembly in the dash. I put the driver's side defroster vent back in (had to use my old trick of a long Philips-head screwdriver with the screw taped to the end) and replaced the defroster hoses. Then I put the speedometer back in. I've had to pull and replace the speedometer several times in the past, and it's always been an angst-ridden process, as I agonized over the fate of the frail wiring I was muscling out of the way to get at the mounting nuts and the cable nut. With fresh wiring, I can stick my hand in with calm confidence!

With the speedometer and the clock back in, it was starting to look like a '41 Cadillac driver's compartment again, this time with a proper finish to the dashboard. So I gave in and put the radio grille back in place to see the full effect. It was amazing. Even my wife was impressed. I couldn't wait to get the windshield back in so I could see the WHOLE full effect with the steering wheel and the chrome garnish moldings!

I replaced the windshield wiper switch link and cut some foam plastic to replace the dried black goop that remained around the circumference of the radio speaker. The next evening I sat on the edge of the front seat and coaxed the radio up behind the dash and into its appointed position behind its grille. Once I'd gotten the volume and tuning knob shafts through their holes, I was able to screw the retaining nuts down and secure the radio in place. I fastened the bolt that sticks out from the driver's side of the radio case to the dash-to-firewall brace that helps stabilize the (heavy!) radio against road bumps. Fastening the escutcheon plates over the tuning and volume knob shafts involved the familiar exercise of snaking my hand up behind the dash to slip the washers and nuts into place and wrench them down tight. Two set screws secured each knob in place. Once the antenna cable was plugged back in, the feed wire fuse case was hooked together and the dial light feed was connected, the radio was reinstalled.

At this point I was praying and hoping that the wiring was all properly connected. Not until I'd gotten the engine running again and begun testing the lights would I know for sure if I was going to have to remove the dash and go back to that body harness connector for more surgery. So, on Tax Day, 2004, I decided to start experimenting. For the first test, I made sure all switches were off and the doors were closed. Since both clocks were disconnected, I should have been able to hook up the battery and have no current flow. I should have been unable to make a spark as I touched the cable end to the battery terminal. So I leaned over the right front fender and brought the loose battery cable slowly up to the terminal. No spark jumped, no matter how many times I bumped the cable end to the terminal. That was a very good sign.

I left the battery disconnected and hooked my battery charger up to both of the car's battery cables to begin testing the electrical system. This was a technique Bill Sullivan suggested I use. If there were a short or incorrect hookup, the battery charger wouldn't put enough oomph through the system to rapidly fry the wires or start a fire, the way the battery could. With the charger running, I opened the rear door and happily watched the courtesy lights flash on. That meant that at least one connection on the headlight switch was correct, and most importantly, it meant that at least one of the wires in that confounded body harness connector was properly hooked up! Opening the front door switched the dome light on.

I walked around to the driver's seat and pulled out the headlight switch to the first click. The parking lights came on (driver's side was dim, though) and the taillights and license plate light glowed nicely. Two more correct headlight switch connections, and another correct one for the body harness connector. I couldn't tell if the instrument lights had come on, though, and that was a little bit worrisome. It might mean that a light switch connection was incorrect or loose. The heater control glowed correctly when I moved the switch from the "off" position. Since I had seen no evidence of a short or fire hazard, I moved the charger connection from the loose battery cable to the battery terminal while I went inside to get the ignition key.

When I returned, I removed the charger and hooked the battery up to the car. I put the key in the ignition and turned it. Immediately I heard the hum of the radio beginning to warm up. I pushed the radio's "off" button to save power, but brightened at the evidence that the radio had been installed and connected correctly. When I turned the key I also heard the old familiar "ping" as the instruments sprang to life. The fuel gauge needle jumped to the "almost half a tank" position. That meant that yet another connection in the body harness connector was right. I couldn't get the turn signals to work, and that was a disappointment. A large part of the motivation to go ahead and replace the wiring harness was the shorted turn signals. I was going to have to work on this challenge.

I pressed the "start" button and the starter spun eagerly. I thought "Why not?" and began pumping the accelerator to start the engine. But the car wanted to be playful, and that pesky joint between the accelerator pedal and the throttle linkage let go. So I switched the ignition off, got out and snaked my arm down between the windshield washer bottle and the gear shift linkage to put the joint back together. When I again engaged the starter, the car caught happily after the carb bowl filled up. It still worked! After three months of idleness, the engine was running again, and very smoothly. I was momentarily surprised by the rush of air through the empty windshield opening. The ammeter showed that the generator was charging strongly. I tried the headlights, and the driver's side glowed dimly, while the other lamp shone brightly. I made a mental note to check whether I'd tightened the connections at the fender-mounted junction strip on the left-hand side.

I still couldn't see the instrument lights, so I twisted the knob alternately one way and the other. Not since I had installed the correct headlight switch in 1968 had the rheostat that lets the driver dim the panel lights been included in the circuit. I had already installed the switch (risking crusty, crumbling insulation on the wires as I disconnected each from the old switch and hooked them to the new one) before I found out that I was supposed to run a wire from the terminal that goes to the taillights to one side of the rheostat, and to hook the instrument lights wire to the other side of that rheostat. So at the time I just left things as they were, with the instrument lights hooked directly to the taillights terminal (on-off, no varying the brightness). Gratifyingly, twisting the knob established real, if somewhat uneven, contact. But only the speedometer, clock and radio dial lights came on, and the instrument cluster stayed dark. Another factor that had persuaded me to redo the wiring was my inability to get the instrument cluster light to come back on after I took the speedometer out shortly after the car reached Virginia.

After I'd run the engine for a while, long enough to warm it up (and incidentally prove that the temperature gauge was hooked up correctly), I shut it off, got my drop light and went under the dash. One thing I have noticed is how much easier it is to see what is what behind the dash, as compared to the way things were with the old wiring. You can see the color coding and everything is cleaner. There are no loose bands of old electrician's tape scattered about and wires take smooth paths from one point to another, easily followed by the eye. It didn't take long to see that the bulb and socket for the instrument cluster light was out of place and hanging by its wire. Oh, goody! A *simple* problem! I snaked my hand up through the wires and cables and gently replaced the socket in its hole. When I pulled the headlight switch out, all of the dash lights lit up together for the first time in 30 years.

Now for the turn signal problem. I located and examined the bakelite connector that joins the three wires from the steering wheel hub turn signal switch to the flasher, the feed wire and the wire to the little red indicator light on the speedometer face. I made sure all of the connections were tight and that they were properly sorted out. Everything matched the wiring chart, but when I turned the key and tried the signals again there still was no response. I was brooding over what could be responsible for the absence of function when my wife came out to see the new dash installed and in place. She was enormously impressed with the transformation of the driver's compartment, even without the steering wheel (awaiting installation of the new windshield). She was puzzled why I wasn't elated over the car's return to functional status.

Then something occurred to me. The old wiring for the turn signals had included a 9-amp fuse in a metal tubular fuse holder. The new wiring harness had the same sort of fuse holder, and I had simply put a 9-amp fuse into it. A 9-amp fuse is noticeably shorter than a 10-amp fuse, and if the new fuse holder was not designed to hold a 9-amp fuse, the turn signals might not be getting any electrical power at all. So I located a 10-amp fuse and swapped the 9-amp fuse for it. Then, when I turned the key and tried the turn signals they operated beautifully, front and rear. This meant that one more of the body harness connector wires was correctly joined! The left front turn signal was dim, just like the left front parking light. That strongly suggested a poor connection at the back of the lamp unit, and sure enough, when I checked I found the connector not fully seated. Once I twisted it back into place, both the parking light and the turn signal behaved as intended.

For one last test, I turned off the garage light and my drop light, closed the garage door, opened the driver's door and stuck my foot in to depress the brake pedal. Still standing outside the car, I looked back to see the brake lights putting a pool of red light on the inside of the garage door. Ah, the feeling of relief to know that the body harness connector had been replaced correctly, and I wasn't going to have to take the dash apart again to rework it!

With that I finally allowed myself to believe that the new wiring harness had been successfully installed. Everything that worked before still worked, and a list of things that didn't work now performed properly or better—turn signals, dash lights, brake lights. And best of all, the wiring was much, much safer, with no potential short circuits due to exposed wire, brittle insulation and tired repairs with old electrical tape. The dash looked new. The turn signal switch now operated smoothly. And a lot of cleaning of instrument bezels and other detailing had been done.

15. Windshields, Weatherstrip and Worn Gears

Windshield Replacement

Shortly after I removed the dashboard, I also took out the windshield. As noted before, sometime during the limousine's long sleep at my parents' house, the driver's-side half of the windshield had been cracked. It wasn't broken through, but five or six meandering cracks radiated from a spot near the rearview mirror. Apart from being unaesthetic, this was the sort of thing that would prevent passing a state inspection, should I want to get a regular registration for the car someday. Another "issue" with the windshield was a fairly common feature of these old GM cars—significant leaks at the lower outboard corners of the windshield halves. The grommet that seals the windshield to the car body is a rubber channel with a squared-off "U" cross section into which the edge of each windshield pane fits. At the lower outside corner of each glass pane, the outline of the glass, and the channel that encases it, take a sharp bend, rounded, but a sharper-than-90-degree change of direction. The natural tendency is for the sides of the channel to bulge away from the glass at this bend, and even with the garnish molding holding it to the glass from the inside, and the pinch-weld molding holding it to the glass from the outside, it is very easy for the channel to allow water to get past the edge of the windshield and enter the car. That's why so many of these cars have water tracks down the dash under those outside corners, where the dash finish has been streaked or dissolved.

After discussing the theory of it for the umpteenth time with my friend Harry Scott, I finally just set about removing the windshield. First I started tentatively peeling back the old rubber grommet that held the driver's side (cracked) pane around its top, outboard and bottom edges, and

I progressed to using a utility knife on the inside edge of the grommet, cutting it back even with the edge of the glass. After a while, only the inboard edge of the pane was still held by the separate rubber piece bound to the divider strip that separates the two halves of the windshield. Standing on the running board with one hand inside the car, I thumped the glass from the outside until the outer upper corner began to move away from the rubber. Then I sat on the front seat and pried the glass towards me, slipped it out of the groove in the center rubber strip and removed it from the car. The glass had come out in one piece (though cracked) and I had a good pattern for a replacement.

I examined the rest of the channel, especially where it joined the separate rubber piece that holds in place the stainless steel reveal molding that frames the windshield as part of the car's exterior trim. I had nursed a faint hope of separating the windshield grommet from this separate piece (known as the "pinchweld seal") and thereby being able to leave in place the stainless molding, which several people had told me was difficult to remove without crimping or otherwise permanently damaging it. But it rapidly became clear that the two rubber parts were too difficult to pry apart successfully. So, I just pulled, chipped and scraped the windshield rubber channel out, all the way to the center post.

I knew I was going to have to remove the stainless reveal, at least on the driver's side, and I knew that to do so required removing the exterior stainless piece that covers the center vertical windshield divider bar. That stainless piece was originally put into place by snapping it over a rubber retainer piece that was first fitted onto the divider strip. By this time I had resigned myself to removing the intact passenger-side windshield pane as well as the cracked pane. Not to do so could mean a very noticeable mismatch between the new driver's-side glass and the original passenger-side glass. Moreover, arranging a leak-free seal between the new rubber for the driver's-side glass and the remaining original rubber holding the passenger-side glass in place would be iffy, at best.

So, I began unscrewing the bolts holding the inside chrome strip to the divider bar. I successfully removed all but one without breaking or ruining the bolt. I mangled the slots of that last bolt and the last ⅛ inch of it broke off and stayed in place. Oh, well. I took off the chrome strip with the attached rear view mirror and set it aside. Next I pried loose the rubber piece that separated the two glass panes. Going over to the passenger side of the front seat, I removed the other glass pane, set it aside and pulled out the rest of the windshield grommet material.

The divider bar (really a 1-inch wide strip of steel with embedded nuts) had two rubber pieces that had to be removed and replaced. The rubber on the inside surface of the divider bar had a squashed capital letter "I" cross-section, embracing the inboard edge of each of the windshield panes and holding them in a "V" configuration. The outside piece was hollow and roughly tubular with a letter-C cross-section. The ends of the "C" were sandwiched between the inside rubber piece and the metal strip, with the stainless trim molding enveloping the round part of the "C." Needless to say, both rubber parts had to be removed and discarded. The exposed metal strip had some rust, but not a great deal.

Where the windshield had been there was now a gaping hole, split by the center divider strip. The perimeter of the hole was defined by the pinchweld. When the body shell was manufactured at the Cadillac plant, the piece that forms the inside of the cowl, windshield pillars and "header" was welded to the cowl and exterior windshield frame by pinching the edges of both pieces together all the way around the windshield opening and welding them together—hence the term "pinchweld." Besides holding the sheetmetal pieces together, the pinchweld also serves as a frame for the windshield to be anchored against, as well as something for the stainless steel reveal molding to hold onto.

I took the windshield panes to the local auto glass place and asked them to replicate both in clear safety glass. Meanwhile, I ordered from Steele Rubber Products a new rubber channel with the center slotted strip, all vulcanized into a single unit. The theory was that the windshield could be put in with the complete grommet, all at once, with a reliable seal. I also went over the windshield opening to remove the vestiges of the old channel and the old pinchweld seal. I sanded the rust from the center strip, and whatever rust there was on the pinchweld. And I painted the exposed areas of the pinchweld with black Rustoleum paint. I did the same for the center divider strip. Drilling out the broken bit of bolt from the divider strip was a fairly simple job.

I put a query out on the Cadillac-LaSalle Club message board, seeking advice on installing the windshield, specifically, whether the dashboard should be in place before the windshield is installed, what kind(s) of sealant goop should be used and how and where each type should be applied. The consensus of the two gentlemen who replied to my question was that the dashboard should be in place before installing the windshield, and that the best results are achieved when one finds and hires an old-timer auto glass repairman. Both said that the latter was well worth the price.

The week after Easter (by which time I had reinstalled the dashboard), Harry Scott brought me a copy of a page in the Fisher Body Manual that included instructions for replacing 1941 windshields. The text described the procedure in some detail. It specifically called for the use of "cementing compound F.S. 655" and "F.S. 638 sealing compound." My best surmise was that F.S. 655 would be equivalent to 3M weatherstrip adhesive and that F.S. 638 would be equivalent to 3M windshield sealant that comes in caulking gun tubes. With that in mind, the exercise would go like this:

1. Put weatherstrip adhesive on the pinchweld all around the windshield opening.
2. Install the pinchweld rubber seal.
3. Install the rubber piece that surrounds the center metal divider strip and put something (adhesive? sealer?) where the edges of this piece meet the pinchweld rubber seal.
4. Install the right- and left-side reveal moldings. (Note: the instructions do NOT appear to envision putting weatherstrip adhesive in the groove of the pinchweld rubber seal where the reveal molding sits.)
5. Install the center division stainless cap molding.
6. Pack the angle where the inside surface of the (installed) pinchweld rubber seal meets the inside cowl surface with windshield sealer over the entire perimeter of the windshield opening.
7. Pack the space between the edges of the (installed) divider strip rubber piece, where the inner surface of the metal divider strip remains exposed, with windshield sealer, extending the sealer at top and bottom to the bead you just put around the perimeter.
8. Quickly and efficiently insert into place the windshield halves in their grommet (likely a two-man operation involving some serious effort).
9. Replace interior garnish moldings to hold glass and grommet in place, and replace the interior chrome strip with rear view mirror so you can...
10. ...stuff weatherstrip adhesive in between the front flap of the windshield grommet/channel and the windshield glass.
11. It also appeared that the instructions called for stuffing weatherstrip adhesive between the center section of the windshield grommet and the divider strip rubber piece, but that seems like an ungainly and not very profitable operation.

On the evening of April 22, I set about cutting the pinchweld rubber seal to fit. I worked it onto the pinchweld (without any adhesive) all around the windshield opening in such a way that the ends of the long rubber extrusion met and crossed at the base of the windshield center divider strip. I notched the rubber on either side of the spot where it crossed over the upper end of the divider strip, and I cut out enough rubber so that the seal would lie flat across the divider strip and remain engaged with the pinchweld on either side of the strip. I did the same thing with the free ends of the seal at the base of the divider strip and then trimmed the ends so that they would butt up together.

I stepped back and looked at the provisionally installed seal, and thought I would see if the reveal molding was going to be easy or difficult to fit. As I held the molding up to the pinchweld seal it gradually became clear that I was wrong about placement—the seal was inside out. The side of the molding that was supposed to be facing the inside of the car was, indeed, facing the inside of the car. But the wrong groove of the "S" cross-sectioned rubber seal had been fitted over the pinchweld. Thoughtfully, Steel Rubber had molded the seal in such a way that one of the grooves was wider than the other. The thin groove embraces the edge of the correspondingly thin stainless reveal molding, and the wider groove matches up nicely with the pinchweld (two thicknesses of body sheetmetal). Properly oriented, the seal holds the reveal molding snugly against the body sheetmetal. Fortunately, it was just a matter of removing the seal and flipping it. The trimming I had done previously worked just as well in the correct orientation. (Cue for a sigh of relief!) I was very glad I had dry-fit the seal before gluing it in.

Now I knew I could get the car ready for the actual windshield installation. The reveal molding was still going to be a bit tricky, wrestling it into position over the pinchweld seal, and putting the stainless center divider piece back in place over its rubber retainer promised to be an interesting activity in its own right. But the steps in the procedure were now clear.

The next evening, I decided to glue the pinchweld seal in place. I taped paper towels to cover the dash and catch any drips. Starting with the driver's side, I pulled the rubber seal off of the pinchweld where I had dry-fit it. I took my tube of 3M weatherstrip adhesive and applied a layer to both sides of the pinchweld where the rubber seal seats. Then I replaced the seal on the adhesive-daubed pinchweld and repeated the whole process on the passenger side. Once the pinchweld seal was in place, I couldn't stop myself from getting the driver's-side half of the reveal molding and holding it up to the windshield opening to think about how it was going to go in and how easy or difficult it would be. Some people advise removing or at least loosening the windshield wiper mounts that sit about ¼ inch away from where the reveal molding sits when installed. I decided to see if I could get away without going back under the dashboard to do that.

I could see that the fit was going to be snug. The molding has an outer lip that forms a shiny ¾" wide outline for the windshield, and an inner lip that grips the pinchweld from within the car. Between the molding and the pinchweld is the rubber seal, which also folds back over the inner lip of the molding to meet the rubber channel that holds the windshield. Once the rubber seal is in place, the trick is to slide the molding over the rubber seal without seriously dislodging it. It's an art and not a science—to judge by my car, the original installation at the factory was not always absolutely perfect. I'd heard a lot of warnings and horror stories about kinking, bending or otherwise ruining the reveal molding in the process of removing or installing it. For one thing, the inevitable petrified state of the rubber after years of aging makes even beginning to get the molding off a real trick. For another, the molding has to be flexed significantly to work it out of the opening, and to work it back in when installing it. So there was an undertone of suspense throughout this adventure.

When I was a grade school student eagerly assembling plastic models of airplanes, military vehicles and cars, I was always very impatient. I generally ignored the instruction "and set aside to dry." And I would start fitting the pieces together long before I opened the instructions, sometimes even gluing things together as I went. On more than one occasion, I found to my regret that I'd skipped a step, preventing some nifty action feature from functioning correctly. That sort of experience only tempered and didn't cure my impatience.

As I held the reveal molding, the itch to start putting it into place overcame thoughtful prudence. The "U" shaped piece had come off of the car starting where the center divider meets the roof. That leg of the "U" was pulled downward and toward the center of the car, drawing the upper outer corner off of the pinchweld. That allowed the lower corner to be pulled free and the whole piece to be removed from the car. So to put it back, I started with the lower leg of the "U", fitting the molding over the rubber seal along the cowl and coaxing the lower corner into the lower outer corner of the windshield opening. I squeezed the legs of the "U" together enough to sneak the upper corner of the molding into the upper outer corner of the windshield opening and began pulling the base of the "U" into place along the side of the windshield opening. As that part of the molding settled in, I worked on the legs of the "U" along the cowl and the roof header. After a bit of persuasion, the ends of the "U" could comfortably fit into the corners where the center divider met the cowl at the bottom and the roof at the top. The piece was installed and it looked pretty reasonable.

I went around to the passenger side with the other half of the reveal molding and did the same workout on that side. Once both reveal molding pieces were replaced, only the center divider remained. The stainless steel cap molding that covers the divider strip is held in place by snapping it over a hollow rubber piece that covers the strip itself. The rubber piece has a "C" cross section and the ends of the "C" embrace the divider strip, with the belly of the "C" pointing up and out in front of the car. The decorative stainless piece clips over the belly of the "C" and embraces it and the strip in a single assembly. I put adhesive on the inside surfaces of the rubber piece where it would contact the metal strip, and worked it into place over the strip. Convincing the stainless piece to clip onto the rubber piece took a significant amount of wrestling, but as with a lot of these tasks, persistence eventually paid off. And there it was, looking very correct. I sat down inside the car and examined the inside of the reveal molding where the pinchweld seal folds over onto it. There were a couple of areas where the inside surface of the stainless molding was exposed, so I took the leftover ends of the seal material and cut narrow strips to fill these gaps, gluing them in with weatherstrip adhesive. Now to see about hiring an old-time windshield glass man. Harry Scott had mentioned such a fellow who lived in Stafford, Virginia and who might be willing to help out.

On Saturday April 24, Harry came over to see what I'd done putting the windshield reveal molding back in, and to discuss and explore the process of putting the new windshield into place. That morning I had purchased a 15-foot coil of 3M Windo-Weld(tm) Molded Sealant and a caulking gun–style tube of 3M Windo-Weld(tm) Sealant, and I showed these to Harry. He agreed with my thought that these products could fill in for the "cementing compound F.S. 655" and "F.S. 638 sealing compound" called for in the Fisher Body manual.

I showed Harry the reveal molding installation including the couple of spots where the rubber pinchweld seal had been displaced, and my efforts to remedy those spots with scraps of seal material. We talked about how the two sealing products ought to be applied, and concluded that the preformed coiled product should be packed down the middle of the center divider strip (between the edges of the rubber piece that holds the center stainless piece in place) and around the perimeter of the windshield opening in the angle that accommodates the squared-off edge of the windshield rubber channel. The stuff in the tube would go on the pinchweld rubber seal where the seal would press against the installed windshield channel.

Harry wanted to see how the rubber channel and the windshield glass would go together, so we took the new glass and channel into the house, spread the channel out on the floor so it assumed the shape of the windshield, and worked each glass pane into the channel. The fit was just right— snug, but not strained. And the assembled windshield could be handled (gently) as a single piece. The center rubber part had two lengthwise slits on one side, one on either side of the bolt holes, to allow for the "V" angle of the windshield when installed. Absent instructions from the rubber manufacturer, I decided that the slotted side should face the inside of the car. When we picked the windshield up and folded it to the approximate angle it would assume when installed in the car, it complied nicely and even stood up on its own when placed on the floor.

We decided to "dry-fit" the windshield, putting it into the car without adhesive in order to figure out the best way to do the job once all the sealing products had been applied. We had wondered whether it would be best to place the bottom corners first and pivot the windshield into the opening, or to locate the top of the windshield first and swing the lower part into place. This was a way to find out how things would work *before* there was a whole lot of sticky goop to deal with. We taped an old tablecloth in to protect the dash and the steering column. Harry got in on the passenger side and I passed him the windshield through the driver's door and climbed in myself. When we brought the windshield to the opening, it became quite clear that a direct approach was the only possibility. And even then, it *looked* like the windshield was too big to fit into the opening. Harry suggested fitting one side at a time, and he worked the passenger-side pane in while I held the driver's side. Then, as Harry pushed the center towards the divider strip, I tried to cajole the driver's side glass into the opening. It came close, but not close enough to push it in.

The thought occurred to us that if we did get the windshield in, it might be extremely difficult to get it out again without damaging the glass, the rubber or both. So we decided to put the glass aside, set our various sealing compounds in place, and then, as long as we'd made it this far, we'd do the installation for real. One additional preparation step we took was to remove from the door pillars a piece of the retaining material for the door windlacing that was interfering with putting the windshield into the opening. The windlacing was going to have to be replaced anyway, so this was an acceptable measure to ease the windshield installation.

We started with the coiled pre-extruded product. It was like nothing so much as a single strand of ⅜" thick black sticky spaghetti. When handled it was quite pliable and very tacky. It behaved like a sticky, more elastic Silly Putty. If you tried to pull off a piece, it stretched extensively, but if you pulled suddenly, the piece you wanted would snap off. The picture from the Fisher Body manual called for a significant build-up of sealing material down the middle of the center strip and around the perimeter where the corner of the windshield channel rests. We packed this putty-like compound in those locations, trying not to use so much that the windshield channel would be kept from seating fully against the cowl and the reveal molding seal. Once we thought we'd completed this step, I got the caulking gun with the tube of sealer, and Harry and I took the windshield outside and squirted sealer in between the edge of the windshield glass panes and the inside surface of the channel. Then back in the car, I put a bead of sealer all along the exposed flap of the pinchweld seal and down the driver's side edge of the center strip. Harry did the same thing on the passenger side, and I swapped the caulking gun for the windshield, handing Harry the passenger side end as before.

Once again, Harry put his end in place first and we began urging the assembly forward toward the center strip, and got a wide putty knife to help push the driver's side end of the windshield past the door pillar. It took a fair amount of steady effort from both of us before the windshield finally slipped into its hole. There were a couple of spots where I had to do some manipulating with my putty knife to make sure that the channel was properly seated (where the channel had been pushed out of position in the process of pushing the windshield into the opening). Real progress!

With the glass and rubber in place, it was time to replace the inside garnish moldings. Two of these mimic the reveal moldings, running across the top, the outer edge and the bottom of each windshield pane. Two small keystone-shaped pieces connect the two larger pieces. And a vertical chrome strip covers the center divider and carries the rear view mirror. These decorative pieces are also vital retaining devices to hold the windshield and its channel in place. It took some coordinating to get the perimeter pieces in place and joined properly at the top. And some trial and error was required to start the screws in the proper holes and in the proper direction to pull the moldings down into place. We realized after we'd gone this far that we had to loosen the moldings again to put the center piece with the rear view mirror in place. Ooops! Replacing the bolts that hold the center piece was tricky, but not as hard as it could have been. The rubber windshield channel had holes punched to allow these bolts to pass through, and for the most part, these were where they needed to be. In several instances though, I had to lever the bolt to pull the hole through the rubber into place so that the bolt could find its nut in the steel divider strip. Only a couple of days before we began this adventure, I received in the mail a replacement for the bolt that had broken when I took the windshield out in the first place. Finally, I screwed the keystone-shaped pieces in place at the top and at the bottom of the center divider.

Tightening the garnish moldings down squeezed little bits of sealing compound out of the windshield channel and out from between the channel and the pinchweld seal. But the material had not set up at all, and cleaning it up in liquid form promised to be more messy than leaving it and waiting to see if it congealed after a day or so. So it wasn't until the next day that I worked on trimming the overage. Sure enough, the material was much easier to remove neatly after it had had some time to set up. Once that was done and the glass was cleaned off and wiped down, The job was finally complete. And the car looked fabulous with its windshield and reveal molding back in place—*and no cracks in the glass!!* I put the steering wheel back on and twisted the horn button into place to complete the reassembly.

Now, for the first time, I could sit in the driver's seat and see what the driver of a brand new 1941 Cadillac Series 75 would have seen, with a crystal clear windshield framed in chrome, a creamy white steering wheel in front of a gleaming burled wood dash with sparkling chrome accents and trim. That's a nice feeling.

Door Weatherstrip Replacement

On May 8, 2004, I took the limousine out for its first drive since I started performing major surgery on the wiring system. My wife rode beside me on a leisurely drive through our neighborhood. We honked and waved at neighbors and enjoyed a beautifully mild Spring day. The car drove well and all systems operated correctly. I stopped to chat with one of my neighbors who noticed and appreciated the new dash. Afterwards, I parked the car in our driveway and tackled the passenger-side door weatherstripping.

Late in the previous Fall, I had begun replacing the long sponge rubber strips that go all around the edges of the doors to keep water, wind and other unwanted events from slipping in between the closed door and the body opening it fills. This was another job I had wanted to do since I bought the car. The original weatherstripping had hardened, cracked and fallen off in spots. When the fellow I bought the car from repainted it, the weatherstripping was painted over, further reducing its appearance and effectiveness. But until Steele Rubber Products began remanufacturing the rubber parts for these cars, there was no way to know with any certainty whether any generic weatherstripping product you purchased (from J.C. Whitney, for example) was going to fit, look right, or even do the job. So it wasn't until 2003 that I ordered replacement weatherstripping for the doors.

That Fall, I had pulled, pried, scraped and dug the old, congealed rubber and adhesive out of the angle between the inner surface of the panel that forms the outside "skin" of the door, and the perpendicular surface that forms the edges, top and bottom of the door. That old weatherstripping had a cotton cord running through it, which sometimes helped in the removal process and at other times only made digging out the old stuff that much harder. In some spots the old rubber was still pliable. In others it was crumbly or gooey or petrified. Eventually I got it all out from all four doors—I think I got it all, anyway. Then I sanded any rust spots and touched up the door edge surfaces with black Rustoleum paint wherever bare metal was exposed. As long as I was working in that neighborhood, I took the opportunity to clear out all eight door water drains with a 1" putty knife. Quite a bit of fine, tan New Mexico dust was removed during this operation.

I had installed the new weatherstripping on the driver's side doors, and I had learned some useful techniques for doing the installation without removing the doors from the car (which I'll describe later). But by the time Winter and the wiring project had conspired together to keep the car in the garage, I had gotten only as far on the passenger side as removal of the old weatherstripping and preparation of the door surface for the installation of the new material. Since the doors had to be opened all the way to apply the adhesive and place the new rubber, the car's confinement to the garage had made it impossible to complete the job.

So with the car outdoors for the first time that year, and plenty of room to swing the doors wide open, I retrieved the new weatherstripping from the trunk of the fastback, got my 3-M black weatherstrip adhesive and some paper and masking tape (to protect the fender and hood surfaces while daubing adhesive onto the forward edge of the front door). I cut off a length of weatherstripping long enough to make it all the way around the front door with about 6 inches extra just to be prudent. I lined the rubber up with the door so that the ends would meet (or cross) about halfway across the bottom edge under the door. Then I moved the weatherstrip aside and applied a thin coat of adhesive across the top of the door along the vertical and horizontal surfaces that form the angle in which the weatherstrip is supposed to sit. This process involved moving the nozzle of the tube of adhesive back and forth and from side to side, along the area to be covered while gently squeezing the tube to keep the product flowing steadily. Not actually smearing it along with my finger or another tool minimized the annoying thin strands of adhesive produced each time a finger or tool was withdrawn from the liquid adhesive. It's like a super-gluey, black version of mozzarella cheese, and the strands settle on (and adhere to) anything and everything. Besides, you need at least two hands for this procedure, and if one hand is full of goop, you must be very careful indeed. Also, this is definitely a great job to do *before* you reupholster your car.

Then I put adhesive on the corresponding surfaces of the weatherstrip. The principle is much the same as a contact cement, where glue is applied to both surfaces to be joined, and after the glue sets up a bit, the surfaces are pressed together. The adhesive set up pretty quickly in the warm sun and I placed the glued section of the rubber so that its profile matched the diagram that came with the product.

I followed the same process to attach the weatherstrip down the latch side of the door and about halfway across the lower edge of the door. Then came the tricky part. Even with the front door wide open, the hinged side of the door was really too close to the fender and the rear corner of the hood to apply the adhesive by just squeezing it out of the tube as the spout is drawn across the door surface. One way to apply the adhesive is to put some on a finger, reach in between the door and the body, and apply the adhesive that way. But I had figured out something better. I pulled the point and ink tube out of a clear plastic ballpoint pen and slipped the barrel onto the spout of the adhesive tube, making a 6-inch extension that could reach into the narrow space.

To protect the fender and hood surfaces I used painters tape to attach a couple of pieces of typing paper to cover the paint. Then I poked the nozzle extension in and applied a coating of adhesive where the weatherstrip needed to go. I applied adhesive to the weatherstrip itself, and then carefully threaded the long rubber snake in front of the hinges and between the door edge and the hood and fender until I was ready to press it into place on the door. The trick was to keep the glued surface of the weatherstrip from (a) mucking up painted surfaces on the way into place and (b) touching the glued surface of the door until it was correctly lined up. After that exercise, there remained only the matter of attaching the loose end of the weatherstripping to the underside of the door. Then to finish up by snipping the excess off so that the two ends of the weatherstrip mated up nicely.

The first closing of the newly-weatherstripped door was extremely gratifying, and you have to know some history of the car to know just how delighted I was. Ever since I bought this Series 75 sedan, the front passenger door was a tricky item. Unless it was shut gently and carefully, it would start to rattle loudly as I drove. These doors predate the elaborate exercises that car makers have engaged in over the years to prevent unexpected door openings, whether during ordinary driving or on impact. No geared sprockets, hooks that grab onto metal posts and so forth. The doors on a 1941 Cadillac are held shut by a simple chisel-shaped bolt, not unlike the average closet door in a residence. There is an adjustable striker plate that the bolt locks against, but no secondary catch. If the striker plate is out of adjustment in one direction, the bolt doesn't catch behind it and the door doesn't shut. If it's out of adjustment in the other direction, the door rattles. If someone shut the front passenger door with the amount of force ordinarily used in closing a car door, it would bang loudly, and rebound against the striker plate with enough force to pull it out of adjustment. That's when the rattle would start, and I'd have to unscrew the bolts that hold the striker plate and reset it. I don't know how many times I cautioned a passenger not to slam the door (with or without success). Nor do I know how many times I took screwdriver to striker plate afterwards. I do know that many times I insisted on reaching across the front seat and closing the door myself.

But with the weatherstrip in place, everything was different. Now, the door required a normal amount of force to shut it, and the sound it made when it was shut was that of a respectable classic car, and not a painful metallic indication that something was wrong. So, I shut it again. And again. And I called my wife out to observe the new phenomenon. I had had occasion to caution Barbara about the front passenger door only a couple of times, so she didn't fully appreciate what a big deal this was. But she understood that it was a big deal to me, and she expressed an appropriate enthusiasm (what a sweetheart!). Buoyed by this massive improvement, I went to work on the remaining door (rear passenger), and that went smoothly and uneventfully. The nozzle extension came in handy there, too.

The weatherstripping on all four doors had now been replaced. The only adequate response was to take another drive around the neighborhood! So I started the engine and off I went, enjoying the breeze and the late afternoon sunshine in my 63-year-old luxury car.

Steering Surgery

On July 25, 2004, I replaced the bearing at the end of the steering column. During the trip last Fall to the local upholstery shop for an estimate on replacing the limousine's tattered seat surfaces and door panels, I had noticed that turning the wheel to the right was a little bit harder than turning it to the left. There was just a hint of binding. The wheel didn't actually stick or require effort to unwind it after a turn, but there was not the same smooth lubricated feel that I felt when turning to the left.

This difference in steering effort between one side and the other brought back memories from years ago, when I had had to take the end off the steering gear box and replace a mangled bearing. Driving to and from high school I had noticed the increasing stiffness on right turns, until one trip home, when each right turn had required substantial force to return the wheel to the straight-ahead position. Once I got home, I crawled under the car and set to work on the steering box. The lock nut was pretty easy to knock loose, and then I unscrewed the round threaded end plug of the steering box that serves as the race for the bearing at the end of the steering shaft.

Under normal circumstances, the bearing consists of eleven rollers, each about ¼ inch in diameter and ⅜-inch long. A stamped steel frame or cage holds the rollers in position to contact the gently tapered end of the steering shaft. The whole apparatus rests in the hollow of the end cap, lubricated by the 200-weight oil that is supposed to fill the steering box at all times. Above the tapered end of the shaft is a worm gear that acts more or less like a screw. A sector gear is mounted on a shaft perpendicular to the steering shaft such that the teeth of the sector gear mesh with the threads of the worm gear. The gear box holds this arrangement in place and bathes it in oil. (This description is simplified. There is a system of ball bearings that ease the friction between the threads of the worm gear and the teeth of the sector gear.)

The worm gear at the end of the steering shaft acts like a screw, moving the sector gear up or down, depending on which direction the wheel is turned. The sector gear, in turn moves the steering arm in an arc, which moves the tie rod from side to side and steers the front wheels. When the steering wheel is turned to the right, the worm gear pushes against the end bearing and pulls the sector gear up, which pivots the steering arm, which moves the tie rod to the left and points the car's wheels to the right. Turning the steering wheel to the left "unscrews" the worm gear, which now works against a bearing at the top of the steering gear box. The steering arm pivots in the other direction and the wheels point to the left.

The main trouble with the steering boxes on these cars is that they almost always leak, and keeping them filled requires diligence on the owner's part. My diligence as a pretty normal high school student was somewhat spotty. When I removed the end cap from the gear box to find out what was hanging up the steering, I saw that the bearing cage had been twisted and broken, and the rollers had parted company with it. Each successive right-hand turn had jumbled and mashed the parts until there was no option but repair.

Phone calls to auto repair places and parts shops had failed to turn up a new bearing for my car, so I had turned to the recycled parts industry—the local salvage yards. By this time, early '40s Cadillac parts cars had become rare to non-existent in junk yards. The '46 hearse I used to visit on North 2nd Street had been cut up for scrap. The brown '41 sedan in a South Coors Road yard had been retrieved for restoration by a truly intre-

pid soul. But I got lucky. On Atrisco Road, S.W., I located a 1942 Series
62 Cadillac sedan, and my brother Phillip and I headed to the South Valley for some mechanical surgery. Getting access to the end cap of the steering gear box on a junked car with little or no access from below involved
a lot of loosening bolts and manipulating and ultimately removing the
steering column. But eventually I had a usable bearing (and some other
parts including nice pedal pads and two round 1942 Cadillac turn signal
lenses) to take to the counter man and pay for.

Back at home, I had put the bearing in place in the end cap, screwed
it back into the gear box, adjusting it by feel and intuitive guess before
tightening down the lock nut, and filling the gear box with some gear oil
from the neighborhood Texaco station. I test drove the car around the
block, and sure enough it steered normally again. That was about 35 years
ago.

Before diving back into the steering box once again, I called Cooper's
Vintage Auto Parts and ordered from their catalog a nice new bearing.
What a luxury! To be able to order a new bearing from a catalog, with no
need to call around to all the junkyards, determine if one of them had a
usable car they would let me cannibalize, go there and remove the bearing, hope it's okay and not worn out, install it on my car and hope for the
best.

The bearing arrived in due course and looked very familiar when I
unwrapped it. I didn't get around to opening up the gear box for a couple
of weeks, but when I did, the old bearing fell out in pieces. The cage had
lost the ability to hold the rollers in place, and it was easy to understand
why the steering felt wrong. The end cap is a hollow cylinder about an
inch and a half in diameter and about an inch and a quarter long. The outside of the cylinder is threaded for its entire length and one end of the
cylinder is closed and slotted on the outside so you can use a (large) screwdriver to turn it into place. The open end of the cylinder is beveled so that
the rollers of the bearing can roll between the beveled surface and a corresponding surface on the end of the steering shaft.

I wiped out the inside of the end cap, where the bearing is supposed
to rest, to make sure no foreign matter like metal shards remained. When
I put the new bearing in place it fit well and rolled freely, so I felt confident
in proceeding with the job. I filled the cup of the end cap with chassis
grease, put the bearing in place and made sure that the lubricant was worked
in between each of the rollers. With the bearing held in position by the
grease, I took the assembly underneath the car and carefully screwed it back
into the steering gear box.

I turned the end cap until I couldn't turn it any more by hand, and then I backed it off a quarter turn. The service manual details an involved procedure for adjusting the end cap and adjusting the play in the steering arm, all in the same operation. It involves disconnecting the tie rod from the steering arm and using a spring gauge to measure the force required to move the steering wheel at a particular point in its turning range, while setting the appropriate adjustments on the steering gear box. I confess I chickened out. Between not having a spring tension gauge and my reluctance to take the car apart any more than absolutely necessary, I elected to postpone indefinitely carrying out the procedure outlined in the service manual.

A few days later, I drove the car around the neighborhood and the steering worked as smoothly as it did when I first got the car.

16. The Fastback Lives!

During the year and a half following the first effort by Harry Scott and me to start the fastback's engine, the car had remained in its berth in my garage. I didn't try again during that period for a number of reasons—mulch in the driveway, time demands of household projects, unavailability of an assistant, etc. But I did rebuild the carburetor and I sent the stock fuel pump out to be rebuilt. And when I thought of it, I would insinuate some oil into the cylinders and run the starter to keep things limber.

Then, on the evening of the first of June, 2005, after work, I succeeded in bringing the '41 fastback back to roaring, rambunctious life. After a fair amount of coaxing, the engine caught and ran, noisily but very smoothly. My wife and daughter were properly impressed, and the car's windshield wipers swept back and forth for their added amusement.

The day before, I had charged the battery, taken out the spark plugs, squirted some oil into the cylinders and run the starter to cycle the pistons and help the rings form the best compression seal they could, given the age of the engine and the indeterminate time since the last time it was (if it *ever* was) overhauled. The vigorous puffing of air through the plug holes is always entertaining during this exercise. Then I ran the engine through a few revs with the plugs in. The change in the rhythm and tone of the cranking sounds indicated that at least some compression was being encountered.

As I let the battery recuperate on the charger, I debated bringing over the 5-gallon gas can I use for the lawnmower (and, incidentally, to gas up the limousine), and inserting the end of a length of clear vinyl tubing I had purchased some time ago and had fitted with a brass coupling that matched the inlet of the fastback's fuel pump. It suddenly occurred to me that this plan had a potentially unpleasant flaw in the questionable ability of vinyl to stand up to the solvent action of gasoline over time.

I phoned Harry Scott for a hydrocarbon chemistry consultation, and he affirmed my suspicion that the better approach would be to use neoprene hose. That would avoid the question and the hazard entirely. So I put off further experimentation to another day.

During the day on June 1, I thought about using some of the neoprene tubing I had used to hook up an electrical fuel pump for the almost-successful starting effort that Harry and I had made about a year and a half ago. In the meantime, I had had the fastback's own (mechanical) fuel pump rebuilt. I had also rebuilt the carburetor and (I thought) correctly secured the integrity of the line from the fuel pump to the carb. So the hose I had rigged to the electrical pump was available for my current use, assuming it was long enough. And there might be a way that I could attach the hose to the same brass fittings I had used to make the clear vinyl tubing mate up to the fuel pump inlet.

When I got home, I brought the gas container over to the ledge between the fastback's grille and its front bumper. The neoprene tubing appeared long enough, and although it wouldn't fit through the spout of the gas container, it would fit through the collar that held the spout. Sure enough, the tubing could be fit snugly over the brass fitting, and a small hose clamp placed over the joint made it nicely reliable. I screwed the fitting into the fuel pump and stuck the other end of the tubing into the gas can and below the level of the liquid. I took the spark plugs out again, so that I could work the pump to fill it and the carburetor fuel bowl with gasoline, without making the starter (and the battery) work unnecessarily against engine compression. After a few revs, I started to see gas spurting into the glass dome of the fuel pump sediment filter. Once that filled, I knew gas was going to the carburetor.

Once the improvised fuel system had been primed (improvised to the extent that I was by-passing the car's as yet uncleaned and unsealed fuel tank), I hooked the battery charger back up to make sure that the battery was as fresh and strong as possible for the job of trying to start the engine. I squirted a few drops of oil into each cylinder and replaced the plugs. After a suitable charging interval, I hooked my shunt wire up to the side terminal of the coil that would normally connect to the ignition switch on the dash. Leaning in over the passenger-side front fender, with my left hand I touched the free end of the jumper wire from the negative battery terminal to the solenoid terminal, while I opened the throttle with my right hand. The engine turned over and soon began trying to start. With each revolution, it lurched briefly, beginning to catch, but not getting enough of an impulse to take off. Instead of "ah-ruh-ruh-ruh-ruh" it sounded more like "Ah-ruh-ruh-RUH-ruh-ruh-RUH-ruh-ruh-RUH..." At this point, I noticed that a fine quick squirt of gas was leaping from the spot where the fuel line to the carburetor attached to the fuel bowl each time the fuel pump cycled. So I stopped running the starter, unhooked the battery and turned my attention to this new-found leak.

Sometime before I bought the car, a series of brass fittings had been added to the line from the fuel pump to the carb, apparently to lengthen the line by an additional inch or two. One of these fittings had developed a fine crack, and under the pressure generated by a rebuilt fuel pump against a properly seating carburetor needle valve, this crack was allowing gas to escape in time with the pumping action. I discovered that removing the damaged fitting did not prevent the fuel line from fitting comfortably and sealing well, so I tightened it up and went back to trying to start the engine.

The engine kept trying unsuccessfully to get going, and I tried covering the carburetor air intake partially or completely with my hand to emulate the choke, but I couldn't tell if that helped. I watched the fuel line and it didn't leak anymore, but I noticed that the cap over the needle valve was now wet, and it didn't seem to be due to the previous leak. So I got an open-end wrench and found that the cap could be tightened about a quarter turn. That seemed to do the trick, and after I wiped it off, the outside of the carburetor stayed gas free.

I remembered that I still had a nearly-empty can of starter fluid on the shelf, and I fetched that and sprayed some down the carburetor throat. Not a whole lot, as I'd read other people's warnings on the Cadillac-LaSalle Club message board about possible catastrophic damage to engines from over-enthusiastic use of the stuff. The effect was a noticeable increase in the engine's eagerness to start, but, as yet, the line between trying and succeeding remained elusive. The car was definitely closer to starting, and that was gratifying, but I didn't want to drain the battery excessively, so after a while I hooked the jumper wire on a non-conductive item, reconnected the charger and went in for dinner.

After dinner and a session of recharging, I checked visually for any more fuel leaks. Finding none, I unhooked the charger, reconnected the battery and prepared to resume the starting attempt. I sprayed a shot of starter fluid into the carburetor, opened the throttle and touched the jumper to the solenoid terminal. The engine turned over and immediately roared to life! I withdrew the jumper from the solenoid and kept wiggling the throttle as though I were fluttering the accelerator pedal, to keep the engine well enough fed to keep going. Meanwhile, the blast from the fan was stirring up and sending myriad bits of dust and detritus in my face. I thought I had pretty thoroughly vacuumed the engine compartment and the surrounding frame members and body parts, but apparently there had been a good deal I had missed.

As I let the engine warm up I noticed that, while it was running very smoothly (vibrating the front fender almost not at all), it was fully as noisy as I had remembered it. From my first encounter with this car, the engine had exhibited valve lifter noise. I don't know what the cause was—whether it was because Eddy Horton used to pull a boat on a trailer through the mountains of Colorado with the car or what. I had never had the valves and lifters worked on, and I certainly didn't expect the car's long hibernation to have eliminated the noise. It was just a real treat to have the engine running again, having started with a regular six-volt battery (and not a 12-volt, as Bill Sullivan had resorted to when waking the limousine) and its own fuel pump.

Barbara and Emilyann heard the noise and came to the garage door to watch. I let go of the throttle and the engine maintained a steady idle. The girls were wowed, and congratulated me. It was too late in the evening to clear the driveway and see if the car would move under its own power if I pulled the shift lever into reverse. After a while, I stopped the engine and unhooked the battery and the shunt wire to the coil. Then Barbara told me that they had enjoyed watching the windshield wipers while I'd been under the hood running the engine. I looked and saw the fan-shaped pattern where the light dust on the glass had been cleared.

So, a 64-year-old Cadillac came back to raucous life after not having run for close to thirty years. Repeatedly during that time I had reproved myself for not having properly set either car up for long-term storage before I took off for New York City in 1978. I hadn't even bothered to ensure that a proper level of antifreeze was maintained in the cooling systems, and with the fastback left outside all those years, I'd imagined all the worst broken-block scenarios. Once, when visiting my parents, I had begun arranging to have an old-timer mechanic I'd known in Albuquerque take the fastback's drivetrain under his knowledgeable care and bring it up to a proper level of repair. But my father had dissuaded me and urged me to conserve my financial resources. No matter. Now I knew that the car had not been ruined by my neglect, and the resulting sense of relief added to the sense of accomplishment at having brought about what Bill Sullivan calls "infernal combustion." There was plenty left to do before the car could be driven regularly or safely, but for now it was enough that the engine runs!

I started the car every couple of days after that and ran it for a while, because Bill Sullivan had said that this was good for these cars and because it made sense to let the parts get accustomed, once again, to working together. I was repeatedly astonished at how willing this car was to start, given the opportunity. It had always been like that when I was driving it regularly in Albuquerque—noisy running, but eager to start and very little engine vibration.

Passenger-Side of the Fastback's Engine. This is the "after" version of the view illustrated earlier from when I was trying to free up the pistons and crankshaft. The heads, manifolds and carburetor have been replaced, and the engine runs!

I remembered, I am proud to say, the follow-up tightening procedure that the 1941 Cadillac service manual recommends for cylinder head bolts. The first step, which I had performed when I first replaced the heads, is to tighten each bolt to 70 foot-pounds, beginning at the center of the head and working out to the edges. Then the manual calls for retightening after the engine has been warmed up "thoroughly." Of course, when I first put the heads back on the engine, that wasn't possible, since the engine wasn't running at the time. So a few days after the initial restarting of the engine, I retightened the head bolts and, to my great relief, there was not a single malfunction of bolt or thread. Everything worked the way it was supposed to.

On the day before Independence Day, I invited Harry Scott over to see and hear the fastback's engine run. Before he arrived, I moved the various boxes, parts, garden tools and so on that had found homes next to the car. I thought there was a chance we might want to see if the coupe would move under its own power.

When Harry's truck pulled into the driveway and Chloe, our springer spaniel, began her customary barking welcome, I connected the battery cable, attached the shunt wire to the coil terminal and touched the alligator clip of the other shunt wire to the solenoid terminal. After a few revolutions, and some jostling of the throttle and the choke valve, the engine started and settled into its clattering roar. I still hadn't properly adjusted the automatic choke, so I had to keep working the throttle until operating temperature was reached and the engine could keep running without stalling.

Harry noticed that the car did not smoke as it ran, and that there was very little vibration. With Harry present to lend a hand in case I had to push the car back into the garage, the time was right to see what would happen if I put it into gear. Bill Sullivan had told me about a 1948 Pontiac he had recently resuscitated. That car was also equipped with an automatic transmission and had been dormant for decades. Bill got the engine running and fearlessly tried the transmission out, with the result that the

The Fastback. This is a picture I took in July 2005 after I drove it out onto the driveway under its own power.

car drove off just like it had been parked the day before. I was eager to see if the same thing would happen with this Cadillac fastback.

So I moved the family sedan back down the driveway to make some room. I lowered the fastback's hood, resting the front edge on a block of wood to keep the hose to the outside fuel tank from being pinched. Then I climbed behind the wheel of the fastback and released the parking brake hand lever. The brake pedal gave firm resistance when I pressed it, and that was a good sign. All the work I'd done to free up and rebuild the master brake cylinder and wheel cylinders had not been for naught. I pulled the shift lever one notch to "D" and the engine r.p.m. immediately dipped while the car strained to go forward. So far, so good. The transmission was responding after all these years! Then I pulled the shift lever all the way down so that the pointer touched "R", and the engine promptly stalled.

I put the transmission back into neutral. Then I climbed out and walked briskly around the back of the car to the front end to lift the hood and restart the car. The engine caught right away (Harry was impressed) and resumed running as though nothing had happened. I returned to the driver's seat, and when I put the car into reverse, it obediently moved backwards and out of the garage. For the first time in nearly 30 years this once-proud car was under way. I kept going until we were entirely out of the garage, stopped, put the car in neutral and set the parking brake. For good measure, Harry set a chock behind the right front wheel, as I ran into the house to get Barbara and Emilyann to come see the car actually running. They were duly impressed, and Barbara helped me guide the machine back into the garage. It took a couple of tries to position it so that I'd still be able to move around in the garage.

There it was, once again in running condition, however tenuously. Yes, it was using a jerry-rigged fuel supply. And yes, the car's own wiring harness was unusable and had to be worked around. But the engine was functional and could transmit power to the wheels, and the brakes would stop the car, even if the linings were very thin. One of the first cars ever equipped with an automatic transmission had traveled again, under its own power. Who cares how short the trip was?

17. Still Smitten by the '31s

Even with all this time, energy and emotion invested in two 1941 Cadillacs, I still thought about getting a 1931. When I'd see one for sale, on eBay or in *Hemmings* or in car club newsletters, I'd pore over the photos, picture myself driving the car, inventory things that needed to be done, and wonder how I could afford it. Why, you might ask, was I not happy with what I had? Sam Blaylock had wondered the same thing aloud to my father, years ago when we came for the 1931 cabriolet. The fact is I never lost a real sense of connection, esthetically as well as emotionally, with the '31 model year. I always regretted selling that '31 V-8 cabriolet, even though I knew I was ill-equipped to restore it creditably, and even though I would have preferred it had been a limousine, rather than a convertible.

Although since high school, I have been fond of the entire Cadillac automobile family, more than any other model year, 1931 has consistently quickened my pulse. Friends have spoken up for this or that year, and I had owned two 1941 Cadillacs since the late 1960s. But the special charm of the 1931s has never lost its appeal for me. (I include the 1930 V-16 models, as most of the signature styling features of the 1931 Cadillacs debuted a year earlier on the 1930 V-16s.)

There is something unavoidably jaunty and cheerfully optimistic about the American automobiles produced during the early years of the 1930s. It was as though the car manufacturers had really hit their stride for the first time, technologically and aesthetically. The car as a technology had just become established, and it was just finding acceptance as a regular household appliance. It's almost as if everything up to about 1930 was preparation and everything after that was refinement and consolidation. Until that time, the American public had not really embraced the car. The Model T Ford had convinced people that cars could be affordable, but it wasn't until the Model A's introduction that "Henry made a lady out of Lizzie."

Through unkind coincidence, this was happening at the same time as the stock market crash and the beginning of the Great Depression. But because of the lag time involved in getting automotive designs into production, the first half of the '30s decade saw the flowering of the concepts that were first put on paper during the buoyantly confident days of the late '20s. After those blooms peaked, their splash and glamour would give way to more subdued themes, reflecting a transformed esthetic and economic climate.

The beginning of the twentieth century saw the establishment of the first automobile factories and the incorporation of interchangeable parts and mass production. To the public however, the product was an eccentric novelty, expensive, unpredictable and tricky to operate and to live with. Manufacturers were struggling with basic engineering design problems— how much horse and buggy technology to retain? How to design and arrange controls? How to protect the engine and mechanics from the passengers (and vice-versa)?

As the automobile evolved, things gradually settled into a fairly universal configuration. The engine moved to an agreed-upon spot between the front wheels, with a radiator standing in front of it, flanked by two big round headlights. The driver sat to one side of the front seat, just behind the engine, with a steering wheel in his hands instead of a tiller. The passengers sat beside and behind the driver. And underneath everything was a ladder-shaped frame with a wheel at each corner. Fenders covered the wheels, connected by running boards, and the body flowed from the radiator shell, over the engine and between the fenders and running boards, rising abruptly at the windshield to cover the passenger compartment. It was a logical development from the (engine-less) horse-drawn carriage into something new and previously undreamed of.

During the teens, the nature of the technology began to sort itself out. Gasoline, steam and electricity were still competing on a nearly equal basis for the right to power the auto. But a car was beginning to look more like a car and less like a horseless carriage. Engines became more powerful and more reliable. Chassis design permitted safer operation at speed. Electric lights began to replace kerosene and gas lanterns, and starter motors appeared. The twenties saw the beginnings of the general population's love affair with the car. Affordable automobiles began to be available, some so basic that a farmer could repair the machine in the field with baling wire. In 1924, nitrocellulose lacquer paint was introduced, allowing cars to be made in practically any color, affordably. And in 1927 the first car appeared designed from the start by a stylist.

Then with the end of the twenties and the beginning of the thirties, everything suddenly moves to a new, higher level. The technology leaps forward, with bigger, more powerful engines. Vibrant colors are everywhere, with chrome plating splashed on radiators, wheels, trim and bumpers. And sweeping lines, curves and contours give each vehicle a distinctive personality. And it all speaks in the language of irrepressible optimism. The sparkling chrome, the wide, wide whitewall tires, the ingenious hood ornaments, the often extravagant upholstery, the proliferation of driving lights, parking lights, spotlights and of course, wide shiny headlights. And there is a sense of proportion and symmetry that holds everything together. It's the classic era of automotive design, especially because the classical ideal of beauty finds a clear voice in these fire-breathing, gasoline and oil drinking machines.

More than anything else it's the cheerfulness, the eagerness to go out and tame the road that calls out from these cars. From the plain Model A Tudor sedan to the enormous Duesenberg dual-cowl phaeton. From a Hupmobile coupe to a Bugatti Royale. The statement is purposefulness coupled with a fresh enthusiasm for life. All too soon, the wheels would be covered, the corners would be rounded, the running boards would be swallowed up by the doors, and the radiator shells and headlights would melt into the fenders. Streamlining would spread like a fashion trend, making cars more aerodynamic and efficient, but depriving them of a certain combined visual grace and impact. Oh, yes, there would be many beautiful and impressive and elegant and imposing styles in the years to come, but changing tastes, the changing economy and the changing world would leave the Classic Era inexorably behind.

There have been attempts by many to try to evoke the spirit and essence of the cars of the early thirties using modern chassis and running gear. But the proportions are hardly ever right. The car is too low, or too wide, or the tires are too thick, and so on. There was just a wonderful confluence of proportions, shapes and lines that works only as a system. Compromise it, and the effect is lost (as the old designers well knew).

The Cadillacs of 1931 robustly express the spirit I've been talking about. The styling for that year represents the fullest development of the pre-streamlining philosophy of car design. The headlights would never again be as wide open. The magnificent radiator shell that was every bit as impressive as any sported by a Rolls Royce or Mercedes would soften and disappear in the next few years (shrinking to a narrow "fencer's mask" grille by 1937). The gracefully curved fenders were open and unskirted, shamelessly showing steering links, shock absorbers and leaf springs. Cars had yet to begin concealing in earnest every trace of their mechanical-ness beneath curves and folds of body sheet metal. In 1931, vertical lines made a kind of last stand in Cadillac styling, becoming something to be avoided from then on (briefly returning for an impressive performance in 1965 and 1966).

The word "definition" captures a great deal of what I'm talking about, in the sense that every part of the car is clearly defined and distinct, but unmistakably part of a unified whole. And each part has reached a climax point, from a design standpoint. The "front clip" certainly represents the full expression of what the cars of the late 1920s had been leading up to. And each of the body styles was esthetically balanced and proportioned. 1932 would begin an entirely different styling phase—rounder lines flowing into each other as the blending and streamlining process began.

Fortunately, many authentic examples of these marvelous cars are still with us, lovingly restored, or waiting patiently for their turn at refurbishment. These are the cars that I (and many, many others) love to watch and when we can, to drive and even own. And the affection that the cars inspire ensures that they will never again be written off automatically as good for nothing but scrap metal (as happened in the Fifties). No, they will be valued and preserved (and the prices paid will reflect that!) for many years to come. And with them, that brief era of automotive joy will live on.

18. A Dream Comes
Within Reach

While I was writing this book, just when I thought I had a reasonably complete tale, the story took a turn that still leaves me astonished. The dream I'd had in my early teen years of owning a V-16 limousine slipped out of the realm of pure fantasy and materialized as an attainable goal.

In early 2005, I came upon an Internet site for a business in Wichita, Kansas, that specializes in upholstery and interior trim for private airplanes. The owner has a sideline collecting and selling high-end classic automobiles. His inventory was heavily weighted in favor of Rolls and Bentley, with the odd Ferrari, Packard, Delage, Mercedes, and even some GM cars, including a handful of Cadillacs. It was a picture of a Cadillac that had brought me to the web site in the first place, a beautiful black 1930 V-16 imperial sedan.

The website contained additional pictures of the car, and I found myself transfixed. Here was a shiny, stately V-16 limousine with a very presentable interior and very few missing or incorrect parts. There were silk roll-up shades for each of the windows in the passenger compartment and a roll-up window between passenger and driver's compartments. Instead of full jump seats, there were two fold-down auxiliary seats, popularly referred to as opera seats. If it was anything like what the pictures represented, this was my dream car, pure and simple, the car I had in mind before I ever saw the 1941s or the 1931 V-8 convertible. This took me right back to my initial "high school crush" on the V-16s.

The accompanying write-up described the car as original, except for replating of the brightwork, new tires and exhaust, and detailing of the undercarriage. The writer cautioned that some worn spots existed in the upholstery and on the paint, owing to 75 years of age, but asserted that the car had been very well kept and was so well preserved the purchaser might choose not to reupholster and repaint the car. I carefully pored over the photos, some of which were high resolution and could be enlarged substantially on the computer screen, to reveal remarkable detail.

Sure enough, the upholstery showed some small holes, and the carpets had definitely passed their prime, but the wood trim was lovely, including the inlaid panels below the windows and the curved vanity boxes flanking the rear seat. The glass was clear, with no delaminating or discoloring. The interior of the car was clean and only slightly worn, considering its age. In general, it made you want to climb in and sit down.

I noted that the speedometer had been replaced with a similar but incorrect gauge, so there would be no worrying about whether the indicated mileage was correct! The dashboard cigarette lighter was immediately recognizable as a 1941 Cadillac item. One of the window cranks was broken and at least one other was missing. That led me to recall that the windows on the '31 convertible I had owned refused to be lowered more than a few inches. Perhaps the window regulators on these cars generally required servicing, coaxing or some sort of attention after all the years.

This 1930 V-16 was not the only Cadillac from this period I'd seen pictures of with a broken window crank. There were pictures from an auction for a 1929 seven-passenger imperial sedan, and from another auction of a 1928 imperial sedan. The bad news is the broken/missing parts. The good news is that they are the same size and shape as those on earlier Cadillac V-8s (as opposed to parts exclusive to the V-16 cars, which always sell at a premium).

There were no engine photos, which I thought was odd, considering that with these cars, the engine is the reason for the extra excitement. But the exterior shots showed a straight, nearly complete and truly elegant car, sleek and massive. Fender-mount spare tires were missing the rear-view mirrors that usually sit on top of them. And the twin exhaust pipes did not have the chrome-plated fan-shaped tips. But the flying goddess radiator mascot was there, tossing her hair to the passing breeze.

I e-mailed Harry Scott and Bill Sullivan, telling them about the car and directing them to the pictures, and both agreed it was a beautiful example. Harry called it sharp and unusual. I sent an e-mail to the website contact address, asking about the history of the car, condition of the engine, and, of course, the car's price. The e-mail response from the seller was a short one that directed me to a page with the prices of all their cars, stating that they were too busy to respond to individual e-mails, and inviting me to phone if I was serious about the car. Although the price was not extravagant enough to make me dismiss the notion of purchasing the car out of hand, it was certainly an amount I had never considered paying for an auto of any age. Nevertheless, the fact that I accepted the invitation to call the seller on the phone means I considered myself "serious" about the car.

The gentleman I was handed off to when I phoned, Lawrence Smith, told me that the car "probably came from New England" but he didn't know its history. It had spent most of its life in a garage (which I could have surmised after looking at the pictures). He told me that the previous owner had also owned a 1930 Cadillac V-16 roadster, which he had restored and sold. He had sent the chrome items for both cars out to be replated at the same time. When everything came back, the better parts were put on the roadster and the sedan got the second best. (I took that as a suggestion to expect some minor flaws in the chrome, which looked perfect in the pictures.) He recapped that the car was entirely original except for the replated chrome parts, repainted fenders, new tires, redone engine, new exhaust system, and painted and detailed undercarriage. He said the car was missing the windshield wipers and the spare tire locks, in addition to the items I had spotted. But the car was an example of an already rare breed that was only becoming even more scarce as people took the sedans apart to mount convertible bodies on the V-16 chassis and take advantage of the higher selling prices for open cars.

I thanked Mr. Smith for the information and said good-bye. In the next few days, he added four pictures of the sedan's engine to the display on the website. It was a beautiful blend of mechanics and artistry in a very clean engine compartment. The Cadillac V-16 engine was stunningly styled, in addition to being meticulously engineered. Polished aluminum, black enamel and chrome treat the eye when the hood is lifted, and the wiring and plumbing are discreetly concealed. (The V-16 engine manufactured in 1938, '39 and '40, by contrast, was much more of an "all business, no frills" machine.) This particular specimen wasn't up to strict "show" standard on several points. The exhaust manifolds had burned off whatever paint or other finish had been applied to them, leaving a flaky white residue in places. The radiator hoses were originally a distinctive pattern with fine ribs running lengthwise, and this engine bore generic hoses from an auto parts store. The manifolds were fastened to the blocks with ordinary hex nuts, instead of acorn nuts, and the manifold gaskets were incorrect. The ignition and coil wires were of modern type, and the short rubber conduit to neaten the appearance of the coil wires was absent. But these were things a show judge would criticize, while the average person would likely never notice (except for the flaking on the exhaust manifolds). This was still a gleaming example of a truly magnificent powerplant.

Now I was starting to realize what a bind I was in. Here was a very desirable example of the car I'd always idealized, and the price, while quite intimidating, was not stratospheric (like the partially-restored red V-16 dual cowl phaeton offered at another website for the eye-popping sum of $345,000, with a whole lot of work (and cash outlay) left to be done before it could be shown or auctioned off for big money). So I cast around for reliable guidance to help me either keep my head, or take the wild leap into 16-cylinder ownership.

So I turned to Pete Sanders, a real veteran of the multi-cylinder world, having restored a V-12 and the V-16 Madame X town sedan he currently owns. Pete's Madame X project started with a stripped hulk in a salvage yard that had a tree growing through the engine bay. He did the restoration himself, and now that car is a spotless, award-winning work of art. Pete knows every aspect of the finding, care and feeding of V-16s, and his perspective would be most helpful. I called him and directed his attention to the photos on the website. He said he couldn't believe how well-preserved the car was, and thought it was a splendid Cadillac. He said he thought that a friend of his knew the owner. He offered to contact him, and to see if some kind of a price reduction could be worked out, assuming I was serious about buying the car. Pete suggested I should sell the 1941 fastback, take out a home equity loan and buy the car. Put on the spot, I thanked him for the advice and the offer of help, and said I needed to think about it.

Now, a Cadillac-LaSalle Club member named Yann Saunders has undertaken the mammoth and admirable task of tracking down and accounting for all of the V-16s that have survived to the present day. The (new) Cadillac Database© on the Internet has a wealth of useful, interesting and even trivial information on the entire V-16 phenomenon and Cadillac automobiles generally.[2] Referring to that resource, I found a picture of "my" car and a caption indicating that it had been for sale in the same context since at least 2002. That was very reassuring to me, as it meant I likely had some breathing room in which to come to a decision whether or not to purchase the beast.

Yann had identified the car as a Series 4375. That particular series was the most frequently purchased of all of the different V-16 body styles offered. The big sedans have been described as the "bread and butter" cars of the line. The Series 4375 was a limousine with a leather-trimmed front compartment and a glass divider between driver and passenger compartments as well as full-width folding auxiliary seats. The companion Series 4375S was the same seven-passenger body without the divider window

---

2. In 1999, Yann donated the Cadillac Database to the Museum and Research Center of the Cadillac-LaSalle Club, Inc., of which he is a long-standing member.

Pete Sanders's 1930 Madam X V-16 Sedan. Once a junkyard derelict, this is now a prize-winning show car. The raked windshield, chrome moldings around the windows, and slender windshield and door pillars are hallmarks of the "Madame X" series of Fleetwood bodies.

and jump seats. But the more closely I examined the website photos, the more I felt that "my" car was actually a Series 4330. The 4330 had a slightly shorter body than the Series 4375, being designed for five passengers. Comparing photos of the two series side by side, the slightly smaller rear quarter window in the 4330 car is easily seen. The 4330 had two fold-down "opera" seats (as did "my" car) to accommodate two additional passengers, when needed. The difference, aside from the slightly different appearance, lies in the numbers of each series manufactured. The production numbers for these cars were:

Series 4375-S 501
Series 4375 438
Series 4330-S 394
Series 4330 50

So, the car I was looking at was a pretty rare bird. There weren't that many V-16s made in the first place, but there were only 50 Series 4330 cars

Series 4375 Imperial Sedan. This is a beautiful example of the Series 4375 seven-passenger body style. The difference between the Series 4375 and the Series 4330 (to which my car belongs) can easily be seen by comparing the portion of the body above the rear wheel. The body of the Series 4375 is extended rearward to make room for the full-width jumpseats in the passenger compartment. From the radiator shell back to the rear door hinge pillar, both bodies are the same. The wheels on this Series 4375 are the "standard" wooden "artillery" wheels that were almost always upgraded to the optional wire-spoke wheels. The picture was kindly provided by Mr. Scott Eckenhoff, the car's former owner.

produced. I debated whether to tell Yann that he had probably misclassified the car, but I demurred, fearing that someone might decide to buy the car out from under me as I dithered. I ultimately did tell Yann, and he kindly said he would wait before making the correction to give me time to decide whether to buy or not.

19. Acquiring the Car of My Dreams

In early May 2005 I called a couple of appraisers to see what they would charge to evaluate the sedan, and darned if one of them didn't post a message on the Cadillac-LaSalle Club message board asking where to find values for Series 4330 1930 Cadillac V-16s. I had only mentioned to this appraiser that I was thinking of buying a 1930 Cadillac in the Wichita area. Now this fellow was asking about the specific body style of the car I was interested in. He must have figured out which car I was considering, and he may even have gone to look at it and speak with the seller. I'd been waiting to contact the seller until I had the money to buy the car and hopefully, an indoor place to put it. I wanted to keep whatever bargaining position I had, and not give myself away immediately as having fallen for the car. My friend Harry Scott told me if he were thinking of buying that car, he'd ask *me* to appraise it. At that point I figured I was going to find out as much information as I would need just by showing up and examining the car myself.

Towards the end of June, Barbara asked me to call our favorite mortgage broker about the possibility of refinancing our home and including in the new loan balance money to buy the 1930 Cadillac. I was at once thrilled at the idea that owning the car might be possible in a way that didn't involve potential interest rate hikes (as with a home equity loan), and filled with gratitude for my wife who was encouraging me to pursue this dream. John Ragano outlined several possible approaches and we settled on a new 30-year loan at a rate almost ½ a percentage point lower than what we had. I quickly completed and returned the documents required to get the process in motion. In due course, an appraiser visited our house, and we waited patiently for word that a closing could be scheduled.

I put the 1941 fastback up for sale first, and delayed selling the lim-

ousine. Right away a gentleman from Wisconsin called expressing interest in buying the fastback, and he asked for pictures. I drove the fastback
out of the garage and onto the driveway for a photo shoot, and ended up
having quite an adventure.

By now the process of starting the car had become fairly routine, and
I was beginning to take it for granted. I figured I would start the car and
back it out onto the driveway, where I could photograph it from a variety
of angles, and take pictures of the engine and the interior as well, unhin-
dered by the tight quarters and dim light of the garage. So, after I'd purchased new batteries for the camera, I hooked up the jumper wire to the
coil and touched the other jumper wire to the solenoid terminal and
cranked the engine until it started and warmed up.

I moved my wife's Mercury sedan well back down the driveway, and
set a 2 × 8 board across the driveway about halfway between the garage
and the street, with boards underneath its far edge so that it would serve
as a wheel chock to backstop the fastback's somewhat feeble parking brake.

I climbed into the driver's seat, stepped on the brake pedal and pulled
the shift lever through first and low, feeling the car's eager forward lurch
as it went into gear. When the lever reached reverse, the eagerness to move
switched directions, and we began moving back out of the garage. I steered
gently down the driveway and eased into the improvised parking block I'd
set up. Then I shut the engine off in the now-customary way by unhook-
ing the jumper wire from the coil.

For the better part of the next hour, I removed the items that had
found storage space on the fastback's seats and floors over the years, I vacuumed the car and I took a couple of dozen pictures. Before I began clicking the shutter, I removed the red plastic container that was substituting
for the car's fuel tank. And rather than include the 2 × 8 board in the pictures, I put the car into reverse (the equivalent of "Park" with the early
automatic transmissions) and moved my boards out of the frame.

When I was sure that the pictures had downloaded successfully to my
computer, it was time to put the car back in the garage. So I replaced the
books, folded sheets and shop-rags-to-be, car parts and so on that I'd
removed earlier, put the shop vacuum away and went upstairs to see if Barbara was available to signal me as I guided the car into its berth. She was
resting, so I figured I could probably do it alone without much difficulty.

I brought back the plastic gas container and put the hose back into
its mouth. Then I hooked up the coil wire, touched the other wire to the
solenoid terminal, and worked the throttle, confident that the car would
start right up, having just been run an hour ago. And away it went. Literally! To my utter shock and chagrin, the car immediately began running

backward down the driveway! I had forgotten that I'd left the transmission in reverse. And in by-passing the unsafe wiring harness of the car, I had also by-passed the interlock that prevents the driver from starting an automatic transmission-equipped car in reverse. Still bent over the right front fender, I frantically grabbed at the coil wire and successfully stopped the engine. But the car was in motion and I was sure that it was going to meet the front bumper of our Mercury before it slowed and stopped. My right knee was next to the front wheel, and I could feel the wheel rubbing my pants leg. I found to my relief that if I pressed with my knee, the friction was enough to slow the car down appreciably. So I pressed with great emphasis, and the motion stopped.

As I straightened up and looked around, my heart skipped a beat. The car had described a graceful right-hand turn and had come to rest with the right rear wheel a couple of feet off the driveway in the grass. If it had come straight back, the encounter with the Mercury would have been unfortunate. As it happened, an angel averted that disaster.

I got a couple of boards to place behind the rear wheel before I put the transmission into neutral (as I should have done in the first place!) and replaced the coil wire (and the Number 7 spark plug wire that I had also pulled loose). I restarted the engine, climbed into the car and drove it into the garage, backing and reentering a couple of times until I was happy with the positioning. It was with great relief that I stopped the engine. I thanked God and my guardian angel that the extent of the damage was the rope burn on the inside of my knee and the tire track on my trouser leg. Then I went inside to send those pictures that could have been rather expensive, if things had turned out a little bit differently.

My prospect thanked me for the pictures and said he wanted to come (from Wisconsin) to see the car, but that the earliest he could do it would be mid–August. He asked me to keep him posted whether the car had been sold or not. But on July 20, he called to say that his wife didn't care for the fastback body style, so they were going to pass.

Then on July 21, I cranked up my computer at work and like any red-blooded car nut, went to the ebaymotors.com website. There under "Cadillac" was "my" car, the 1930 V-16 sedan!!! The listing was for ten days, and the starting bid amount was $40,000, showing that the reserve had not been met. I suspected that the seller had figured out, from my call early last Spring, and from that appraiser snooping around, that there was an interested buyer out there, and he was trying to smoke that buyer (or any other potential purchaser) out. From my point of view, he'd only succeeded in putting me in a bind. The home mortgage refinance had not closed, and I hadn't freed up either of the spaces in the garage, so I had nothing to bid with and nowhere to put the car if I won the auction. As one of my professors used to say: "Ah, the vicissitudes of life!"

The same day, I got an e-mail from Lawrence Smith, the seller, addressed openly to those who had in the past expressed interest in the 1930 Cadillac, announcing the eBay auction and informing us that the reserve was significantly lower than what he had previously been asking. I called John Ragano about the status of the mortgage refinance, and he said we could close on Monday July 25 (and fund on the following Friday) or we could close during the day on Friday the 22nd (which was "tomorrow" at that point) and fund on Wednesday the 27th. We elected to close on the 22nd so that funding would not coincide with the end of the eBay auction, when everything gets crazy.

I called Pete Sanders, but I only reached his answering machine. Harry Scott volunteered that Pete was likely at his New England vacation place. Good for him! But now I knew that I was on my own as far as negotiating a deal to buy the 1930 Cadillac.

Harry Scott was a great help during this process, hand-holding, encouraging and offering tactical advice. I considered flying to Wichita to examine the car, but I quickly realized that it was extremely unlikely I would find anything there that would change my interest in having it. I'd been holding off calling Mr. Smith until I had tried getting whatever deal Pete Sanders might have been able to arrange, and until I had a supply of cash to negotiate with. But events were overtaking me and the game plan urgently needed amendment. On Friday the 22nd, I bit the bullet and called Lawrence Smith to tell him I was indeed interested, and to ask him what it would take to buy the car now. He told me the amount that he felt was the minimum he could accept for the car. I was overjoyed! Immediately I said that was a price I would be glad to pay. The relief in my voice must have been crystal clear over the phone line. Mr. Smith went on to say that he really wanted to get a slightly higher amount. He said he had more than that in the car and that he'd "like something to show for it." I relished the idea of paying the lower amount and having some extra money left for things like a correct speedometer, spare tire locks and mirrors, and so forth. But I also knew this was a very rare and special car, and that I'd come to the deal prepared to spend significantly more. I told him I would see what I could do, that I had to get the money from my broker and that I would call him back. I was going to need wire transfer instructions, in any event, as that was the only payment method the eBay write-up said would be acceptable (according to Harry, a lot of fraud has been perpetrated with cashier's checks churned out on high quality laser printers and copiers).

When I told Barbara about the conversation with Mr. Smith, she said "Oh, you should pay him the higher amount." I decided I'd use that as the opening of my next conversation with Mr. Smith.

We closed the refinancing later that day, which meant that the money would be wired on Wednesday July 27 (once the three-day last-chance-to-back-out period had expired). That left a weekend and half of the following week to anticipate, fret and second-guess myself.

When we got home and Barbara checked the mail, there was a letter from a book publisher saying that yes, they would be happy to see my book manuscript. Barbara and Emilyann congratulated me and I savored the momentary adulation.

After we'd been home for a while, I called Mr. Smith to tell him that my wife had said I should pay him the second price he'd quoted. He caught me up short when he said he'd been offered $5,000 more by someone else. Without an instant's pause, I said I'd meet that offer. He acknowledged that no one would be able to wire money until Monday, and said that the car would go to the one who got the money to him first. When I objected that I wouldn't be able to wire before Wednesday at the earliest, he asked if I was sure I could have the money to him then. I said "Yes," and he agreed to wait. I asked for the wiring instructions and he asked me to call back in the morning, because he was away from his office.

After that phone call, my wife gave me a well-deserved critique of my Pillsbury doughboy negotiating skills. She didn't believe that there actually was another buyer, and she thought I had just bargained us out of $5,000. She did concede that I'd been willing to pay even more from the outset.

The next morning, in the middle of my daughter's swim team meet, I called for the wire transfer instructions. Barbara and I had scripted various scenarios for how this conversation might go, with an eye to anticipating any additional "wrinkles" like the competing bidder. But it was Mr. Smith's grandson who answered and took down my e-mail address. He relayed a message from his grandfather that as long as I had the money to them Thursday morning, I could have the car for the price we'd agreed to and they would end the eBay auction. With a great deal of relief, I thanked him, returned to Emilyann's swim meet and resumed my apprehensive anticipation.

Monday and Tuesday were fully taken up with work on the basement of our home, taping and "mudding" the drywall and getting the fireplace properly installed. The exertion and distraction were probably a good antidote for the stress of waiting for the refinance to bear fruit. I'd hoped to find time call to Lawrence Smith and ask to see a copy of the car's title, but that wasn't possible until Wednesday morning. The title he faxed to me was an Oklahoma document in the name of the fellow from whom Mr. Smith had acquired the car. On the back, it was signed over to Creative Interiors, Inc. A couple of phone calls to my local DMV disclosed that Virginia would only issue me a title if I presented an existing title in the name of my immediate seller. The exception is if I bought from a dealer, in which case, DMV would accept an assignment of title. Lawrence Smith confirmed that his company officially was a dealer, so the title question resolved itself.

Also on Wednesday morning, I called Vince Taliano, director of my regional chapter of the Cadillac-LaSalle Club, and asked him to help me put the '41 fastback on eBay. Just the day before, a '41 fastback similar to mine had been sold in an eBay auction for $7,200. That was $1,700 more than my asking price for my fastback. Harry had suggested that if I put my car on eBay right away, the unsuccessful would-be buyers of the other car might snap it up. So I sent Vince a bunch of the pictures I'd taken of the car, and we worked up a descriptive text for the ad. By the mid afternoon, Vince had done a fine job of composing an attractive ad and it had been posted on eBay.

Through the course of the day, Wednesday, I kept calling the settlement company to see if the money from the refinance had been wired into our bank account. My earnest hope was to head over to the bank branch near my office as soon as the money was there and to wire the purchase price to Lawrence Smith. That way, the Thursday morning deadline would not be a nail-biting stress test.

In the early afternoon, the settlement company said that the documents were at the courthouse being recorded, and once that was done, the money would be transferred to my account. A little after 3:00, the fellow who'd done our closing told me that the wire transfer had been sent to our account, and I began calling our bank's bank-by-phone number to try to catch the moment that the money from the refinance arrived. 4:00 came and went, but not before I'd visited the bank branch to see if their computers were more up-to-the-moment than those I could reach by the phone line, and to be there if there were any chance to get a wire transfer to Mr. Smith's bank before the Fed wire closed for the day. (I'd been given various answers when I asked how late one could send a wire transfer—4:00, 4:30, even 5:00. But 4:00 PM was the most often mentioned time. My bank branch had recently extended its operating hours to stay open after 3:00, or I wouldn't have been trying this.)

Back at the office, I kept checking the account balance with no sign that the money had been moved. I called Mr. Smith to let him know that it was looking increasingly unlikely that I could wire the money Wednesday. I said that in any event, the wire transfer would be done first thing Thursday morning. He expressed concern and said that he had told another person that if I didn't get the money to him by noon, he would sell the car to the other buyer. He thanked me for calling to keep him informed.

Then something occurred to me. Earlier in the day I'd opened a selling account with eBay as part of setting up the '41 fastback auction. One of the items of information called for was the bank routing number for my checking account, and I'd discovered that the routing number on the checks I was using came up as invalid. My bank had recently merged with another bank, and even though they'd let us keep using the old checks, apparently the routing number printed on them no longer corresponded to the number for the merged bank. It dawned on me that the cancelled check I'd been asked to bring to the refinance closing last Friday was the roadmap that would be used for directing the wire transfer to my account. If the routing number on that check was wrong, that could be why, at 4:30 PM (1½ hours after the settlement company wired the money to me), it still had not shown up in my account.

A call to the bank confirmed that a wrong routing number could indeed thwart a wire transfer, and it produced for me the correct routing number. A call to the settlement company followed in which I gave them the right number. The next call to the bank's check-your-account-balance number told me that, just like magic, the money had reached the account!

It was 4:40 when I dashed over to the bank branch, on the off chance that a wire transfer to Mr. Smith could still be accomplished that day. At first it looked like it might happen. To his surprise, the clerk was able to access the bank's wire transfer computer program, and he began entering the account and routing numbers. But the system generated an "invalid date" message, and wouldn't accept any other date. So the clerk began looking for the paper form for requesting a wire transfer, which, for some reason, proved elusive. I was beginning to worry about catching my van ride home, and whether I'd have time to return to my office first and retrieve my jacket and briefcase. He located a form and we filled it out so that the wire transfer could go first thing in the morning. I just had time to retrieve my things (and turn off the coffee maker) before dashing to the van.

When the bank branch opened in the morning I spotted my wire transfer application on the desk Antoine had occupied the day before, and I watched as the fellow who relieved him entered the information into the computer and sent the money on its way. I returned to my office and e-mailed Mr. Smith that the wire transfer had been done at 9:15 AM, EDT. A couple of hours later, he e-mailed me back that they had received the money, asking how I wanted the car titled and asking what arrangements I'd made for transporting the car. He added that there were five books he would send with the car.

Although I had spoken with a number of transport companies, I had not as yet selected one or arranged for a pick-up. I reviewed my file and settled on a company that had drawn enthusiastic comments from several Cadillac-LaSalle Club members on the message board. After I called and made the arrangements (door-to-door shipment in an enclosed trailer), I e-mailed Mr. Smith and gave him my full name for the title and the information about the shippers, including their phone number. He e-mailed me back to say that the "haulers" would be picking the car up at 9:00 the next morning. He also asked for my mailing address for the title. When I responded with the address, I asked how I could contact Jim Bradley, the man he had bought the car from. In addition to the name and phone number of Mr. Bradley, he gave me the names and phone numbers of two gentlemen who had been willing to pay several thousand dollars more than I'd paid for the car in case I decided I wanted to sell it. At that point I knew Mr. Smith had treated me very honorably indeed. He had sold the car to me for the price we'd settled on, in spite of two better competing offers. I replied expressing my appreciation for selling me the car and telling him that owning a V-16 limousine had been my dream since the age of 14, a dream I'd all but given up on. I assured him the car would find a warm welcome at my house.

That evening my wife and daughter congratulated me on my purchase. When they asked me how I felt, I could only say that I was stunned. The reality would take a while to sink in. I tried to call Mr. Bradley. His wife said he was at his shop and gave me the number, but the phone kept ringing. I would try again the next day. Did I dream about the car? Yes, I did.

On Friday, August 29, I watched the clock, knowing that the 1930 Cadillac was scheduled to be picked up at 10:00 AM, my time. The day before, the fellow from the car transport company had said, when I asked him how I would pay for their services, "Oh, you can pay by credit card. Just call after the car has been picked up and give us the information." So, in the early afternoon I called, and the fellow I'd been dealing with was out for the day. I dialed the number his voice mail referred me to and the woman who answered said "Oh, that pickup has been held up pending payment." Visions slipped past my eyes of Lawrence Smith waiting in vain for a promised pickup and the company rep telling him "Oh, Mr. Cummings got confused on the payment terms," and the rescheduled pickup not taking place until sometime the next week. I told her what the fellow had told me the day before, but she only said he should have known that wasn't correct. I gave her my credit card information and asked her to rearrange a pickup as soon as possible (and not to make it sound as though I was the one who messed things up). She agreed to do that.

After the phone call as I was trying to calm down, I received an e-mail from Mr. Smith "Your haulers picked up the car this morning." Whoa, there! Back on the phone with the transport company, the woman I'd just spoken to was out to lunch. The woman I was speaking with now couldn't verify that I'd left my credit card info, but agreed to call off any efforts to reschedule a pickup that had apparently taken place after all. P.S.—the first woman called back to say that a server error had foiled the entry of my credit card info, so would I please give it to her again.

Later that evening, the eBay listing for the fastback got its first bid, at the minimum initial amount of $1,500. I hadn't started that car since I'd taken it out for pictures, and I wanted to make sure it would start promptly if someone came to inspect the car. So I put the hose to the fuel pump back into the plastic gas container, connected the coil wire and set about trying to start it. I got no results at all. Not even a whiff of gasoline from the carburetor throat. Pulling a plug wire and cranking the engine showed that the plugs were sparking. But it seemed as though no fuel was reaching the carburetor and I couldn't understand that, since the fuel pump was newly rebuilt. Meanwhile the cranking was depleting the battery, so I stopped and hooked up the charge. I checked to make sure that the hose was below the surface of the gas in the container, and then I saw it. When I'd taken the gas container to use it with the lawnmower, I'd stuck a red plastic plug into the end of the hose to stop gas drips. This evening, I'd forgotten to remove the plug when I put the hose back into the gas. So through all that cranking, the fuel pump had been sucking against a plugged hose, instead of a reservoir of gasoline. No wonder it didn't start! I took the plug out and the car started, relieving me of the sickening suspicion that something was broken. I hate it when I'm too clever for my own good.

On Monday, a fellow from Germany e-mailed me. He'd seen the eBay listing and wanted to know if I had a problem with selling the car overseas and if I had additional pictures of the places where cars are prone to develop rust. That evening I took some more pictures for him. Another fellow called and told me about the three old Cadillacs he had, and how much he'd like to buy mine, but his wife was telling him he had too many. Nobody challenged the lone bidder the listing had attracted.

On Tuesday, the title and bill of sale for the 1930 V-16 arrived, with the title signed over to my name and notarized. Now I had everything necessary to have the state of Virginia issue me a title to a V-16 Cadillac. Also arriving in the mail was my invitation to the Fall Car Show of the Cadillac-LaSalle Club Potomac Region. The theme this year was to be V-16 and V-12 Cadillacs, and the club director had sent out personal invitations to owners of such cars residing within reasonable transportation distance of the show location just north of Washington, D.C. As a new member of the multi-cylinder fraternity, I had just been invited to show my car.

Throughout Monday and Tuesday, the eBay auction for the fastback was static with only one bid showing. The process of moving the 1930 from Wichita was uneventful as well, with the car waiting at the transport company's Wichita terminal. Tuesday evening, a garrulous gentleman called from Florida. Owner of a 1941 Cadillac coupe of the non-fastback variety (Series 62), and a retired paint and body man, he was intrigued by my car with an eye to performing custom bodywork on it. We chatted very pleasantly, but I got the impression his wife wanted him to have fewer cars, and not another one.

On Wednesday, it wasn't until mid-day that the auction action warmed up. With a little over 3 hours left in the auction, someone bid $2,100, which topped the first bidder's (undisclosed) maximum bid. Then with two hours remaining, a third bidder stepped in, topping bidder Number 2. With less than one hour left, it took Bidder Number 3 a couple of tries to top Number 3 with a bid of $2,506. The bidding war died down, though, but a fourth bidder at $2,556 showed up right before the auction ended.

Also on Wednesday, Barbara began giving me definite indications that she really wanted us to keep the fastback. The same Federal Express deliveryman who had brought the 16" wheels and wide whitewall tires for the '41 limousine had delivered the title and bill of sale for the 1930 V-16, and he and Barbara had discussed the cars. He suggested to her that the fastback could readily be sequestered in an open area in the woods on the front of our property. He spoke of pouring a concrete floor with a cloth or plastic shelter that would be weather resistant and inconspicuous to the neighbors and passersby. Barbara began asking me to run down the cost of the improvements necessary for the fastback to be driven reliably and presentably. Then she considered what she could do around the house with the sale proceeds if I disposed of that car. Both of us considered it entirely possible that the failure of the fastback to sell might be providential. I considered the added factor that a wife who is also interested, in a practical way, in the old car hobby is an invaluable asset to an old car guy.

Consequently, I didn't relist the fastback on eBay right away. Harry Scott and Vince Taliano were in Des Moines attending the Grand National

Meet of the Cadillac-LaSalle Club. And besides, my home Internet connection was out, due to the service provider's technical difficulties. A couple of people e-mailed me after the close of the auction to ask how much I wanted for the car or to request photos.

On Friday, the transport company's website indicated that the status of my car was "to be loaded." When I called for further information, I was told that the car had been assigned to truck number 600145, and that it was expected to arrive in Manassas on August 8. That news was at once exciting, and helpful, since the original arrival date (August 11) coincided with a doctor's appointment, and the revised scheduling simplified things. I would know with more precision when I could expect to see my car after I called the transport company the next Monday.

Come Monday, a phone call to the transport company disclosed that the scheduled arrival of the 1930 Cadillac in Manassas would be Tuesday at 7:50 A.M. The fellow I spoke with was less than convinced that such a precise arrival time was meaningful. Nor was he certain that the car would be delivered to my home the same day it arrived in Manassas, even if it was expected early in the morning. He suggested that I phone the local business that acts as the transport company's depot, and express to them my sense of urgency (which I did). I renewed the online listing for the '41 fastback on the *Hemmings Motor News* website. And no sooner was the listing confirmed than an Air Force Lieutenant Colonel phoned and asked if he could come to my home and examine the fastback.

When I arrived home Monday afternoon, I called Bill Sessler and arranged to bring the 1941 limousine to his place, so I could park the 1930 Cadillac in my garage. Plan A, to use the fastback's slot, had to be shelved until that car was sold. One by one I moved the cars that occupy our driveway—the '75 Datsun 280Z I drive to and from my van pool pick-up site each work day, and the '04 Mercury Grand Marquis that is the family's workhorse. But when I turned the key to the '90 Sable station wagon we've hung onto for utility use, there was no response from the starter. The poor car doesn't get used enough, and it shows its resentment periodically by going on strike. If it insisted on staying in place, it would be a relatively minor obstacle to removing the '41 limousine from the garage. But it might pose more difficulty when the 1930 arrived and I had to drive around the station wagon to get the new arrival safely into the garage.

I started the '41, backed it out of the driveway and set off for Bill Sessler's shop. It was a pleasant trip, particularly since the rain had paused and people coming home from work were noticing the shiny, elderly car passing by. I pulled up to one of the overhead doors at Bill's and left the engine running while I went inside to find Bill and see if that was a good spot to park.

Bill asked me to move my car over one door, and I shut the engine off and joined him for a ride back to my house in his 1946 Cadillac convertible.

Bill's '46 is a truly unrestored original. It is very driveable, but the convertible top is almost all gone but the bows. As we started out, I saw right away the attraction of these open cars. The world was passing by but everything had an immediacy that doesn't happen in a closed car. Unlike a small convertible sports car, there was substance and gravitas to this car and it was really fun to travel in it. About halfway back, the heavy clouds kept their promise. First some small drops appeared on the windshield, but very soon big drops began plopping on the glass. Coincidentally, we began slowing down to make a left-hand turn at the light at Hoadly Road. As we waited for the turn arrow, the heavens opened up and our open-air ride rapidly became aquatic. When we turned onto Hoadly Road, we discovered that it was being repaved. One lane of two was blocked off, and the other had been milled to a coarse surface. The cars in front of us were proceeding slowly and cautiously on the uneven roadbed. That meant we were unable to travel fast enough for the slipstream to carry the rain over our heads. Instead, the water poured onto our heads, shoulders and laps, and the comical aspect of our drenching was unavoidable. At least Bill was wearing a wide-brimmed hat that kept the rain out of his eyes. When we got to the turn at Purcell, we briefly debated waiting out the rain under the shelter of the gas pump islands at the 7-11 store, but we decided to go on. Through the occasionally-wiped windshield I directed Bill to my house and bid him good-bye, much more grateful for the ride than I was irked by the dousing. The next day, Bill told me the rain was harder on the way back. Poor fellow! When he got back to his shop, he put my car inside and wiped it off for me.

Tuesday, August 9 dawned overcast and promising more rain. I connected my battery charger to the 1990 Sable wagon, even though I didn't hold out much hope that it could be revived without a new battery. If there was a chance I could clear the driveway before the 1930 sedan arrived, I was going to try. All my experience had been that once the battery had run down to the point that the car couldn't start, jump starting or recharging the battery rarely worked, unless the jump start was from an AAA-dispatched tow truck. The optional big engine required a large number of cold cranking amps to fire it up. The tow trucks were usually able to deliver substantially more current than any passenger car I could hook up to.

The transport company's local depot said that the car had not arrived in Manassas yet. Meanwhile, I cleaned the newly-vacant garage stall and prayed for a period without rain to coincide with whatever time the 1930 Cadillac arrived in the driveway. And I waited some more. Then the Air

Force officer who had called about the fastback called and asked if he could drop over during his lunch break to see the car. So I removed the folded shop towels, notebooks, and other items I'd grown accustomed to storing in the passenger compartment, and I fired up the car and ran it for a while so it would be easy to start for my visiting sales prospect.

I called the transport company and its local depot several more times with inconclusive results, until a fellow at the local depot allowed that the car was being unloaded and as soon as the paperwork was done and it was entered into the computer, he would arrange for delivery in the afternoon. That was encouraging. The fairly steady sprinkling rain was not wonderful old car delivery weather in my book, but I really wanted to see that Cadillac securely ensconced in my garage. A little after 11:30 AM, the prospect for the fastback arrived, and I showed him the car, started it, and answered questions about it and about what would be involved in making it a presentable driver. He was very interested, and I left him with copies of some pictures I'd taken that he could show his body man to get a better idea of the expenses he might be undertaking.

Just as the lieutenant colonel was leaving, I glanced down the driveway and saw a flatbed truck passing slowly by, with the most gorgeous black classic car perched regally on it. I called into the house to Barbara "It's here!", and quickly backed the Grand Marquis out of the driveway while Barbara and Emilyann (camera in hand) and Emilyann's visiting friend Katherine Mantoni walked briskly down to the street to meet the new arrival. The rain was still a light sprinkle and the car wore beaded droplets over its entire surface. But it was magnificent and everything I'd hoped for. I dashed back up the driveway to take a chance that the Mercury Sable wagon had actually taken enough of a battery charge to start. It would be really nice to have it entirely out of the way, but perched in the driveway's turnaround, it posed a navigational challenge, rather than an outright obstacle. Wonder of wonders, it started and I was able to back it out of the driveway and onto the street.

When I returned to the 1930 Cadillac, the tow truck driver was angling the bed so the car could be rolled off, and in our conversation he was surprised to learn the large displacement of this car's engine, and the fact that V-16 sedans were capable of speeds of 90 m.p.h. He said it had taken ten minutes to start the car at the depot and he wanted to get the car onto level ground before trying here. Lawrence Smith had kindly included a sheet of starting instructions with the car, and the tow truck driver now repeated those to me. Reach under the battery compartment on the passenger side under the front running board and turn the battery cutoff switch. From the driver's seat, switch the (non-original) toggle switch on

the lower right-hand corner of the instrument cluster to the "up" position. Push the starter pedal in with the toe of your right foot and start the car. The customary ignition switch on this car was currently a decorative feature. I later noted that the transmission lock feature built into the stock ignition switch was also nonfunctional.

The starter motor whirred quietly and briefly before the engine began running with a very quiet hum you had to be listening for, and that could barely be called a rumble. I signed for the car and the tow truck driver turned it over to me so I could take it into the garage (and out of the rain).

Behind the Wheel for the First Time. Taking delivery of the car I drove it into the garage and out of the rain. My daughter Emilyann snapped this shot from the back seat as I familiarized myself with the shift pattern. The chrome item to the left of the dome light is the speaker for the owner-to-chauffeur communication system.

Opposite top: The design and its execution produce a large car that is simultaneously majestic and graceful. The compartment under the front door edge contains the car's battery. The rear compartment door is decorative. In between is a courtesy light that glows when the rear door is opened.

Opposite bottom: Introduction. Barbara and I meet the 1930 Cadillac V-16 for the first time. It has just been lowered off the rollback and started up. Lawrence Smith had included handwritten starting instructions.

The Goddess. Tossing her hair to the breeze, this lady graces the radiator caps of the 1930 through 1932 Cadillacs. An alternative was a stylized heron, or just a plain radiator cap. This is another shot my daughter took when the car arrived at our house.

As I climbed into the driver's seat, Barbara invited Emilyann and Katherine to get into the rear seat for the ride up our 150-foot driveway. I put in the clutch and got the feel for the shift pattern before putting it in reverse so I could aim it up the drive. The shift mechanism was precise, and each position was clear and easy to find. I moved the lever to reverse and backed out carefully on the clutch. I noticed that the friction point of the clutch was closer to the floor than with my '41 limousine. The engine responded willingly to the accelerator pedal with a deceptively slight increase in sound volume. We backed up and I applied the mechanical brakes, which controlled the car just fine. Shifting into first, I turned the big wheel to point us up the driveway. Meanwhile Barbara walked ahead of us to help me guide a large and, as yet, unfamiliar automobile into our garage for the first time. Emilyann was taking pictures and even a video of the brief trip with our camera.

Once the car was in position in the garage, I put it into neutral and

Top: Most V-16s were ordered with dual side-mount spare tires and with wire wheels, although the "standard" selections were a single rear-mount spare tire and wooden "artillery" wheels. The compartment under the driver's door was for tool storage. As on the right side, the rear panel is decorative. *Bottom:* Classic lines and refined elegance characterize the entire car.

Top: The five-passenger sedan body is impressive without being overwhelming or ungainly. From this point on in Cadillac styling, the characteristic lines and shapes of the coaches and carriages of the past would fade away as the new streamlining age began. *Bottom:* A "face" that held its own against the best the competition had to offer. The effect of the so-called "LeBaron sweep," the curved sculpted line that arcs across the top panels of the hood and into the cowl sides, can clearly be seen. Everything works together in a harmonious whole.

Top: Detail of the Front End Ensemble. The parking light echoes the shape of the headlight (the largest diameter headlight any Cadillac would carry). There are so many vertical lines in the overall design, yet everything about the car says that it is eager to run. *Bottom:* A Fair-Weather View of the Goddess. In two years, Cadillac would take the radiator cap into the engine compartment. But the goddess would stay on top of the hood (in various stylized incarnations) through the 1956 model year.

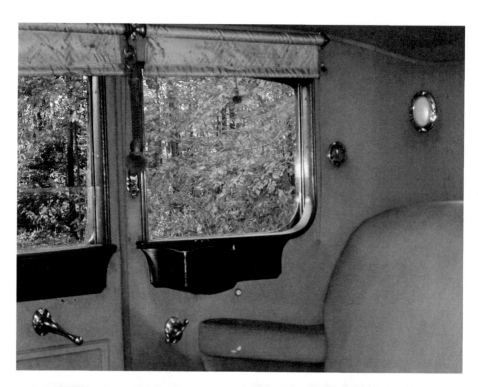

The Passenger's View. This is the perspective from which the man or woman who could afford a new 1930 Cadillac V-16 limousine would see the world. In the distance is the goddess perched atop the radiator.

Opposite top: Rear Quarter Window. The mother-of-pearl button below the window sill smoking set is for contacting the driver. The intercom microphone is to the right of the window. The switch to the left of the window turns on the running board courtesy lights. The handle to the left of the armrest rolls down the quarter window for ventilation. Pulling on the small tassel hanging to the right of the window shade releases the lock and lets the roller retract the shade.

Opposite bottom: Imperial Division. This partition with the roll-up window separating driver from passengers was known in this era of automotive history as an "imperial division." The oval hole next to the door jamb is for stowing an umbrella. The left-hand opera seat has a back and when open, faces the passenger-side door. The other opera seat has no back. The only other Series 4330 I have ever seen has wooden trim strips on either side of the divider window, instead of the fabric-covered trim on this car, and was built without the lap robe belt seen here.

The Driver's Controls. The steering wheel and accelerator pedal are like new. The translucent gear shift knob was an option. The frailty of old pot metal castings is evident in the broken window crank. The front seat in cars with an imperial division typically was fixed in place and could not be adjusted. This car was special-ordered with cloth in the driver's compartment instead of the customary leather upholstery.

set the hand brake so I could get out and look at the engine. I lifted the hood and watched the gleaming assemblage of polished aluminum, porcelain and enamel as it ran, smoothly as cream, only the spinning of the fan telling the eye that this wondrously engineered marvel was working. After a bit of marveling I switched the engine off. I helped my passengers Katherine and Emilyann out of the back seat, and Barbara brought me several rolls of soft paper towels to blot off the raindrops.

   In a box in the back seat, Lawrence Smith had included with the car some nicely made reproductions of the 1930/31 Cadillac service manual, the V-16 owner's manual, the Fisher Body service manual, and the Cadillac parts list. I called Mr. Smith to thank him again for selling the car to me, and he said that since then thirty people had called seeking to buy it. I realized I had been very fortunate in terms of timing and Lawrence Smith's consideration. This car could easily have gone to someone else.

The Dashboard and Front Seat. The levers on the steering wheel hub are the head- and taillight switch and the manual throttle control. The speedometer has been replaced with a similar but incorrect instrument and the three toggle switches on the lower right corner of the instrument cluster and underneath the dash are not original. A prior owner attached a map case to the driver's door panel.

Because of the rain, there was no impromptu cruise around the block as I'd imagined there would be—just the trip up the driveway. But Emilyann did get to hear the horn. And I found out what the other two toggle switches at the bottom of the dashboard were for. One was the headlight switch and the other was the switch for the instrument panel lights. Some day in the future I might rationalize the eccentricities I was discovering in the electrical system. Harry Scott came by later that day in the afternoon and marveled at the car. He thought it looked much better in person than the pictures indicated. Bill Sessler visited while I was barbecuing chicken for the family dinner and he took some pictures. I was only beginning to really know that a dream from my early teens had come true, fully and entirely.

I took the next day off from work, mowed the lawn and got to know my car a bit better. My prospect for the fastback called to tell me he would pass, even though it was just the kind of car he was looking for. He was

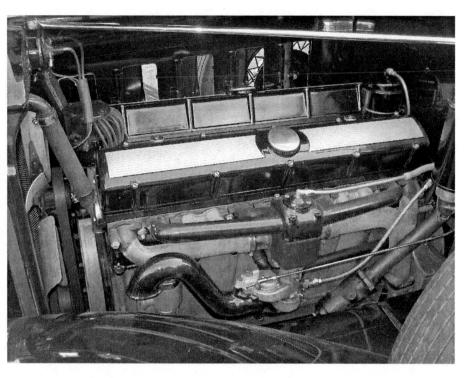

Left Side of the V-16 Engine. Owen Nacker designed the powerplant to be appealing to the eye, and "styled" the engine to conceal much of the plumbing and wiring. V-16 experts will notice items that would need attention for perfect authenticity, including correct radiator hoses and clamps, acorn nuts to hold the manifolds in place, re-porcelained exhaust manifolds and so forth.

Opposite top: Rear Seat and Vanity Unit. Beneath the rear quarter window is a vanity unit that once held a mirror and still sports a wind-up clock and an ash receiver. The overhead light is also a ventilator that communicates with the outside by means of a weatherproof outlet on the roof. The rear corner reading lamps are controlled by the switch to the right of the quarter window.

Opposite bottom: The Spacious Passenger Compartment. The elegant appointments of the Fleetwood interior include silk window shades, a ceiling-mounted cargo net for small items, separately adjustable seat back and bottom cushion, passenger-driver intercom, reading lights and movable cushioned footrests.

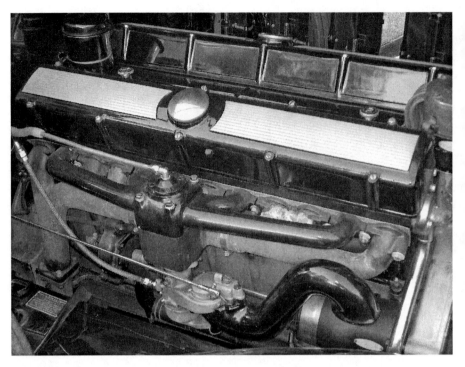

Right Side of the Engine. At 452 cubic inches and 175 horsepower, the Cadillac V-16 was effectively two straight-eight engines sharing a common crankshaft and distributor. There were separate carburetors, fuel pumps, coils, ignition points and manifolds for each bank of eight cylinders. Cadillac developed a special tool for synchronizing the two carburetors.

reluctant to face the significant costs of restoring the car. I started the 1930 again and marveled at the subtlety of this 75-year-old work of art and science. When the starter is engaged it makes a very subdued steady whirr, not the rhythmic "tuh-ruh-ruh-ruh" sound modern starters make. After a couple of seconds the starter sound is joined by an only slightly louder, slightly more guttural sound that is the engine beginning to run. The car transmits to the driver almost no physical indication that the engine is running. The smoothness is uncanny. And the view down that long hood over the shiny headlights, parking lights and of course, that flamboyant lady on the radiator cap tossing her hair to the breeze, leaves the driver feeling like a king.

I called Pete Sanders, who was delighted to hear I'd bought the 1930 imperial sedan. He told me that the fellow he had promised to contact, in hopes of getting me a good price on the car, turned out to be unfamiliar with it. I thanked him for his help and encouragement.

The Standard of the World. With the advent of the V-16, Cadillac could confidently repeat the slogan it had adopted in 1908, after it pioneered interchangeable parts in automobile manufacture.

I thought it was deliciously ironic that several first experiences with a V-16 Cadillac—the first time I got to see one running, to freely touch one, to ride in one, and even to drive one—all happened with my own car.

20. Musing About the Meaning of Things

So what does it all mean? From a hobbyist's point of view, I now had a car I could happily put in car shows, irrespective of the existence of minor imperfections. The extent to which the car remained original, even with the refurbishments that had been done (chrome, some paint, etc.) is a noteworthy feature and bragging point in and of itself. That the upholstery is still usable and presentable after such a long life is something people like to see and marvel at. I can either leave the car just as it came to me, or rigorously restore it, and no one could fault me either way. Of course, the question of showing the car necessarily raises the question of getting it to the location of the show. The favored solution is an enclosed trailer, to save on wear and tear to the car and to obviate any question of safety equipment (turn signals, seat belts, and so on) and distraction of other drivers. And of course, a trailer requires a towing vehicle capable of hauling the trailer *and* its 3-ton cargo. Needless to say, these were not near-term purchase items!

From a preservation standpoint, as long as I own the car, it will not be subject to the depredations of those folks who want to take a roadster or phaeton body from a another car and graft it to the chassis of a V-16 sedan to produce a V-16 convertible where there was none before. Yes, that way someone gets an exciting "ragtop" to enjoy (for a very steep price, mind you!). But a beautiful specimen in its own right of the coachbuilder's art is lost forever.

On one hand, a high-end classic automobile such as this one is a luxury item, and buying and owning one can be seen as frivolous, impractical and self-indulgent. On the other hand, if I take care of the car, it is not going to depreciate. In fact, it is as likely as any long-term investment in the financial markets to appreciate in value. Cadillac is not going to be making any more cars like this one (even if they have experimented with a contemporary version of a V-16 luxury sedan show car, one that would theoretically compete with Bentley, Rolls Royce and Mercedes's Maybach cars). The factory only made fifty of this particular body style, and only some lesser number of them have survived. Finally, this is a singularly well-preserved example of a car that was made with unstinting attention to elegance, detail and quality. Moreover, the market for this car (unlike the market for, say, muscle cars from the 1960s) is not in the grip of a speculative boom that could as easily crash as continue. So, a reasonable case can be made that this is a good investment. (That makes my conscience happier!)

Paradoxically, it is now almost a duty for me to enjoy my elegant sample of the best that the Classical era of automotive history had to offer. When those near to you have gone along with an elaborate enterprise for your benefit, they have a legitimate expectation that you will be pleased and grateful once the goal has been achieved. So I will be taking many opportunities to appreciate this automobile and my great good fortune in being able to keep it in my garage with my name on the title.

Epilogue—The Car That Followed Me Home

So now, you the reader may be wondering what *The Car that Followed Me Home* means, and whether I should have chosen a different title consistent with a tale involving several cars. I started out with the 1941 Series 75 sedan in mind, the car I always thought of as "my limousine." But as the story progressed, I brought in the 1941 coupe and the 1931 convertible. And then the 1930 V-16 showed up and demanded a place on the stage. I had picked the title to evoke that familiar image of a child showing up accompanied by an animal he'd dearly love to keep as a pet, pretending to be surprised that the creature has appeared at the door with him (and not volunteering that some earnest coaxing and persuasion was also involved). The more I thought about it, the more I felt that each one of the automobiles in these pages fit that title in one way or another. In the beginning the limousine was a straight-forward acquisition by a young man looking for his first car. But after my parents' deaths it surprised me by following me to Virginia despite my decision to sell it as part of the estate. My wife and everyone I spoke with had pleaded on the car's behalf. I wound up with the fastback because my father had, in effect, brought it home and begged for us to keep it. The 1931 cabriolet was closer to the title metaphor. It found me when that fellow from Gallup stopped to talk to me about the limousine and brought up the subject of a certain "1930 LaSalle roadster" he knew about. I urged, wheedled and cajoled my parents intensely to allow me to keep that one. And finally, there's the V-16. That was the car I had wanted all along. And it was the one I had to work the hardest to make a case for keeping. This time instead of a little boy entreating his parents, a grown man had negotiated with his conscience, the family finances and his responsibilities to his family.

Ultimately, then, the story is about me as much as it is about any or all of the cars. For years my little girl would come up to me and cheerfully say "Daddy, tell me a story about your little life." I would plumb my memory for a little vignette I thought she might find amusing, and I'd tell it to her with as much drama as I could supply. But I always worried that she had a right to more of a picture of who her father is and what makes him tick than a few isolated anecdotes from my early childhood. I started writing down some of the old car experiences to keep Bill Sullivan and my uncle updated, after all they did to restart the 1941 limousine. I was pleasantly surprised to see that Emilyann was fascinated with the stories. So it only made sense to put them all together and this is how it turned out.

Index